# HANNIBAL'S WAR

'. . . this laughter you condemn springs not from a happy heart, but from one which is almost beside itself with its misfortunes. . . . The time to weep was when our arms were taken from us, our ships were burnt and we were forbidden foreign wars . . .'

Hannibal, as in Livy, xxx, 45

# HANNIBAL'S WAR

JOHN PEDDIE

SUTTON PUBLISHING

First published in 1997 by
Sutton Publishing Limited · Phoenix Mill
Thrupp · Stroud · Gloucestershire · GL5 2BU

British Library Cataloguing in Publication Data

A catalogue record for this book is available from the British Library

ISBN 0 7509 1336 3

TM  ALAN SUTTON™ and SUTTON™ are the
trade marks of Sutton Publishing Limited

Typeset in 10/14 pt Sabon.
Typesetting and origination by
Sutton Publishing Limited
Printed in Hong Kong by
Midas Printing.

*To My Dear Dodi*

# CONTENTS

# PICTURE CREDITS

The author and publisher would like to thank the following for the loan of and permission to reproduce photographs:

Air Photo Library, University of Keele, p. 78; Alinari, p. 5; Ian Atkinson, pp. 54, 109, 203; H.C. Randall, pp. 27, 28, 29 (above and below); Bridgeman Art Library, London, pp. 13, 25, 136, 168, 180, 194; British Library, pp. 44–5, 123; British Museum, pp. 2, 3, 11, 22, 39, 57, 111, 115, 120, 125, 170, 182, 183, 193, 208 (below); Roger Day, pp. 20, 24, 64, 195; Jonathan Falconer, pp. 19, 21; Imperial War Museum, p. 210; Italian State Tourist Board (E.N.I.T.) London, pp. 32, 41, 50, 61, 89, 105, 132, 143, 160; Mansell Collection, pp. xvi, 7, 36, 51, 52, 59, 72, 74, 96, 99, 130, 148, 188, 192, 204; MAS Ampliaciones y Reproducciones, p. 10; The Royal Collection © 1997 Her Majesty Queen Elizabeth II, p. 167; Spanish Tourist Office, pp. 101, 151, 165; Mary Spiller, pp. 172, 173.

# LIST OF ILLUSTRATIONS

# FOREWORD

'Hannibal was an indomitable soldier,' writes John Peddie. 'For him there was never a task too difficult nor a problem incapable of solution.' It is a measure of Hannibal's impact that both military commanders and historians have written admiringly about him. Amongst generals, Napoleon compared him to Frederick the Great and Alexander, and Montgomery wrote of his 'tactical genius', while amongst historians Theodor Mommsen called him 'a military genius of heroic status' and John Keegan saw him as a commander 'of outstanding ability'.

Such comments should come as no surprise, for Hannibal was a figure of colossal stature. His crossing of the Alps, at the head of an army which included war-elephants, hampered by poor weather, hostile tribesmen and unreliable guides, is a remarkable feat of leadership; his victory at Cannae (216 BC) is a striking example of the destruction of a larger army by a smaller, and his almost succeeding to maintain the struggle against Rome in Italy for sixteen continuous years speaks volumes for his determination.

The real strength of this admirable book lies in its author's ability to weave the weft of history into the warp of practical military experience. Hannibal's exploits are not simply described, with painstaking use of classical sources like Polybius and Livy, but are subjected to penetrating military analysis. What was the campaign's objective or, as a Gulf War strategist might say, its desired endstate? What was the proportion of killed to wounded on an ancient battlefield? What sort of elephants did Hannibal use, and how were they managed in battle?

This blending of the historical and the military enables us to make a balanced assessment of Hannibal. He excelled as a tactician, and deserves particular credit for his unpredictability and innovation. At Lake Trasimene (217 BC) he sprung an ambush on a grand scale, and at Cannae his centre deliberately collapsed, luring the Romans into a trap.

His touch was less deft at war's higher levels. He invaded Rome from Spain before his base was secure; he failed to maintain offensive momentum after Cannae; and when fighting spread to Sicily he did not change his chain of command to reflect the island's strategic importance. Yet no general can hope to succeed if he is denied resources and support, and John Peddie proposes that there is at least a case for suggesting that Carthage was responsible for its own military misfortunes.

Perhaps his subordinate Maharbal was right to tell him: 'Assuredly, Hannibal, you know how to win a fight but you do not know how to use your victory.' Yet few generals have won battles with Hannibal's masterful style, or kept a disparate army together so well in the face of such adversity. He was a man indeed, and in this soldierly account he is equitably assessed.

RICHARD HOLMES
September 1997

# ACKNOWLEDGEMENTS

I am deeply grateful to Professor E.R. Holmes OBE, TD, MA, Ph.D for finding time, in what I know to be a very busy schedule, to write a foreword for *Hannibal's War*. Richard Holmes taught military history at the Royal Military Academy, Sandhurst, for many years and now lectures at the Royal Military College of Science. He has written many books on military subjects, most recently *Riding the Retreat*, published by the Imperial War Museum. He is also the author and presenter of the popular BBC TV series, *War Walks*. I am also indebted to Mrs Susan Gole, chairman of the International Map Collectors' Society, for her assistance in the selection of the ancient maps of Rome and Syracuse on pp. 44–5 and 123 respectively; to Mrs Tracy Pryor of the Graphics Department of the Army Training Centre, Warminster, for the preparation of the illustrative maps; and to the Chief Librarian and the staff of the Wiltshire County Library and Museum Service for their unstinting help.

Extracts of translations of the writings of Pliny the Elder, Polybius and Livy, published under the title of Penguin Classics, are reproduced by permission of Frederick Warne & Co. as follows: from *Natural History, A Selection* by Pliny the Elder, translated by John F. Healy (1991), copyright © John F. Healy, 1991 (on pp. 44, 46); from *The Rise of the Roman Empire* by Polybius, translated by Ian Scott-Kilvert (1979), copyright © Ian Scott-Kilvert, 1979 (on pp. 81–2, 135, 210, 217, 227, 228, 245–6, 248–50, 255–6, 388–9, 399, 408–9, 428); from *The Early History of Rome* by Livy, translated by Aubrey de Sélincourt (1960), copyright © the Estate of Aubrey de Sélincourt, 1960 (on pp. 83, 401); from *Rome and Italy* by Livy, translated by Betty Radice (1982), copyright © Betty Radice, 1982 (on p. 66); and from *The War with Hannibal* by Livy, translated by Aubrey de Séincourt (1965), copyright © the Estate of Aubrey de Sélincourt, 1965 (on pp. 99–100, 106, 113, 125, 129, 138–9, 148–9, 171, 180, 210, 236, 254–5, 370, 376, 379, 407, 417, 456, 465, 490, 601, 638, 644).

Finally, I must express to my publisher and his staff my indebtedness to them for their expertise and help in the production of this volume.

JOHN PEDDIE
September 1997

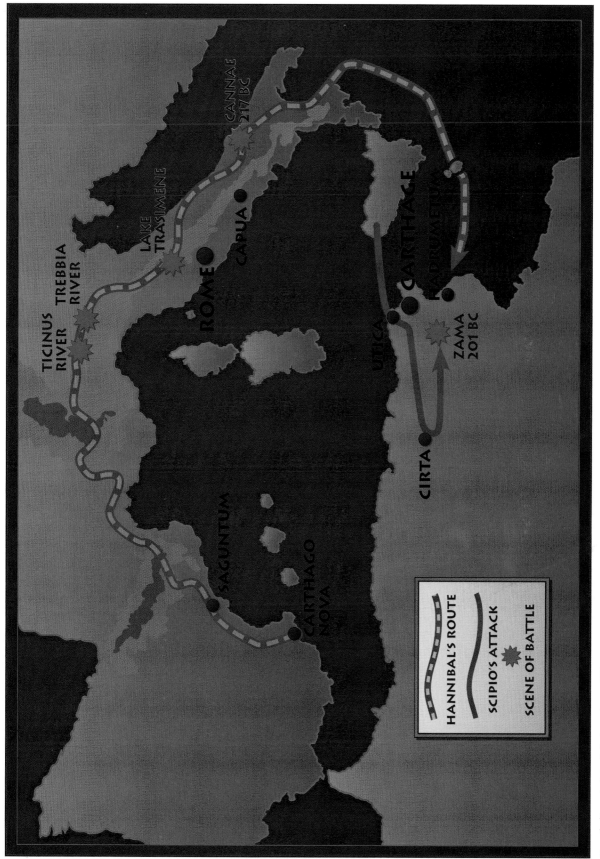

Hannibal's route into Italy (see also p. 12).

# CHRONOLOGY
# 246–183 BC

| Year BC | Carthage | Spain | Italy | Sicily |
|---------|----------|-------|-------|--------|
| 246 | Hannibal born, son of Hamilcar Barca | | | |
| 237 | | Hamilcar takes over the governance of Carthage's Spanish province | | |
| 230 | | Hasdrubal, his son-in-law, succeeds Hamilcar | | |
| 221 | | Hasdrubal assassinated and Hannibal, son of Hamilcar, succeeds him | | |
| 219 | | Hamilcar lays siege to and captures Saguntum | | |
| 218 | Roman delegation declares war on Carthage | Hannibal's War begins<br><br>Hannibal marches from New Carthage and crosses the Pyrenees<br><br>Gnaeus Scipio lands in Spain | Publius Scipio sails for Spain and reaches Marseilles<br><br>Hannibal crosses the Alps and reaches Italy<br><br>Publius Scipio returns to Italy and arrives in the Po valley<br><br>Battle of the Ticinus and the Trebbia | |
| 217 | | Roman naval victory off Ebro | Carthaginian naval squadron off Pisa<br>Battle at Lake Trasimene<br><br>Fabius appointed dictator by Roman Senate | |
| 216 | Carthage sends reinforcements to Spain<br><br>Hannibal's brother Mago arrives from Italy to ask for reinforcements and money | Hasdrubal stopped by Carthage from leaving Spain to join Hannibal | Romans routed at battle of Cannae<br><br>Capua secedes to Hannibal<br><br>Hannibal rebuffed at Nola | |
| 215 | Reinforcements sent to Hannibal under Bomilcar | Roman successes in Spain<br><br>Mago arrives in Spain with reinforcements | Philip V of Macedonia allies himself with Hannibal but envoys intercepted at sea<br>Bomilcar arrives at | Syracuse breaks alliance with Rome |

| Year BC | Carthage | Spain | Italy | Sicily |
|---|---|---|---|---|
| | | | Locri with reinforcements for Hannibal | |
| 214 | | Rome recaptures Saguntum | First Macedonian War begins | Marcellus arrives in Sicily |
| | | | | Roman siege of Syracuse |
| 212 | | Roman army in Spain routed – Scipio brothers killed | Romans besiege Capua; Hannibal captures Tarentum | Marcellus takes Syracuse – Hippocrates and Himilco die in city plague |
| | | | Hannibal feints at Rome | |
| | | | Capua surrenders; Scipio (Africanus) volunteers for Spain | |
| 210 | Roman raids commence on Carthaginian coast | Scipio lands in Spain | | End of war in Sicily – Hanno and Epicydes abandon the island |
| | | Scipio captures New Carthage | | |
| | | Scipio's victory at Baecula | Fabius recovers Tarentum | |
| | | Carthaginian generals in Spain agree Hasdrubal's departure for Italy | | |
| 208 | | Hasdrubal marches for Italy via western Pyrenees | Death of Marcellus | |
| | | | Hasdrubal arrives in Italy and is killed at battle of Metaurus | |
| 207 | Successful Roman raid on Utica, Carthage | | | |
| 206 | | End of Carthaginian resistance in Spain | Scipio returns to Rome | |
| 205 | Laelius raids the Carthaginian coast | | Mago lands at Genoa and marches north | |
| 204 | | | | Scipio (Africanus) sails with expeditionary force for Africa |
| 203 | Naval battle off Carthage | | Mago defeated in northern Italy and wounded | |
| | | | Mago and Hannibal recalled home but Mago dies at sea | |
| | | | Death of Q. Fabius Maximus | |
| 202 | Battle of Zama – Hannibal defeated by Scipio | | | |
| 201 | End of Second Punic War | | | |
| 183 (circa) | Hannibal kills himself at court of Prusias of Bythnia | | | |

CHAPTER I

# INTRODUCTION

Put Hannibal in the scales: how many pounds
will that peerless general mark up today?

Juvenal, *Satire X*[1]

The reasons for the Punic Wars are to be found in the worst characteristics of man: greed, fear, pride, passion and dishonesty. Rome and Carthage had, by a series of treaties, each long recognised the trading ambitions of the other. Probably the most significant of these documents was signed in 348 BC, for it confirmed the sphere of influence exercised by Carthage in North Africa and Spain, safeguarded Rome's trade with Sicily and guaranteed the immunity of the Italian coastline from raids. This agreement lasted for nearly 150 years, until, in 306 BC, another document was signed which reduced the concessions earlier agreed with Rome and restricted the amount of Roman shipping permitted to trade in the southern waters of the Mediterranean. The resources of Rome, at that moment, were being heavily expended in a war with the Samnites and she doubtless felt she was in no position to argue for a better deal.

Some thirty years later, Rome and Carthage were thrown together to rebuff the Pyrrhic invasions of Italy and Sicily. If the eyes of the Roman people had not already been glancing in that direction, this was an incident of such a scale that they could not have failed to notice the economic and military importance of the island, lying within a stone's throw of the toe of Italy, and the threat it would pose to their well-being if held in hostile hands. Its proximity provided an ideal stepping-off point for an invasion of the Italian mainland, as later centuries were to prove. Moreover, its position, in the narrow waters of the Mediterranean, gave it command of a busy maritime crossroads. The strategic importance of Sicily to both protagonists, and to our story, is fully expressed later in the book. I shall not, therefore, say more at this point other than that the island now provided the spark which triggered the First Punic War and set these two great trading peoples at conflict with each other.

It was a confused incident, well in line with the equally confused politics of Sicily at that moment. Some Campanian mercenaries, the Mamertines, had been summoned, from across the Straits of Messina, to serve Agathocles in a dispute against the Carthaginians. When, however, their services were no longer needed, instead of returning home to southern Italy they occupied the city of Messina

*Opposite*: Bust of Hannibal. (The Mansell Collection)

Naked warrior on a
Messanian coin. (© British
Museum)

itself. Hiero II, king of Syracuse, at once moved to eject them, seeing their
presence as a threat to his kingdom. The Mamertines responded by appealing for
help both to Carthage and to Rome.

Carthage moved to their assistance without delay but Rome paused before
making a decision, doubtless appreciating the inevitable conflict with Carthage
which would follow. When she finally intervened, perhaps because she sensed
danger in what she saw as a Carthaginian attempt to extend their influence
closer to the Italian mainland or because she saw an opportunity to secure her
hold on the Straits of Messina, she landed a contingent under the tribune Caius
Claudius Cadix. He employed no half measures. The Carthaginian commander
was arrested, and later executed for cowardice and inefficiency by his own side,
his army was ejected from the town, and the city state of Messina was occupied
by Roman troops. This display of determined and well-drilled action by the
Romans, coupled with the fact that the influence of this mainland power was
now spreading to his very doorstep, persuaded Hiero II to abandon Carthage as
an ally and to join Rome, now revealed to him as a powerful neighbour and,
consequently, a desirable friend. Hiero II of Syracuse, in fair times and foul,
proved a loyal and valuable ally to Rome for many years.

Thus, in 264 BC, the First Punic War began. It resulted in the defeat of
Carthage in 241 BC and peace was agreed by a treaty through which, in a series
of sweeping concessions, Rome was yielded the whole of Sicily, as well as the
islands lying between Italy and Sicily. Additionally, Carthage was prohibited
from sailing quinquiremes into Italian waters, as well as from going to war
against Syracuse or any other allies of Rome: she was required to surrender all
prisoners without claiming the traditional ransom, and she was also required to
pay Rome, over a period of ten years, a total sum of 3,200 talents of silver. An
effect of these agreements was that a large number of Carthaginian mercenary
soldiers were evacuated to North Africa. When, upon arrival, they were
confronted not only with disbandment but also a threat of a cut in the rate of
pay they had initially been promised, they mutinied. For the next three years,
Carthage found herself immersed in war with this faction until, in 239 BC,
Hamilcar Barca, who had commanded many of them in Sicily, and was the father
of Hannibal, raised the siege of Carthage which they had imposed and massacred
some 40,000 in a final encounter near Tunis.

This event is only significant to our tale because of its impact upon the future
of the island of Sardinia, which had continued to remain in Carthaginian hands
after the First Punic War, for, in a strange aberration, Rome, when drafting the
detail of the post-war treaty with Carthage, had seemingly ignored the danger
the island posed, both to her security and to her ambitions to extend her
influence. If held in enemy hands, Sardinia was ideally situated to threaten not
only Italy's western coastline but also Rome's coastal and deep water shipping
lanes connecting with her armed forces in both Gaul and Spain. She now saw fit
to do something about it. She passed a decree declaring war on Carthage and
arbitrarily added a clause to the treaty document, requiring the Carthaginians to
evacuate Sardinia forthwith: if this were not sufficient, she also humiliatingly

demanded of Carthage a further 'fine' in the sum of 1,200 talents of silver. In view of the nature of things to come, and the military importance of keeping open her shipping lanes, the seizure of Sardinia assumes the complexion of a thoughtful piece of offensive forward planning. Carthage was powerless to resist: her mercenary garrison on the island, disaffected by events in North Africa, surrendered without striking a blow.

Hasdrubal Barca on a coin.
(© British Museum)

Hamilcar Barca had been responsible for the strategically important north-west corner of Sicily during the First Punic War and had sailed to take over his duties there in 247 BC. It is likely that Hannibal was born just before his departure to the war. Upon his return home, Hamilcar was appointed to command in Spain, where Carthage had already established a considerable foothold in the valley of the river Baetis, the present-day Guadalquivir. He at once set in hand, with notable success, a programme of territorial expansion, designed to re-establish Carthaginian fortunes. Hamilcar died in battle, probably during the winter of 229/228 BC, and was immediately succeeded by his son-in-law, Hasdrubal, who proved as successful as his predecessor, if by less aggressive, more persuasive means.

Hasdrubal was the founder of the city of New Carthage, modern-day Cartagena, which fast developed into an important trading and military base. Inevitably, such a speedy Carthaginian renaissance caught the attention of Rome. She, herself, already had established many useful trading contacts in southern Gaul as well as in Spain, west of the Pyrenees, extending to the banks of the Ebro. Indeed, one of these, the walled town of Saguntum, was situated some 87 miles beyond the south bank of the river, and its people, sensing the threat of nearby, ambitious Carthage, had eagerly accepted a Roman offer of protection. To this end, Rome negotiated a treaty with Hasdrubal in 225 BC which, according to Polybius,[2] contained two important clauses: namely, it 'provided that the allies of each power should be secure from attack by the other', and it contained a Carthaginian undertaking by which 'they agreed not to cross the Ebro in arms'.

We may feel entitled to presume, from the brief account left to us by Polybius, that the intention of the treaty was to define and restrict the areas of military influence of both protagonists. On the other hand, Polybius makes great play of the fact that Carthage 'agreed not to cross the Ebro in arms' but, contrarily, makes no mention of any similar commitment by Rome. Indeed, such a commitment would have been irreconcilable to a treaty of this nature if the protection promised to the people of Saguntum were to be honoured. We are thus left in the dark as to the true purpose of what was intended, as much, seemingly, as the Carthaginian senate, who claimed, at a later date, that they had not been consulted by Hasdrubal before the document was signed.

Hasdrubal was assassinated in 221 BC and was succeeded by Hannibal, who thus continued the self-established suzerainty of the Barca faction in Carthage's Spanish empire. Livy[3] comments that, from the very first day of his command, Hannibal 'acted as if he had definite instructions to take Italy as his sphere of operations and to make war on Rome'. In view of later uncertainties about who authorised the declaration of war, this is an interesting statement. Certain it is, however, that Hannibal, upon taking up his duties, immediately opened a series of campaigns designed to extend Carthaginian influence in Spain and bring neighbouring fractious tribes under control. Equally, according to Livy, he deliberately created tension against the Saguntine people, who at last became so concerned that they sent envoys to seek the support of Rome. Rome responded by sending a delegation to Carthage to demand that Hannibal be restrained but it proved a time-wasting gesture. The delegation returned to Rome to report that the Carthaginians had refused to negotiate and to find that, in the meantime, Hannibal had besieged and seized Saguntum.

The Roman Senate had already prepared military plans for this eventuality: they now passed legislation authorising the raising of six legions for the current year, 218 BC, amounting to a total of 24,000 infantry, 1,800 cavalry and 40,000 allied troops. They also enhanced the strength of the fleet to a total of 200 quinquiremes and 20 light craft. It was already their intention, in the event of war, to carry the offensive to Carthage, both in North Africa and Spain, as well as simultaneously to despatch a task force of two legions to northern Italy, to watch over the troublesome Cisalpine Gauls. For this purpose, they appointed two consuls, Publius Cornelius Scipio, the father of the celebrated Scipio Africanus, a young man yet to distinguish himself in battle, and Tiberius Sempronius Longus. Scipio was forthwith despatched to Spain and Sempronius was sent to Italy, with 'instructions to cross into Africa if his colleague proved strong enough to prevent Hannibal from entering Italy'. But Rome was ill prepared for war, as Livy[4] points out, and, despite his words, she was as yet unaware of the extent to which the situation had deteriorated:

> Their recent campaigns against Sardinia, for instance, or Corsica, or Istria, or Illyria, had been only minor affairs, mere pin-pricks, and no real test of Roman arms, whilst their engagements with the Gauls had been more in the nature of casual skirmishing than of regular war. Carthage was a very different matter. She had long been an enemy to Rome, and her troops, trained in 23 years of hard and consistently successful warfare in Spain, and accustomed to obey a commander of supreme enterprise and skill, were now crossing the Ebro, fresh from the destruction of a powerful and wealthy town . . . War was coming and it would have to be fought in Italy, in defence of the walls of Rome . . .[5]

The Roman plan of a two-frontal attack on Carthage in North Africa and Spain, an example of the 'strategy of the indirect approach', as it was to be termed by Liddell Hart,[6] the eminent twentieth-century military historian, provides us with an early glimpse of the formula which, together with the *Fabian Strategy*, we will meet in later chapters. Ultimately, it was to enable Rome to defeat Carthage in this second of the Punic Wars, but for the moment their plans were thwarted by the speed of Hannibal's advance from the Ebro, after the collapse of Saguntum.

The causes of the war, Hannibal's War, as it is sometimes termed, are obscure. Polybius, a Greek statesman, an ancient historian of note and, significantly, a longtime friend of the Scipio family,[7] ponders upon them at length in his *Histories* but, although a contemporary, he provides no clear solutions. He cites the justifiable anger of the Carthaginians at the manner in which Sardinia was wrested from them as a possible origin but nevertheless considers Carthage was both needlessly provocative in the matter of Saguntum and, again, by her treatment of the Ebro treaty. He sees the success of the Carthaginian enterprise in Spain as a contributory cause, in that it provided her people with the resources and the confidence once again to confront Rome. He might have added that the growing strength of Carthage also provided a cause for Rome to strike pre-emptively at her enemy before the latter's increasing presence in the western Mediterranean became commercially and militarily too challenging. Finally, he quotes the traditional tale of Hamilcar, who, when performing a ceremony of sacrifice before sailing with his army to Spain, is said to have led his young son, Hannibal, to the altar 'and commanded him to lay his hand upon the victim and swear that he would never become a friend to the Romans'.

Polybius. (Alinari)

In such a complex atmosphere, Polybius, with most of his contemporaries, appears to have considered war between Carthage and Rome to have been inevitable once Hannibal had been appointed to command in Spain: but even in the circumstances of the extraordinary political power of the Barca family, it would surely have been unusual for Hannibal to declare war on Rome without the authority of the Carthaginian senate. Nor can there be any doubt that they gave that authority, for when challenged about affairs in Spain by the Roman envoy Fabius, and asked to declare whether they wanted peace or war, the senators opted for war and vowed 'to fight it to the end'.[8]

If the origins of Hannibal's War were clouded, so indeed was its purpose. Wars, historically, wear many different complexions; they may be ideological or defensive, punitive or vengeful. They may be fought for economic or social causes or for reasons of aggrandisement. But however they may arise, of one thing we may be certain: they cannot be successfully fought without a clear-cut, grand objective, within which will lie other, minor, objectives, each one a stepping stone, culminating, hopefully, in victory.

A first glance at Hannibal's War reveals no such clear-cut purpose. After crossing the Pyrenees and the Alps, he sweeps into Italy with all the authority of Juvenal's 'peerless general', devastating the countryside and laying waste the cities in his path. If it were his purpose to besiege and capture Rome, he veers away from it, perhaps deterred by the size of the task. Then, having destroyed the flower of the Roman army at Trebbia, Trasimene and Cannae, and having himself suffered severe losses, he now assumes the role of a twentieth-century Chindit commander, playing cat and mouse with his enemy as he marches and counter-marches across the southern half of the peninsula, creating strongholds, laying ambushes, and generally withstanding the vast quantities of enemy military resources thrown against him. Next, as his own resources diminish, he is to be found in the extreme south of the country, acting the role of a guerrilla leader, a sort of Che Guevara. Ultimately, after sixteen long years of combat, he is 'holed-up' in Bruttium, in the toe of Italy, awaiting the call to return home to Carthage, soon to be brought down by Scipio Africanus.

This wastage of Hannibal's strike power, albeit over a prolonged period of years, is reminiscent of the scenario said to have been depicted by Napoleon to his secretary, de Bourrienne, when questioned whether, when encamped with his Grand Army on the cliffs above Boulogne, he had genuinely intended to invade England in 1805. The great man responded by saying:[9]

> Those who believe that are blockheads. They do not see the affair in its true light. I can doubtless land (in England) with 100,000 men. A great battle will be fought, which I shall gain; but I must count upon 30,000 men killed, wounded or taken prisoners. If I march on London a second battle will be fought. I shall suppose myself again victorious. But what shall I do in London with an army reduced three/fourths and without hope of reinforcements? It would be madness.

Likewise, it might be asked, what could Hannibal have done in Italy, with his potential reinforcements contained in Spain, driven under Roman pressure to the far, south-east corner of the country and denied the opportunity of bringing him the help he so sorely needed? Increasingly, we are forced to ask, what was Hannibal's aim? How did it come about that a man so often described by historians, both ancient and modern, as 'a military genius' and 'a brilliant tactician' should have plunged so deeply into a situation which, almost inevitably, was destined to fail? Did Maharbal, his second-in-command and his Master of Horse, speak with justification when, after Cannae, he remarked to him: 'Assuredly, Hannibal, you know how to win a fight but you do not know how to use your victory.'

In the pages which follow I address these questions, whilst taking a military glance at Hannibal's campaign. For this purpose I have drawn upon the histories of Polybius and Livy, both of whom made full use of the writings of contemporary annalists, much of whose work is no longer identifiable and, indeed, has since almost completely perished. For his part, Polybius, a distinguished Greek, born *c.* 200 BC, was fortunate during his lifetime to have developed a strong friendship with the young Scipio Aemillianus. adopted son of Scipio Africanus and grandson of another prominent player in the drama, the consul L. Aemilius Paullus, who fell on the battlefield of Cannae. His work therefore benefited from sources of high quality.

Livy, on the other hand, a Roman citizen, was born in 59 BC at Padua. When he was aged about thirty, he commenced writing his *History of Rome*, a lengthy work consisting of 142 books, of which 35 survive, a total which fortunately includes those crucial to the Hannibalic War. He was gifted with a strikingly vivid, descriptive style. The works of both Polybius and Livy largely complement each other. Their merits, differences and shortcomings have been widely studied and commented upon by eminent modern-day scholars, notably by F.W. Walbank, in

Livy, from a sixteenth-century engraving.

his *Historical Commentary on Polybius*, and by Arnold J. Toynbee, in his very comprehensive study of the period entitled *Hannibal's Legacy*. J.F. Lazenby's book *Hannibal's War* is another invaluable work devoted to an analysis of the campaign, and benefits from the author's personal exploration of the war zone.

Lazenby's modest description of his 'impertinence' as an armchair historian, who had never experienced battle, undertaking an assessment of 'one of the great commanders of history' provided me with the encouragement to take a professional glance at the Hannibalic War, despite his later, somewhat illogical, footnote,[10] that generals who 'pronounce upon ancient warfare' without 'first-hand knowledge' are equally impertinent. Regrettably, I have never been a general! However, I have always agreed with the view, expressed by Liddell Hart, that 'war is a science which depends upon art for its application'; that history, as a study of past events, is a record of human affairs in which, sadly, warfare plays a major role; and that comment by the professional soldier on many of these matters can frequently be helpful. I have not, therefore, allowed myself to be deflected from my task and ask only that it should be accepted in this spirit.

## CHAPTER II

# THE LONG MARCH

Cry 'Havoc', let loose the dogs of war!

Shakespeare, *Julius Caesar*[1]

No plan of operations can look with any certainty beyond the first meeting with the major forces of the enemy. The commander is compelled . . . to reach decisions on the basis of situations which cannot be predicted.

General Field Marshal von Moltke[2]

As soon as Hannibal took up command in Spain it became clear from the measures which he then set in hand that his purpose was to declare war on Rome and to waste little time in doing so.[3] This fact appears to be universally accepted. There is less certainty as to whether Hannibal, in going to war, was acting independently, in the manner of Hasdrubal, who, according to his masters, signed the Ebro treaty with Rome without consulting the senate in Carthage; or whether he had been acting under instructions from Carthage; or, alternatively, whether the Carthaginian senate, taxed by a delegation from Rome about Hannibal's aggression in Spain, had felt compelled to support him by force of circumstances. However it may have been, the Carthaginian senators, when addressed by the Roman envoys and given the option of peace or war, threw back the choice to Fabius, their challenger: and when the Roman chose war, so Livy recounts,[4] they accepted his declaration unanimously and vowed 'to fight it to the end'. There can thus be no doubt about their open support for Hannibal but the shadow remains as to whether it was willingly given.

The annals left to us by Polybius, an eminent contemporary statesman and historian, offer little help in reaching a firm decision. Hannibal, upon taking up office, he relates, at once set in hand a programme of events with the purpose of preparing for war. He planned for this, the Second Punic War, to be fought on the Italian peninsula. He proposed to exploit the discontent of the Celtic tribes of the Po valley, who for some time had become increasingly restless with the constant expansionary pressures being exerted against them by Rome. Primarily, the thrust of his measures was directed at ensuring the security of Carthage and its Spanish province during his absence. To this end, he conducted a series of brief forays against potentially troublesome neighbouring tribes, then, when these had been successfully quelled and brought to order, he turned his attention to Saguntum, a

Saguntum from the east.
(Ampliaciones
Reproducciones MAS,
Barcelona)

fortress city of the Edetani and a prosperous trading centre, initially founded by Greek colonists. It possessed a dangerous friendship with Rome.

Saguntum was situated on the western bank of the Rio Palancia. It lay on the coast, 87 miles south of the Ebro, deep in the territory recognised by Hasdrubal's treaty as being subject to Carthaginian influence. The city had close trade relations with Massilia, modern-day Marseilles, a city state lying in the Rhône estuary, closely linked by trade to Rome. Doubtless, both would have made full use of the coastal shipping lanes to Rome from which the threat of a Sardinia occupied by Carthage had but recently, and controversially, been lifted. Saguntum, for its part, in about 228 BC, had seized an opportunity to conclude an alliance with Rome, which provided her people with an undertaking of protection, should the need ever arise. In view of the history of war between Carthage and Rome, it is thus unsurprising that Hannibal viewed the Saguntines with considerable suspicion. From the moment of his appointment as provincial governor he had unsuccessfully applied heavy pressure upon the city elders to bring their town firmly under the Carthaginian wing. If Hannibal were going to war with Rome, which was his intention, we may be sure he recognised the folly of leaving Saguntum, a walled and fiercely independent city seaport, astride his lines of communication and free to offer succour to his enemy.

Hannibal laid siege to Saguntum in the spring of 219 BC and its inhabitants resisted with fierce determination for a period of some eight months. There is no need, in these pages, to discuss the action in detail. It is notable, however, that a justifiable and consistent criticism of Hannibal by military historians has been the ineffectiveness of the siege warfare he later conducted during his Italian campaign. This is a charge which cannot be levelled in this instance. The Carthaginian assault upon Saguntum was resolute, skilled in siege tactics and well equipped with a variety of siege machinery.[5] When Hannibal found it necessary to leave the scene for a brief spell to lead a punitive expedition against the Carpetani and Oretani tribes, Maharbal, whom he left in command and was later to be his Master of Horse, carried on the assault 'with such vigour that Hannibal's absence was hardly noticed'. The ferocity of the fighting was remarkable. In the final assault, Hannibal had issued instructions that no man of military age should be spared. It was, writes Livy, a barbarous order; but, he asks, how would it have been possible to show mercy to men who, in desperation, either fought to the death or set fire to their own houses and burned themselves alive, together with their wives and children?

Coin showing Hannibal in 219 BC. (© British Museum)

As soon as the occupation of Saguntum had been completed and its plunder and prisoners distributed, much of the loot being despatched to Carthage as a sop to those senators hostile to the war, Hannibal set about preparing for his departure to Rome. His first act was to grant leave to his Spanish troops. They were given orders to return by the spring, 'in order that, with God's help, we will begin a war which will fill your pockets with gold and carry your fame to the world's end'.[6] His next action was to instruct his elder brother, Hasdrubal, on how Spain was to continue to be administered whilst he was away and what preparations were to be made for 'the defence of the province against the Romans', in the event of their arrival before his return. For this task he provided Hasdrubal with 11,850 Libyan infantry, supported by 2,550 cavalry, together with a force of 300 Ligurian targeters, 500 Balearic slingers and 21 elephants. In addition to this land force, he also left with Hasdrubal a substantial navy, comprising 50 quinquiremes, 2 quadriremes and 5 triremes. Finally, 'he made arrangements for the security of Africa' by cross posting to Carthage some 15,000 cavalry and infantry recruited from Spanish tribes in exchange for an equal number of African soldiery.

When all this had been done, and the necessary administrative arrangements had been put in place, Hannibal set forth on his long march. Before we follow him, however, it is necessary that we turn our gaze to Cisalpine Gaul, for this was the hinge pin of the first phase of his campaign. He had been promised support by the major tribes of the region. It was here that he proposed to 'winter' in the coming season and he looked to them to satisfy his logistical and reinforcement requirements upon his arrival.

The Italy which Hannibal would have seen, and which would have provided the model for the preparation of his plans, may be divided into three sectors. The first and most northerly of these was Cisalpine Gaul, a fertile and populous region. It lay broadly between the Alps and the north-western reach of the Apennine range. It was famous for the quantity and quality of its foodstuffs, particularly millet and acorns, and for the very large number of pigs it provided each year, both for domestic consumption in Italy and as a general supply for the

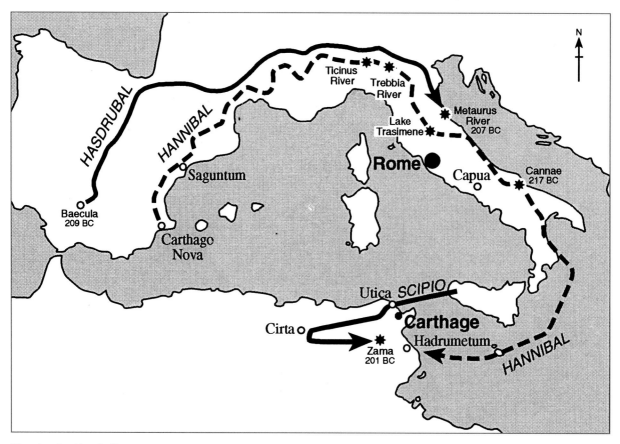

Map showing Hannibal's
march into Italy and
ultimate withdrawal to
Africa

Roman army. Polybius[7] saw the Cisalpine area as shaped like a triangle, 'the
northern side being provided by the Alps themselves, and extending some 250
miles in length, the southern by the Apennines for a distance of some 400 miles,
and its base by the coast of the Adriatic, its length from the city of Sena to the
head of the gulf amounting to more than 280 miles. The combined length of the
three sides of the plain thus amounted to some 930 miles.'

It was an area where, prior to 219 BC, Rome had exerted little more than
outside influence but in that year she commenced the extension of her physical
occupation yet further northwards. She established two strategically sited
'colonial' towns, thus introducing an armed presence into the region, one at
Placentia, dominating an important, tactically valuable routeway through the
Apennines to the seaport at Genoa, and thence to Rome by sea or land; and the
other at Cremona, on the northern bank of the Po. Both were carefully sited to
watch over the territories of the Boii and the Insubres, two particularly
troublesome and influential Celtic tribes with whom Rome had been at war
seven years earlier. Understandably, these two peoples saw this move as a
dangerous incursion and a threat to their sovereignty. It caused them to turn to
Hannibal for help and, possibly attracted by news of the siege of Saguntum, they
sent emissaries to him in Spain to put their case.

The weir on the Po. (From a painting by Richard Wilson. Bridgeman Art Library, CH 019515)

The plain which was Cisalpine Gaul is bisected by the Po, the longest river in Italy. It rises in the Monte Viso group of the Cottian mountains and empties into the Adriatic after running a course of some 405 miles. In its upper reaches it is fast and precipitous for the first 22 miles. It then meanders, its course taking it, first, in a south-easterly direction and then north through Turin, before resuming its generally eastward line. Historically, it has constituted a challenging obstacle to many armies but its crossing is not insuperable.

The main channel of the river separated the Celts. On the northern bank, with some minor tribes, were to be found the Insubres, the largest and most powerful tribe of all, and the Cenomani. The Insubres had initially crossed from Gaul via the Taurine Pass. They founded a tribal capital at Mediolanium, modern-day Milan, some 20 miles east of the river Ticinus. They were friendly to Carthage and firmly hostile to Rome, having been defeated by them in a battle at Clastidium four years earlier. Their neighbours, the Cenomani, were declared allies of the Romans. They had supported them in 225 BC in their war against the Insubres and the Boii, and were to do so in 218 BC against Hannibal. Their territory lay around Lake Garda, broadly bounded by the Po, the Oglio and Adige rivers.[8]

On the opposite, southern, bank of the Po, amongst the first Celtic settlers to arrive, were the Anares and, later, the Boii, followed by the Lingones. Livy relates how they came over the Poenine Pass, by Mount Saint Bernard and, finding the northern plain was already occupied, they crossed the river on rafts and 'expelled not the Etruscans only, but the Umbrians as well: they did not, however, pass south of the Apennines'. Originally, a further tribe, the Senones, had moved into this southern area of the Po basin, establishing themselves on the Adriatic coast between Ariminum, today Rimini, and Ancona. The Senones, together with the Lingones, are said to have taken part in the sack of Rome in 390 BC but both peoples were subjugated before the arrival of Hannibal, the Senones capitulating in 283 BC and the Lingones as recently as 224. Their colonisation of Senones territory thus provided the Romans with tactical access to the river waters of the Po, as well as the ability to 'turn' the north-eastern flank of the Apennines and open the way to Placentia by extending the *Via Flaminia*. This strategic highway, completed in 220 BC, connected the city of Rome with Ariminum.

The second sector which Hannibal would have considered when making his operational plans was separated from Cisalpine Gaul by the Ligurian mountains, a rough-hewn and rugged area lying at the western end of the Apennine range, where it meets with the Maritime Alps. This was the home of the Ligurian people, a hardy, warrior hill tribe, already providing mercenary soldiers for service with the Carthaginians both in Spain and North Africa. Some had recently participated in the siege of Saguntum. In the west, their territory reached beyond the foothills of the Maritime Alps, towards the Rhône estuary. In the east, it extended to the Ligurian *emporium* at Genoa, situated at the northern end of the Tyrrhenian Sea. The tribe comprised numerous clans, one of the most important of whom, from the viewpoint of both Carthage and Rome, were the piratical Ingauni who occupied the generally inaccessible coastline between modern-day Monaco and Genoa. It was, by its very nature, bereft of harbour facilities: this fact, together with lack of communications across the mountainous hinterland and piratical dangers at sea, added logic to the Roman seizure of Sardinia.

Hannibal, so we are informed by Polybius,[9] had, in the period leading up to his campaign,

> . . . thoroughly informed himself of the regions at the foot of the Alps and near the river Po, the density of the population, the bravery of its men in war, and above all of their hatred of Rome, which had persisted since the earlier war . . . Hannibal therefore harboured great hopes of the tribes, and had been at pains to send envoys who bore lavish promises to the Celtic chieftains, both those living south of the Alps and those who inhabited the mountains themselves. He was convinced he could only carry the war against the Romans into Italy if, after having overcome the difficulties of the route, he could reach the territories of the Celts and engage them as allies and partners . . .

Hannibal set forth from his base at New Carthage, today known as Cartagena, some time at the end of May or early June, 218 BC. Under his command he had a force of 90,000 foot soldiers and 12,000 cavalry. Livy records that it marched in three divisions, probably in three columns, each following in the footsteps of the other. Neither Livy nor Polybius make mention of elephants at this moment:[10] this may be an oversight but it is equally likely that, due to the distances to be marched, they were carried by sea to Emporiae, a seaport near the Iberian frontier with Gaul, about 75 miles north-east of Barcelona. Initially a colonial foundation of Massilia, it displayed unwavering loyalty to Rome. Today it is known as Ampurias.

Polybius, writing in Greek, quotes all his distances in *stades*, there being 9 *stades* to 1 English mile. He gives the distance from Cartagena to the Ebro as being 2,600 *stades*, roughly 290 miles. Hannibal's marching columns, together with heavy baggage, even given an unopposed advance, are unlikely to have covered much more than 10 miles a day,[11] suggesting that he would have arrived on the line of the Ebro by the beginning of July. None of the ancient historians provide us with any explanation as to how his three 'divisions' were fed. South of the Ebro he may well have depended upon forward supply dumps, created in friendly villages, where he could restock his baggage train. North of the river, in potentially hostile territory, it is probable that he carried a full baggage train and was resupplied by sea at predetermined points. This would have ensured Hannibal a dependable supply arrangement, whilst providing him with operational mobility.

The distance from the Ebro to Emporiae was 1,600 *stades* (about 180 miles). Polybius makes clear that Hannibal's progress, during this stage, was not easy. His determination to secure his lines of communication with New Carthage brought him into conflict with several tribes and he had been compelled to take several cities by storm. He had thus been involved in 'heavy fighting', with resultant 'severe losses', but Polybius opines that, despite all, he made remarkable speed. Nevertheless, these losses, together with the thought of the march which lay ahead, caused a number of his Spanish troops, such as those who had been forcibly drafted from the Oretani and the Carpetani, to become restless and question their participation in an operation for which they had little or no enthusiasm. Hannibal, consequently, chose this moment to do some reorganisation. He delegated to Hanno, one of his senior commanders, the task of controlling, upon his departure, the mountain passes between Spain and Gaul and allocated to him a force of 10,000 infantry and 1,000 cavalry for this purpose. Simultaneously, he returned to New Carthage a contingent of 3,000 mutinous Carpetani, together with a further 7,000 men whom he knew to be restless about the thought of the campaign ahead. Then, having discarded his heavy baggage with Hanno, he pressed forward to cross the Pyrenees. Polybius[12] records that his strength at that moment comprised 50,000 foot soldiers and 9,000 cavalry. If these figures be accurate, the implication must be that he lost 20,000 infantry and 2,000 cavalry after leaving the Ebro and before entering Gaul. This is a large figure and we are left to surmise either that the fighting south of the Pyrenees was more severe than Polybius judged, or that his deserters were more numerous than have been accounted.

The pass by which Hannibal crossed the Pyrenean range is generally thought to have been the Col de Banyuls. This lies at a height of some 1,100 feet, is

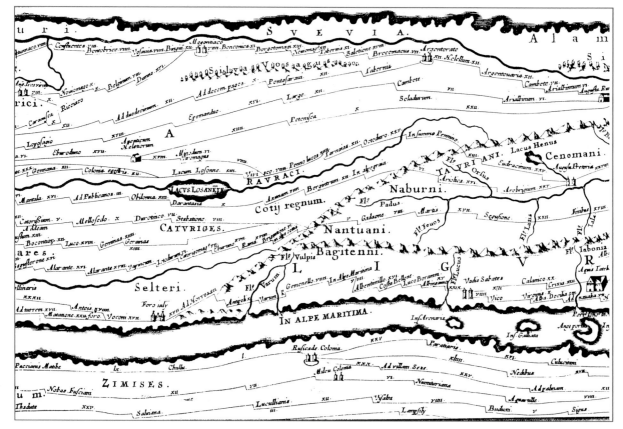

*Above and opposite:*
Peutinger's Map of the
Maritime Alps, and the
tribal areas in the Po valley
of northern Italy.

situated about 23 miles from Emporiae, and 20 miles from Illiberis, modern-day
Elne, where Hannibal is said to have encamped to rest and reorganise before
proceeding further. From here, after satisfying local Gallic chiefs that he came as
a friend and not a foe, he set out to complete the next phase of his march, 1,600
*stades* to the crossing of the Rhône. It is likely that he followed an ancient
trackway, the Iberian Way, which, a century later, was to be overlayed by the Via
Domitia. Today, it passes from the Spanish border through Elne, Perpignan,
Narbonne and Montpelier to Nîmes, at that time the capital city of the Volcae
and a short march from the Rhône crossing at Beaucaire-Tarascon.

At this point it must at once be said that little precise detail is known of the
direction taken by Hannibal across the Alps, neither of his crossing place over
the Rhône, nor of the river valley he is said to have pursued in his climb through
the foothills into the mountains, nor, again, of the mountain pass which led him
down into the Po valley. It is a matter which has been the subject of numerous
studies by generations of eminent historians, including Napoleon Bonaparte,
who, himself, led an army across the Alps. In Appendix A, I have listed some of
the options which have been canvassed and, as my readers will observe, the
variations are many, mostly highly convincing and written by knowledgeable
men, as will be noted from the bibliography. The very number of these works has
had the affect of clouding the discussion, which, nevertheless, still provokes

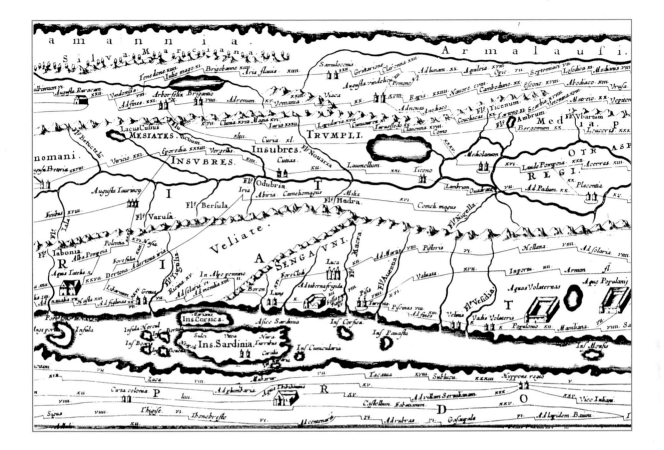

strong debate. It is not my intention to add to it, other than to outline a route
which responds to the military and other facts and which would have brought
Hannibal and his planners to their destination. There were three major factors
which would have limited their choices of direction, namely: the topography of
the land; the spread of the tribal territories, together with their loyalties; and, as
we shall later see, the surprise arrival of Cornelius Scipio in the river estuary,
whilst Hannibal was completing his crossing of the Rhône.

The Rhône, historically offering a gateway to Europe from the Mediterranean,
is the sole major European river to do so. It rises in central Switzerland, near the
Furka Pass, and then flows southwards, first through the Swiss canton of Vallais,
where it is fed from the surrounding mountains, and thence across Lake Geneva,
before cutting its way on a complicated course through the Jura mountains. It
then turns southwards to Lyons, where it receives a major tributary, the Saône.
The Rhône valley remains comparatively narrow until it reaches the coastal plain
near Orange and, again, at Arles, where it forms a delta. In this southern reach
of the river, where Hannibal made his crossing, it receives powerful tributaries
from the Alps, namely the Isère, the Durance and the Ardèche, as well as some
minor tributaries. In broad terms, the rate of flow of Alpine rivers, such as these,
hits a peak between the end of May and early June, when they are fed by melting
ice and snow. Additionally, the Durance also peaks between the end of

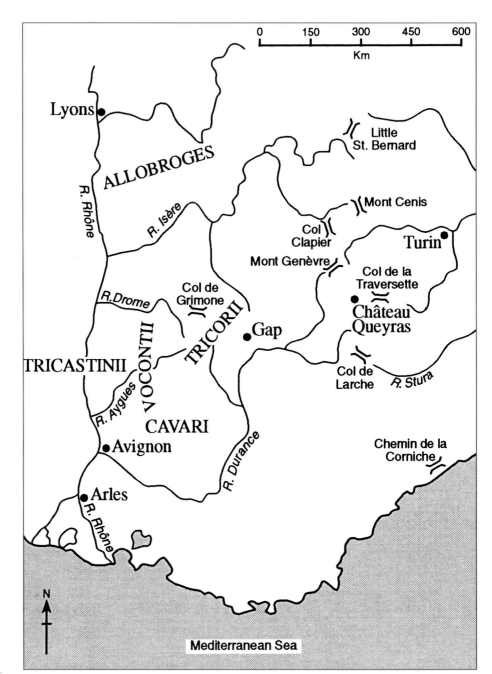

Map showing the rivers of
the Rhône valley.

November and early December in its lower reaches, where it receives a tributary
fed by rain rather than by melting glaciers and snow.[13]

The Volcae, whose territory Hannibal entered as he approached the Rhône,
were amongst the tribes resident at that time along the banks of the river. They
formed a powerful grouping with settlements on both banks, but mainly on the
west. Their homelands extended northwards to Pont Saint Esprit and from there
westwards to Toulouse, the latter being the capital of one of two sub-tribes, the

The amphitheatre at Orange, a city in Cavari territory through which Hannibal marched on his way into Italy. (Jonathan Falconer)

Tectosages. They did not easily accept the arrival of Hannibal and, according to Livy, would have resisted him directly had they felt competent to do so. Upon his approach, the majority of their number, determined to oppose him, crossed to the eastern bank of the Rhône in order to use it as an obstacle and to better obstruct his progress. Those of the Volcae who remained behind, however, proved cooperative and willingly helped with the provision of timber and the construction of rivercraft to assist Hannibal's passage.

Two main tribes occupied the opposing, east, bank of the Rhône. These were, firstly, the Sallyes, whose lands extended northwards from the coast, for a distance of some 50 miles, to the line of the Druentia, nowadays the Durance river. Beyond this, between the Durance and the Isère (then the Isar) lay the territory of the Cavari. The Isère provided the northern boundary of Cavari territory, and its lower reaches separated them from the Allobroges. Upstream, the demarcation line provided by the valley became less clear and was the cause of constant friction between the two peoples, of whom the Allobroges held the reputation of being uneasy, frequently hostile, neighbours. The Cavari were a tribe of considerable consequence. They occupied the whole of the land on the east side of the Rhône, between Cavaillon on the Durance and the confluence of the Rhône with the Isère, just north of Valence. They possessed suzerainty over

The amphitheatre at Nîmes, the capital city of the Volcae and situated a strategically short distance from the Rhône crossing. (Jonathan Falconer)

numerous minor tribes and the central towns of Avignon and Orange, which are generally assigned to them, may have been their capital cities.

Hannibal crossed the Rhône towards the end of September. He had the option, after leaving Nîmes, of heading for one of two crossing places. We are not told which one he selected. It seems reasonable to assume that, with such large numbers and in comparatively peaceful country, he would have used traditional routes to take him to his destination. The first of these, lying due east of the city, would have carried him to Beaucaire, across the Rhône to Tarascon, and thence along the traditional trackway towards Liguria and the Maritime Alps: but there are two arguments which suggest he did not come this way. Firstly, he was about to have a seemingly preplanned meeting with Celtic chieftains, north from here, in Cavari territory; secondly, the Durance, only 12 miles north of this crossing point, would, as we have already seen, have been running in full spate at that time of the year and would have provided him with another obstacle to cross as he made his way northwards. Alternatively, he could have avoided the need of two river crossings by marching north-east from Nîmes to Roquemaure, on the Rhône; from thence, he could have made his way across the river, north of the Durance, in the direction of the Cavaran cities of Avignon and Orange.

His crossing, as we are aware, was opposed by hostile tribesmen, mainly

*Opposite*: Arles, in ancient times probably a Greek trading post, has always been an important communications centre and river port. After Hannibal's War, it fell under Roman influence, the imprint of which may be seen to this day. (Roger Day)

Volcae. Hannibal foresaw that his men could be picked off piece-meal, as they came ashore, if he launched an attack from a frontal position and, for this reason, he determined to pause before forcing the passage. He withdrew and provided one of his generals, Hanno, the son of Bomilcar, with a contingent of infantry, gave him native guides and sent him off on an out-flanking march with instructions to get his party across upstream. Hanno was then to return along the opposite bank and, when ready to assault, was to notify Hannibal by smoke signal. The arrangements worked perfectly. Hanno divided his party into two elements, the larger part to attack the tribal army from the rear and the smaller to set fire to the enemy encampment. His intervention created such confusion that Hannibal was given time and space in which to form up his first division as it came ashore. The enemy, outmanoeuvred, took to flight, allowing the Carthaginians to complete their passage without further interruption.

Hanno's march, with his subsequent return along the opposite bank, is noteworthy, for Polybius records that he marched upstream for 200 *stades* before crossing the Rhône, a distance which, measured from Beaucaire, would have placed him well north of the Durance and separated by it from his master, if Hannibal had opted for the Beaucaire-Tarascon passage. Moreover, if Hanno had been required to negotiate the Durance before getting into his assault positions, his whole operation could have been placed in jeopardy had he been observed whilst doing so. It may, therefore, be judged that Hannibal opted to take the northern passage from Roquemaure. Hannibal camped that night beside the Rhône. The following day was to prove long and eventful.

At first light, he commenced the task of rafting his elephants across the water: jetties, 60 feet long, were constructed, jutting out into the river. The animals were lured on to the structures by cow elephants and, from thence, on to firmly attached rafts, disguised by quantities of earth levelled on their surface. These were then cut adrift and pulled across the water by tow ropes from the far bank. Whilst this work was progressing, the surprising intelligence was received that a Roman fleet of sixty ships, carrying Cornelius Scipio, with a consular army of two Roman legions, together with 14,000 allied foot and 2,200 horse, had arrived in the Rhône estuary. They had sailed from Pisa and were belatedly making their way to Spain, when Scipio received the news, perhaps from Massilia, that Hannibal had crossed the Pyrenees. Scipio, at once anticipating his destination and in the hope of intercepting him, disembarked at the mouth of the eastern Rhône, possibly at Fos-sur-Mer, from where, whilst his heavy baggage was being unloaded, he despatched a cavalry patrol of 300 horse northwards to the Rhône crossing places to seek intelligence.

Hannibal, for his part, upon receiving news of the Roman presence, despatched a fighting patrol of 500 Numidian horsemen to discover the precise whereabouts and intentions of the enemy. The two patrols encountered each other a comparatively short distance from the Carthaginian camp and, after a savage fight, the Numidians fled, being pursued by the Romans until they were in sight of their enemy's gates. They had inflicted a loss of some 200 men upon the Numidians, whilst they themselves had received proportionately the same: they had also located the enemy force. They now returned to Scipio to make

Numidian horseman on a coin (end of third century BC). (© British Museum)

their report. Their timings to and from Hannibal's crossing place suggest that Scipio, with his shipping if he were wise, had followed them upstream. When he heard what they had to say, he marched at once but arrived to find the Carthaginian encampment empty and their army three days' march ahead of him, reportedly heading for the Alps.

Scipio now made a brilliant decision which, despite the fact that the war was yet to last for a further sixteen years, nevertheless was to have an impact on its final outcome. He decided that he himself would return at once to Italy with a small body of men to take command of the army, in northern Italy, currently engaged in a frontier war with the Boii. Upon arrival there, he would then advance into the Po plain, where he would wait for Hannibal to emerge from the Alps. Importantly, however, and despite the fact that he had determined to return to Italy to undertake this particular mission, which in itself was farsighted but doomed to failure, he handed over command of his army to his brother, Gnaeus. He instructed him to continue onwards to Spain, where, upon arrival, he was to carry the war to Hasdrubal, in command of New Carthage and Hannibal's home base.

Meantime, whilst he had been awaiting the return of his cavalry patrol, Hannibal paraded his army so that they might be addressed by the delegation from Cisalpine Gaul, which, headed by Magilus of the Boii peoples, had arrived from the Po valley. They had been awaiting Hannibal's arrival, presumably in townships of the friendly Cavari, and now emerged to offer greetings and advice for the road to their Carthaginian allies. Polybius[14] tells us:

> What most encouraged his men was first of all an actual sight of the envoys who had invited them to come this far and now promised to join them in the war against Rome, and secondly, the confidence they could feel in the promises of the Gauls to guide them by a route on which they would be abundantly supplied with necessities and which would lead them rapidly and safely to Italy. Besides this, the envoys had much to say of the size and the wealth of the country where they were going and the eager spirit of the men who would fight by their side against the Romans.

When Hannibal received news of the cavalry patrol encounter and learnt that Scipio was on the march in his direction, he was tempted, in Livy's words,[15] to give battle to the first Roman force that chanced his way but was dissuaded from doing so by the arrival of the Celts from Cisalpine Gaul, who argued 'that the invasion of Italy should be his sole objective, to be undertaken without any frittering away of his strength'. Livy, however, does not express the full strength of Hannibal's dilemma. From the commencement of his operation, even before his departure from New Carthage, the security of his home base and its ability to get reinforcements to him, even into the heart of Italy, had formed one of the main planks of his operational plan. To this end, he had left Hasdrubal with a substantial army supported by a powerful fleet. He had been heedful to handle the Spanish element of his army with care, sending some home when he reached the Pyrenees, so as to hold out a good prospect of leave, 'not only for those who were serving with him but for those who remained behind, so that if he were ever in need of reinforcements they

A typical view of countryside in the Rhône estuary, where Publius Scipio came ashore in an effort to intercept Hannibal as he crossed the river upstream, east of Nîmes. (Roger Day)

would all enthusiastically respond'.[16] He had also, according to Livy, upon departing the Pyrenees, safeguarded his own lines of communication with New Carthage by leaving under one of his commanders, Hanno,[17] a force of 10,000 foot 'to keep control of the passes between the provinces of Spain and Gaul'. Now, with the arrival of Scipio, he was confronted by a Roman army bound for Spain, where its arrival could upset all these carefully laid arrangements.

Hannibal thus contemplated turning back to engage Scipio. His army, now reduced to 38,000 infantry and 8,000 horse,[18] would still have outnumbered that of Scipio, particularly in the cavalry arm, which was traditionally more skilled as well as more numerous than the Roman. He would, on the other hand, almost certainly have been aware that in Cisalpine Gaul, his allies, impatiently pre-empting his arrival, were already rising, and had indeed defeated troops, under praetor Lucius Manlius, who had been despatched by Rome to watch over the establishment of the new 'colonial' townships of Placentia and Cremona. He decided to avoid combat and commenced his move towards the Alps, with his cavalry arm and his elephants providing a rearguard in case of an unexpected intervention by Scipio. It was a decision which, in later years, he might have regretted.

Hannibal now marched for four days along the Rhône and, when he reached an area of countryside known as 'The Island', the precise whereabouts of which has been extensively argued, he paused, at the request of a local chieftain, to arbitrate in a dispute between two brothers regarding their succession to the throne. In itself, it was a small affair but its importance to Hannibal lay in the large quantities of corn and other foodstuffs which were provided for his army as a reward for his intervention. Polybius relates that the new ruler not only renewed their old and worn out weapons but 'supplied most of Hannibal's troops with new clothes and boots, which were of the greatest help to them in their crossing of the Alps'. Then, as a final gesture of gratitude, he loaned his troops to the Carthaginians to watch over the rear of their column as it passed through the territory of the Allobroges.[19]

This escort of friendly troops covered Hannibal's advance to the foothills of the Alps and then turned back. From that point forward, almost to the summit, which he is estimated to have reached in early November, over a period of about five weeks, Hannibal's column, as it ground its way slowly upwards, was continuously harried by Allobroges tribesmen, with their allies. Their tactic of attacking the marching column in several places at once, on narrow mountain roads flanked with steep precipices, inflicted particularly heavy casualties on both men and animals as they were forced off the road to their deaths. Polybius vividly describes how wounded horses were the chief cause of confusion: maddened by pain, they would wheel around and collide with the baggage mules, whilst others, dashing on ahead and thrusting everything aside in panic, would spread disorder along the length of the column.

Hannibal crossing the Alps. (From a painting by Jacopo Amigoni. Bridgeman Art Library, JAL 61188)

Early nineteenth century engraving showing Hannibal on the summit of his pass over the Alps, pointing out the plain of Piedmont and the direction of Rome. (Istria Romana, 1818)

As they progressed upwards, there now came a fresh fall of snow, which covered the frozen thaw they had been negotiating and added to their dangers. Men and animals alike fought to maintain their foothold on the steep slopes across which they were marching. Those who fell were catapulted downwards, clutching at whatever they could to break their slide and then in order to return, were compelled to make their way laboriously upwards on their hands and knees. The soldiers were near despair but worse was to come. As they approached the high pass, a 300-yard stretch of road had collapsed from the face of the mountain. Hannibal promptly set his men to work building up the path and in one day had made a track wide enough to take the mule train and the horses. It was to take three more days before the elephants could get across. By now, they were in a miserable condition from hunger.

Thus Hannibal's climb to the summit had not been easy. Opposed by hostile tribesmen, misled by untrustworthy guides, beset by the snows of an early winter and finding himself on a mountain path totally unsuited for the passage of his elephants, animal transport and cavalry, he had sustained the morale of his army, recruited from many different races, by a display of remarkable leadership. At last, he made it through the final pass but with a serious loss of both animals and men. Then, in a gesture designed to restore his soldiers' spirit, he gathered them around him, pointed out the direction of Rome and reminded them of the treasures, wealth and other attractions locked up behind its city walls, awaiting their pleasure.

As with every other aspect of Hannibal's route through the Alps, there has been much debate on the whereabouts of the pass through which he and his army finally emerged. Five mountain passes exist which might have served his purpose. These are, from north to south, the Little Saint Bernard, the pass at Mont Cenis, the Col du Clapier, the Mont Genevre and the Col de la Traversette. From a total of twenty-four modern-day historians who have recorded their conclusions,[20] four have selected the Little Saint Bernard as most likely; six, Mont Cenis; five, Col du Clapier; six, the Mont Genevre; and three, la Traversette. Napoleon Bonaparte, who wrote from personal experience, declared for Mont Cenis as Hannibal's pass.

There are two distinctive features of the pass we are seeking. The first is the sloping mountainside upon which Hannibal's column found itself ensnared before reaching the summit and which we have looked at above. Two such places have been identified, one on the Col du Clapier and the other on the Col de la Traversette. The second feature is the view from the summit. Polybius[21] relates that, when Hannibal gathered his men around him, and addressed them in an effort to restore their morale,

> . . . he relied above all on the sight of Italy, which now stretched out before them, for the country lies so closely under these mountains that when the two are seen simultaneously in a panoramic view, the Alps seem to rise above the rest of the landscape, like a walled citadel above a city. Hannibal therefore directed his men's gaze towards the plains of the Po, and reminded them of the welcome they would receive from the Gauls who inhabit them. At the same time, he pointed out the direction of Rome itself . . .

If we are seeking validity for the requirement of a panoramic view, it may be found in Polybius' assurance that on these matters he could 'speak with confidence', since he had 'enquired about the circumstances from eye-witnesses and personally inspected the country' to learn and see for himself. We may judge, therefore, that the description, given by Polybius and quoted above, of the ground seen by Hannibal when addressing his soldiery, was also a description of that seen by Polybius during his subsequent visit and recorded in his annals. The summits of both the Col du Clapier and the Col de la Traversette command a wide view of the plain, which, in each instance, lies some 30 miles distant.

The further north one progresses from these two passes, the greater becomes the distance to the plain. Because of this, the Great Saint Bernard may almost immediately be dismissed from consideration. There are other reasons: it lies on the Italian–Swiss border, east of the Mont Blanc group of mountains and, according to Livy,[22] it is most unlikely that these more northern passes into Gaul would at that time have been open due to the hostility 'of the half German tribes' which inhabited them. The Little Saint Bernard pass, for its part, lies between the Mont Blanc massif and the Graian Alps, and it is known, in ancient times, to have provided one of the main routes over the Alps, frequently used by Gallic tribes in their movements to and from Gaul. Located in the western foothills of

Monument of St Bernard at the summit of Little Saint Bernard. (H.C. Randall)

Little Saint Bernard pass.
(H.C. Randall)

the Alps, confronting the Rhône, it links with the Isère river valley and in the east
with the Val d'Aosta. It is well worthy of consideration as a candidate for
Hannibal's pass but it has to be said that both of the Saint Bernard passes lie
deep in the northern mountains and hills, away from Turin. The scene described
by Polybius would not have been seen from either one of them.

Further south again, and from the earliest times, the Mont Cenis pass was also a
well-used invasion route. Geographically, it links the Arc valley of Savoy with the
valley of the river Susa in Italian Piedmont. It possesses a distinctive plateau near its
summit, which also provides the environment for a large natural lake but no such
features were mentioned by either Polybius or Livy. This apart, Mont Cenis, as we
have already noted, was Napoleon Bonaparte's chosen candidate and therefore
must be considered a contender, for it lies close to Turin and possesses the view
qualification we are seeking. There is, however, yet one more piece of evidence to
be considered, namely, Hannibal's behaviour upon arrival in Cisalpine Gaul.

Hannibal had crossed the Ebro with an army of 90,000 infantry and 12,000
cavalry. The whole march from New Carthage had taken him five months and
the 'actual' crossing of the Alps, fifteen days. Now, if Polybius is to be believed,[23]
as the Carthaginian army debouched on to the Po plain, its fighting strength had
been dramatically reduced to 12,000 African and 8,000 Spanish infantry with
'not more than 6,000 cavalry in all'. The men were demoralised and exhausted
and, according to Livy, 'filthy and unkempt as savages'. Plainly, Hannibal needed
urgent administrative help but, since none of our ancient historians relate where

Col de Cenis. (H.C. Randall)

Lake on the summit of
Mont Cenis, showing the
site of the ancient shelter.
(H.C. Randall)

he went to find it, we can only conjecture. He received none from the Taurini. Livy tells us that they were at war with the Insubres at this moment and, if so, this might have worked to Hannibal's advantage. Polybius is more restrained: he simply relates that, after emerging from the mountains and whilst rehabilitating his troops, Hannibal learnt that 'the tribe of the Taurini, who lived at the foot of the Alps, had fallen out with the Insubres and were inclined to be suspicious of the Carthaginians'. Livy,[24] on the other hand, suggests that Hannibal was at this time reinforced by the arrival of Gallic and Ligurian troops. If this were true, it points to Hannibal's early contact with the Ligures, whose territories extended to the southern boundaries of the Taurini and, significantly, adjoined the Col de la Traversette. Perhaps they also helped him in other, practical ways.

The unfriendliness of the Taurini, combined with his own weakness and the knowledge that a Roman army was operating in the Po valley, must have been a matter of deep concern to Hannibal. There was nothing he could immediately have

The Col de la Traversette,
after Gavin de Beer.

done about it but, as soon as he and his men had been rested and re-equipped, he appears once again to have offered friendship to the Taurini, possibly as a test of their political inclination. When they once more rejected his overtures, he laid siege to their capital city, modern Turin, and captured it within three days, putting to the sword all those who resisted him and setting a fearful example to any others who might have felt fit to emulate their behaviour. This was a brutal act but not unusual when set against the military standards of the day: but brutal or otherwise, Hannibal would have been foolish indeed to have resumed his advance, leaving the Taurini, hostile, unheeded and astride his lines of withdrawal.

The remainder of the Celtic population on the plain, so Polybius relates,[25] had been eager from the outset to join the Carthaginians but 'the Roman legions had advanced beyond the territory of most of them and now stood between them and their would-be allies'. At their head stood Publius Cornelius Scipio.

Scipio had reacted to Hannibal's thrust for the Po valley with remarkable speed. Upon his return to Italy from the Rhône estuary he landed, possibly at Genoa, and thence made his way, probably by means of the river valley linking Genoa with Placentia, immediately to assume command of a body of inexperienced troops still recovering from the rough handling they had received from the Cisalpine Gauls in the recent uprising. He then moved his new command across the Po by means of a boat bridge. When that position had been consolidated he advanced to negotiate the Ticinus. Here he constructed yet another pontoon bridge and secured his retreat by providing it with a block house to guard its western approach. Scipio's action in moving to interpose himself between the Carthaginians and the Ticinus is noteworthy because it underlines what he perceived to be Hannibal's intention at this stage, namely, to get his army across the Ticinus and join forces with the Insubres. Both commanders now advanced to encounter each other, marching along the line of the north bank of the Po.

The so-called battle of the Ticinus was in reality fought out between the cavalry arms of both sides. The Roman horse advanced at a slow pace, with their Gallic cavalry in the van, supported by a contingent of javelin throwers. Hannibal charged the Romans at the gallop, using his heavy cavalry for his main assault whilst his light horse made for the enemy's rear. The Roman spearmen withdrew through the ranks of their horse at their first sight of the Carthaginian cavalry and the encounter was quickly over, with Scipio being wounded in the fight which ensued. Indeed, he would have been captured by the Carthaginians had not his young son, later the famous Scipio Africanus, ridden with his squadron into the heart of the action to extricate his father. Scipio now hastily withdrew, firstly across the Ticinus and then to the south bank of the Po, dismantling his pontoon bridges as he went, but he did not move fast enough. Hannibal followed up his success with such speed that he was able to capture the troops left behind by Scipio to cover his withdrawal. Hannibal's reputation was further enhanced by two other pieces of good fortune. The Roman grain store at Clastidium, modern-day Casteggio, was betrayed to him and no doubt, at this juncture, its contents were gratefully received; and his ranks were one night swelled by the desertion to him of 2,000 of Scipio's Gallic auxiliaries.

Aerial view of modern Turin, the ancient capital of the Taurini sacked by Hannibal in 218 BC upon descending from the Alps into the Po valley. (By courtesy of the Italian State Tourist Board (E.N.I.T.) London)

It is noteworthy that, during his invasion of Italy across the Alps in 1800, Napoleon opened his campaign with almost identical moves to those of Hannibal. First, he thrust at Turin, at that time the headquarters of the Austrian army, whilst another of his columns, under General Murat, seized an enemy bridgehead confronting Piacenza, a *tête-de-pont* which safeguarded an enemy pontoon bridge across the river. This local success gave Napoleon command of the road and river communications linking the Trebbia valley with Genoa, previously used by Scipio in his move to the Po plain. Then, turning abruptly, he marched upon Milan, thus compelling his enemy to concentrate his forces and defend the passage of the Ticinus. It was an intervention which he appears to have brushed aside without great effort. Thus the three places of encounter between Scipio and Hannibal many centuries earlier also featured importantly in the mind of Napoleon Bonaparte. This, it will be recognised, was not fortuitous: rather, it is yet another example of the timeless manner in which the nature of ground dictates military action.

CHAPTER III

# THE ENEMY

Here I should like to demonstrate from the actual facts of the situation how great was the power which Hannibal later ventured to attack, and how mighty was the empire which he boldly faced when he almost achieved his objective, and in any event inflicted great disasters on Rome.

Polybius[1]

'Italy', Napoleon Bonaparte wrote in his Memoirs, 'is surrounded by the Alps and the sea. Her natural limits are determined with the same precision as those of an island'.[2] This very simple definition, written through the eighteenth-century eyes of a master of land warfare, could equally have been applied to Hannibal's Roman Italy: but the Carthaginian himself would probably more truly have seen the land mass as a peninsula, jutting into the warm waters of the Mediterranean and thrusting towards his homeland on the northern coastline of Africa. At this point, it was separated by little more than 85 miles, measured from Lilybaeum on the most westerly coast of Sicily. Lilybaeum, initially founded in 396 BC by Carthage to replace Motya, after the latter had been overrun by Dionysius, was a long-established and important trading port which, under siege both by Pyrrhus (276 BC) and the Romans (250–242 BC), had on each occasion displayed its worth as a formidable and impregnable military stronghold. It was now no longer Carthaginian territory. In accordance with the terms of the treaty she had signed upon the conclusion of the First Punic War, Carthage had ceded her interest in Sicily in favour of Rome, together with her rights in the adjoining Aegates and Liparean groups of islands.

Sicily, because of its influential maritime position in the Mediterranean, not only dominated the sea passage between the peninsula and North Africa but also provided harbourage for shipping plying between the Tyrrhenian and Adriatic Seas. This was important in those early days of sail because of the effects of prevailing winds and currents upon passage times. Thus, the island grew in its strategic importance to the Roman people as they progressively tightened their grip on the Italian mainland and sought to extend a controlling hand to the Po estuary and north-eastern Italy, beyond the Ionian Sea. Moreover, Sicily, with its uncertain history as a home for outpost city states founded upon differing national trading allegiances, was only thinly separated from the toe of Italy; it was almost possible, at its narrowest point, to cast a stone across the straits

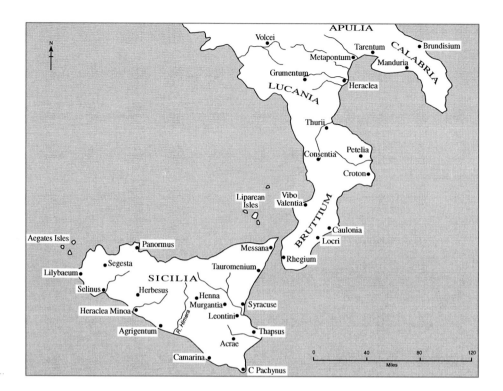

Map showing southern
Italy and Sicily.

between Messina and Rhegium. On this scale, the intervening waters presented
no great obstacle to an invading force.

For all these reasons, Rome became compelled not only to recognise the threat
posed by the island to her security if occupied by a hostile power but also to
appreciate the strategic and economic advantages it would offer if held in her
own hands. To this end, the door was opened for her by Hiero II of Syracuse. He
had initially allied himself to the Carthaginians when Rome availed herself of an
early pretext to seize Messina. However, in the ensuing fighting, the alliance was
defeated. Subsequently, doubtless impressed by her determination and scale of
resources and, indeed, by her very proximity, Hiero came to recognise Rome as a
more dependable ally. He signed a peace agreement with her and, in the event,
the practical support and friendship of the Syracusan people in the early years of
the Hannibalic War provided Rome with a vital key to her ultimate success.
Upon Hiero's death, in 215 BC, Rome annexed the whole of the island for her
own. It was a troublesome year which, apart from her problems with Hannibal,
saw her entering into war with Macedonia and, once again, with Syracuse; but
from both conflicts she emerged successful.

On Rome's eastern frontiers, beyond the Ionian and Adriatic Seas, lay a
worrysome grouping of Hellenistic nations, Istria, Illyricum, Epirus, Macedonia
and Achaea, the powers of many of which at this moment were in decline, a
circumstance exacerbated by an extraordinarily widespread change of leadership
and policies across the Mediterranean. Seleucus III of Syria had been assassinated
in 223 BC. Two years later, Ptolemy III of Egypt had died after a period of

twenty-five years upon the throne. The same year had witnessed the passing of Antigonus of Macedon, who succumbed of a haemorrhage on the battlefield, whilst leading his army against the Illyrians. He was succeeded by Philip V, then only seventeen years of age. The Macedonians, under his youthful leadership, saw advantage in constantly seeking to exploit Rome's political and military difficulties and wasted little time in seeking to ally themselves to Hannibal. Illyricum and Istria had a reputation for piracy. Their activities interfered with Rome's merchant shipping trading in eastern Adriatic coastal waters and, in part, led to the First Illyrian War (229–228 BC). This was followed, some ten years later, in the summer of 219 BC, by the Second Illyrian War, its date coinciding with Hannibal's opening moves against Saguntum, the Roman satellite outpost west of the Ebro. In the words of Polybius,[3] the Senate, foreseeing a war with Carthage in Spain, which they anticipated 'would be both long and hard fought', decided to 'secure their position in Illyria', where Demetrius of Phars was looting and sacking Illyrian cities subject to Rome.

The Adriatic and Ionian Seas provided Rome with a light but important shield against the political and military ambitions of the Hellenic and Greek peoples, who, at an early date, had established a chain of trading posts along the 'instep' of Italy's foot and had thence continued this around 'the toe' and northwards, along her south-western coastline. The danger to Rome, implicit by the presence of these 'colony' towns, was revealed in 280 BC when the military support of Pyrrhus of Epirus was sought by the people of Tarentum, a Greek trading post established on the foot of the peninsula. The Tarentines were concerned with the pressures being exerted upon them by the inexorable march of Roman expansionism. Pyrrhus saw this appeal as an opportunity to extend his empire and was pleased to respond. He landed in southern Italy with an army of 20,000 hoplite mercenaries, 3,000 cavalry and a corps of elephants but enjoyed no great success. After a ferocious two-day battle with Rome at Ausculum in 279, at which he gained what has become known as a 'pyrrhic victory', he withdrew across the straits to Sicily but to little advantage. After a further defeat by the Romans at Beneventum in 275, on the road to Capua, he sailed back home, across the Adriatic. Upon his death, Epirus, exhausted by the energies of his reign, lost its zest for power.

To the west of Italy, in the Tyrrhenian Sea and broadly on a latitude with the central belt of the peninsula, lay the islands of Corsica and Sardinia, separated from the continental mainland to their north by the Ligurian Straits. These latter waters were, as with the Adriatic, troublesome and pirate infested, plagued by the activities of the Ingauni, a coastal tribe of the Ligures and declared enemies of Rome. From the east coast of Corsica, the distance to Etruria on Italian soil was some 50 miles, but the length of the sea passage could have been lessened if the isle of Elba were used as a stepping stone. Since the Italian mainland slanted away from both these islands in a south-easterly direction, the crossing from Sardinia was considerably greater in distance than from Corsica and this distinction multiplied as the island extended southwards. Clearly, any interference with Rome's unfettered use of

Pyrrhus defeating the Romans at the Battle of Heraclea. (By W. Bagdalopulos. The Mansell Collection)

these waters, either the Ligurian Straits or the Tyrrhenian Sea, would have been intolerable, particularly as it would ultimately have closed down her coastal sea lanes to Gaul, Massilia and Iberia. It is thus remarkable that the cession to her of the island of Sardinia had not initially formed a precondition of the Romano-Carthaginian peace treaty after the First Punic War. In the event, the realisation of its importance appears only to have dawned upon her after it had been signed and the seizure of the islands which then resulted appears to have provided a prime cause of the Hannibalic War.

Finally, in our glance at the strategically important features of the Italian peninsula, we come to the Apennine range, often mentioned as the backbone of Italy. We have already looked at its northern element, reaching from the Maritime Alps to Ariminum, modern-day Rimini. From that point, it extends southwards for 500 miles to reach the full length of the peninsula. It by no means forms an unbroken chain but comprises a tangle of mountains, with upland passes and fertile valleys. It boasts numerous offshoots, such as the Volscian Mountains and the Apulian Alps, and in at least one instance, in the shape of Mons Garganus, it includes a solitary mountain divorced from the main grouping. As the mountains descend towards the coasts, on both flanks of the peninsula, there are wide areas of level or near level land through which, in Hannibalic times, the Romans had already constructed important strategic highways radiating from Rome, such as the *Via Flaminia* to Ariminum, and the Appian and Latin Ways, which diverged outside Rome, to come together once more on the Volturnus, north of Capua, before running onwards, through Tarentum, to Brundisium.

The Apennines provide a high watershed area from which rivers flow, in the east, to feed the waters of the Adriatic, and in the west, to meet the Tyrrhenian Sea. They achieve their highest point, 9,650 feet, at the Gran Sasso, in the central massif of the range. In general terms, the mountains are not perennially snow-capped. Thus, in the summer months, many streams either become mere rivulets or dry up completely: but, apart from these, as the allied armies found to their cost in the Second World War, there are other, sizeable rivers originating on its slopes, the Sangro and the Pescara in the east, and the Volturnus, the Garigliano and the Arno in the west, being some of the larger known examples.

Another of these great rivers is the historic Tiber, upon whose banks the city of Rome arose and the benefits of which created the environment essential for her people's development to an imperial power. Livy,[4] the Roman historian, had a clear vision of the river's contribution to her greatness:

> Not without reason did gods and men choose the site of this spot for the site of our City – the salubrious hills, the river to bring us produce from the inland regions and seaborne commerce from abroad, the sea itself, near enough for convenience yet not so near as to bring danger from foreign fleets, our situation in the very heart of Italy – all these advantages make it of all places in the world the best for a city destined to grow great.

Strangely, the geographer Strabo (64 BC–AD 25) allowed no concession to the founding fathers of Rome for the shrewdness of their selection, recognised so clearly by his contemporary, Livy – but we should note that Strabo was of Greek nationality. The site of Rome, he tells us, was a place founded

Altitude in metres

Over 1000

200–1000

0–200

| 0 | 25 | 50 | 75 | 100 miles |

| 0 | 50 | 100 | 150 km |

by necessity (rather) than of choice; for neither was the site naturally strong, nor did it have enough land of its own in the surrounding territory to meet the requirements of a city, nor indeed people to join with the Romans as inhabitants; for the people who lived thereabouts were wont to dwell by themselves, though their territory almost joined the walls of the city that was being founded . . . [5]

Reverse of bronze coin of Antonius Pius, c. AD 150, showing Romulus and Remus being suckled by a she-wolf. (© British Museum)

Nevertheless, the geographical location which Rome occupied, on the Tiber, west of the Apennines, was greatly to her political advantage. She lay not only on a borderline between the Mediterranean maritime city states and a hinterland of relatively backward village communities, but also comfortably beyond the effective range of military aggression from most of her potential enemies. More locally, by chance or by the design of her founding fathers, the selection of her site on the largest river in peninsular Italy brought many benefits to later generations, both economic and military. One of these was its position on the lowest crossing place over the river, from where her people were able not only to control waterborne transport of every size moving to and from the sea and the Italian interior, but also to command the flow of traffic passing over the road bridge linking the two land regions divided by its waters. Pliny the Elder (AD 23–79), in his *Natural History*,[6] has left us a neat working description of the river which rises, he explains,

> . . . in Arretium [modern-day Arezzo], about the middle of the Apennines. At first it is a tiny stream navigable only where its waters are collected together in sluices and then discharged, just like its tributaries the Tinia and the Glanis, which have to be held back by dams for nine days unless rain come to the rescue. And even when it swells to a river, because of its rough and uneven bed for much of its distance, the Tiber can be navigated only by rafts, or more accurately logs. It flows 150 miles, not far from Tifernum, Perusia and Ocriculum, separating Etruria from the Umbrians and the Sabines. But, below the Glanis from Arretium, the Tiber is swollen by 42 tributaries, in particular the Nar and the Anio. The latter is navigable and encloses Latium to the rear . . .

The Tiber valley, as it curves beneath the walls of Rome, forms a deep rift, its edges shaped by steep, weathered cliffs deeply carved from the famous hills of Rome by the tributary streams tumbling down their slopes. It is here, a distance of some 15 miles from the coastal port of Ostia, that the yellow, muddy waters of the river shallow and divide around an island, to create, in either direction, the only ford between the sea and for many miles upstream beyond the city. It remains doubtful whether or not Ostia, by the outbreak of the Hannibalic War, had yet developed into the main seaport for Rome. The economic importance of the town was probably then still confined to the salt-pans created on the silt brought down from the mountains, the produce of which was despatched deep into the Italian interior, largely to the Sabine highlands. Nevertheless, Ostia had long been regarded as a strategic asset of the city state, essential to its future.

*Opposite*: Map of Italy.

Eighty years had already elapsed since its establishment as one of Rome's 'coastguard' colonies, to watch over the estuary. Meantime, Rome met her fast-growing needs for a commercial outlet by using the neighbouring ports of her ally, Caere, north of the colony, on the Tyrrhenian coast.

Northwards from the city, as the line of the river valley reached out towards Arretium, Rome enjoyed two other pieces of geographical good fortune brought to her by the presence of the Tiber. First, its basin provided an ancient highway through the Apennines, to Ariminum and the north-east coast of peninsular Italy, travelling by way of Perusia and Tiberinum and linking with the valley of the Mareschia as it descends the eastern slopes of the mountain range. Second, the western lowlands through which the Tiber flowed contained the major part of the peninsula's agricultural and mineral resources, much of which passed as trade down its waters into the very heart of the city. Conversely, these were resources which had much to offer an invader, a factor which created, over a period, a chain of responses, namely, the construction of the *Via Flaminia*,[7] the establishment of Rimini, an alliance with the Senones in the eastern Po basin and, ultimately, the setting up of two inland 'watchguard' (as opposed to 'coastguard') colonies, at Placentia and Cremona, to cover Rome's advance to the line of the Po and the associated extension of the *Via Flaminia*. In essence, Rome was quietly establishing a firm grasp on the strategically important open, eastern flank of the northern Apennines, an area which was as equally vital to them some 2,000 years ago as it was to the Allies in Italy during the Second World War, when Field Marshal Viscount Alexander and General Mark Clark successfully turned the Apennines and penetrated the Po valley.

Map showing the Po valley and south-east Gaul.

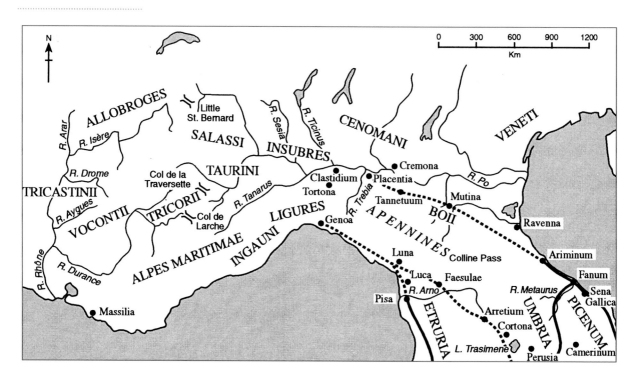

*Via Flaminia.* (By courtesy
of the Italian State Tourist
Board (E.N.I.T.) London)

Rome, thus, lies to the south of the Tiber basin, where the river bends sharply
westwards towards the coast, forming a cul-de-sac edged on one side by the
Tiber itself and on the other by the Tyrrhenian Sea. The city's defences were
bolstered by fortifications of formidable strength. Many of its most ancient walls
are traditionally attributed to king Servius Tullius, who died in 535 BC but
uncertainty is sometimes cast upon this claim. In the early 1980s,[8] a trench dug
at the foot of the Palatine hill revealed a high wall, about 5 feet thick and fronted
by a ditch, which, on good archaeological evidence was dated to 730–720 BC
and declared by many to be the original *pomerium*, marking the sacred boundary
of the city. Livy,[9] writing about Servian times records that, since the population
of Rome had become so great Servius decided to extend the city boundaries. He
accordingly took in two more hills and strengthened the city defences

> . . . by constructing trenches, earthworks and a wall. This involved extending
> the 'pomerium' – a term which needs some comment. By derivation the word
> is taken to mean the strip of ground 'behind the wall'; more properly, however,
> it signifies the strip on both sides of the wall: this ground the ancient Etruscans
> used to consecrate with augural ceremonies when a new town was to be
> founded . . . Its purpose was to keep the walls on their inner side clear of
> buildings (which nowadays are, as a rule, actually joined to them) and at the
> same to leave, on the other side of the walls, an area unpolluted by the use of

man . . . Whenever, with the growth of the city, it was proposed to increase the area enclosed within the walls, this strip of consecrated ground was pushed outward accordingly.

The remains of these workings reveal a simple earthen wall about 15 feet thick and 25 feet high, the exterior strength of which was yet further emphasised by a deeply dug defensive ditch. In part, the purpose of this rampart was to deter an enemy attack across the plateau from the north, where an area of level ground provided a platform from which to mount an assault. Its later development embraced five Roman hills, as well as the fortified Capitoline hill, and was designed to follow the contours of the high ground upon which it was erected, exploiting rock faces and sharp hill slopes wherever they existed. It was also sited to block the head of the valleys leading into the city from the interior of Latium. Despite the effort and thought put into these works, they were unsuccessful in preventing the sack of Rome, *c.* 387–386, when it fell to an army of 30,000 Celts from Cisalpine Gaul, under their king, Brennus, and a large area of it was burnt. As a consequence, eight years later, a massive new wall was constructed of volcanic stone from neighbouring Veii, but on this occasion its scope was enlarged to include the historic Seven Hills. The city's walls now encompassed an area of over 1,000 acres, were some 7 miles long and contained twelve gates, the sites of some of which remain conjectural. The whole works have since become recognised as one of the great defensive fortifications of the age and, when it comes to judging Hannibal's military intention upon invading Italy, it is important that this assessment of the city's defences should be remembered.

Napoleon Bonaparte, when regarding his Italian campaign of 1796, mentioned his unease at the possibility of finding himself trapped between the Po and the Trebbia, with his line of withdrawal across the Alps to France severed by his opponent. He was expressing the sensible fear of every commanding general under such circumstances. The terrain we have been examining, where the approach to Rome from her northern frontiers pursues a course through the western segment of the Tiber basin, would have presented a similar threatening possibility to Hannibal's army. Brennus, whose Celts sacked Rome in 386 BC, was successful in his operation because Rome had not yet accumulated the military resources she later possessed and because her commanders lacked faith in the walled defences of the city of the day.

By 218 BC, these defences had been improved and were considerable. By their very scale, they demanded much of an attacking force in terms of manpower and capability. Such a force would have had two alternatives: either to undertake a prolonged siege or to conduct a swift and overwhelming assault. If the first option were adopted, unrestricted time would have been an imperative, together with manpower of sufficient quantity to circumvallate and contain the city. In either case, possession of siege equipment, siege artillery and engines, with secure access to supplies of food, would have been essential. Even more importantly, if victory were achieved, a clear plan of subsequent action would have had to be in

place if the hunter were not to become the hunted. The sheer size of Rome, with her environs and the network of defensive arrangements she had created for herself, would have done little to ease these concerns in the mind of an invading general.

There were two other safeguards which Rome had set in place over the years, within her system of territorial defence, which were to play an important part, both offensive and defensive, in the operations yet to come. The first of these was a pattern of 'city state colonies', outposts with a garrison of varying size, but normally comprising some 300 men. [10] These were otherwise known as *coloniae civium Romanorum*, the community forming the settlement itself being frequently raised from time-expired soldiery with their families. Roman citizens were allowed to volunteer for garrison duties in these *coloniae*, whilst at the same time retaining their full rights as citizens of Rome. By this means, they were absolved from normal legionary service but, in exchange, they undertook a task, frequently in an exposed position, which was both dangerous and difficult.

*Coloniae* were 'planted out' for a variety of purposes but generally with the intention of solidifying local loyalty. In 311 BC, for example, a colony was established on the Pontian Islands in order to cover the seaward flank of the Roman army if its land communications were cut and it were required to move by sea. In 263 BC, other colonies were 'planted' in the heart of Samnium territory so as to separate their three troublesome cantons, the Cautini, the Samnites and the Hirpini. In 244 BC, Brundisium, an important colony, was set in place to command the Straits of Otranto from the Italian side. Again, in 218 BC, as we have already seen, Placentia and Cremona were created to provide a Roman presence in the Po plain, and doubtless with the dual role of giving military cover for the coming north-westerly extension of the *Via Flaminia*. Placentia, particularly,[11] lay in the heart of rich farm land, producing grain, cattle and wine in abundance, thus providing a third reason for its 'planting'. Other colonies, set up throughout the old Latin Confederation, were maintained as a visible sign of Roman support, with the aim of lending stability to the territory. Additionally, between the years 338–245 BC, Rome established ten 'coastguard' *coloniae* along her shores, with the duty of safeguarding harbour facilities for her use and keeping a watchful eye on her vital coastal sea lanes.

The second safeguard mentioned above comprised a pattern of treaty arrangements, effected with her Latin and non-Latin allies and observed with rigid application on both sides. These contained mutual emergency guarantees of military and material support based on population ratios. In 266 BC, these associated territories occupied some 80 per cent of the total area of the peninsula and their population amounted to about 71 per cent of the whole. In essence, it was agreed that, whenever Rome went to war, all her allies and non-allies alike would provide contingents of troops to be brigaded with the Roman army or navy, whichever might be geographically appropriate. Broadly, they were expected to surrender their control over foreign policy. In other respects, the sovereign rights of each state taking part in the arrangement would be generally respected and, although their units might be

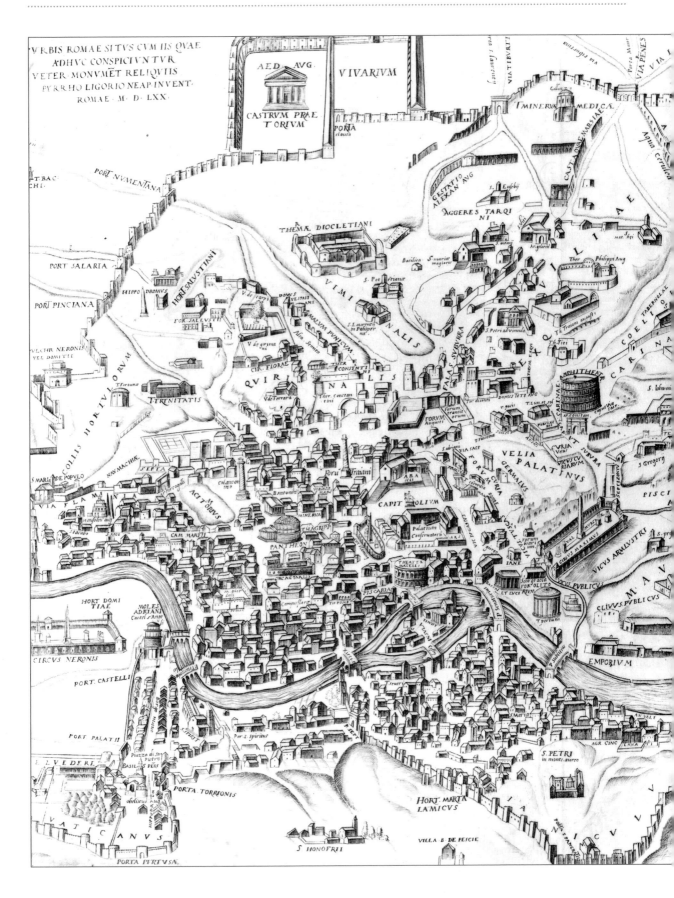

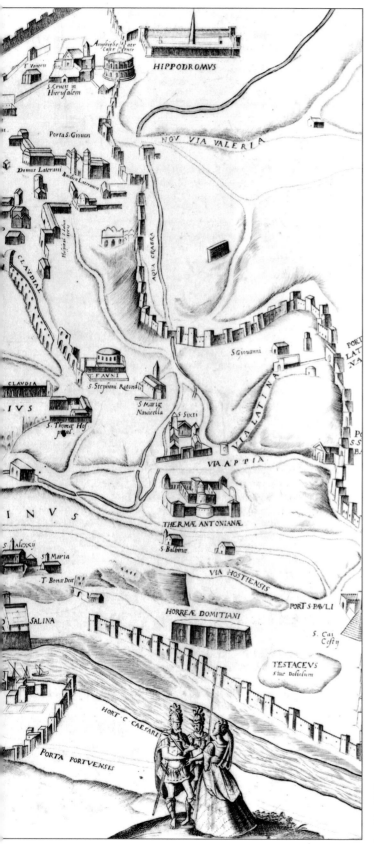

Map of Rome by
cartographer Joannis
Jansson, 1690. (BL. Maps
13.e.17 page 1)

embodied within a Roman formation, their soldiery would serve in self-contained national units under national officers. It was also agreed that each contingent would be raised as a specified proportion of a count of able-bodied men revealed by a periodical local census, undertaken by each of the states concerned. There is no clear evidence that Rome ever called for more than this agreed number but there is a hint that something of this nature may have happened in 209 BC when twelve Latin colonies, harried by Hannibal and taking concerted action, refused to raise any more men or money for their contingents.

An example of this mobilisation scheme in operation occurred in 225 BC, when a Gallic army of 50,000 infantry and 20,000 cavalry invaded the Italian peninsula. Rome at once invoked the treaty arrangements and called for an immediate return from each of the signatories, with details of the strengths they were expecting to contribute. According to Polybius,[12] all concerned responded without a moment's hesitation. They recognised that this was no instance of being asked to make a stand simply for Roman interests. On the contrary, as fellow inhabitants of the peninsula, they saw themselves under threat and as deeply involved as Rome herself. Help came pouring in without delay, 'stocks of corn, of missiles and other warlike stores were collected on a scale which exceeded any such preparations in living memory'.

An estimate of the total military manpower capable of being fielded by the Roman Commonwealth at this moment has been provided for us by Polybius.[13] He commences his detail with the statement that each of the two Roman consuls had entered the field against Hannibal with two legions 'of Roman citizens', each consisting of 5,200 infantry and 300 cavalry: he then adds that,

> . . . besides these, the allied forces for the two consular armies numbered 30,000 infantry and 2,000 cavalry. The cavalry of the Sabines and the Etruscans, who had rallied at once to the support of Rome, numbered 4,000 and their infantry over 50,000. The Romans formed these levies into an army and posted them on the Etrurian frontier under the command of a praetor. The Umbrians and Sarsinati, hill tribes of the Apennine mountains, raised a force of some 20,000, and with them were a further 20,000 men provided by the Veneti and the Cenomani. These troops were placed on the frontier of the Gauls' territory, so as to create a diversion by invading the lands of the Boii. These were the forces which protected the boundaries of Roman territory.

In addition to these manpower totals, Polybius lists the strengths of infantry and cavalry contingents undertaken to be provided by others of Rome's Italian allies[14] and points out that, taken all together, 'the number of Romans and their allies able to bear arms totalled more than 700,000 infantry and 70,000 cavalry, whereas Hannibal invaded Italy with an army of less than 20,000 men'. This latter strength is considerably smaller in number than the total he quoted as being the Carthaginian strength on the Trebbia in the previous year and we must

Table 1: Roman and Allied forces deployed 218 BC.

1. In the field:

| | | |
|---|---:|---:|
| 4 Roman Legions, each with 300 cavalry | 22,000 | |
| Allied force, including 2,000 cavalry | 32,000 | |
| Sabines and Etruscans in Etruria | 50,000 | |
| "              "        cavalry | 4,000 | |
| Umbrians and Sarsinati | 20,000 | |
| Veneti and Cenomani | <u>20,000</u> | 148,000 |

2. Strategic Reserve (Rome):

| | | |
|---|---:|---:|
| Roman citizens – infantry | 20,000 | |
| "              "     – cavalry | 1,500 | |
| Allies           – infantry | 30,000 | |
| "                 – cavalry | <u>2,000</u> | 53,500 |

3. Reserves – Sicily and Tarentum:

| | | |
|---|---:|---:|
| 2 Roman Legions | 8,400 | |
| Each with 200 cavalry | <u>400</u> | 8,800 |

4. Tribal lists:

| | | |
|---|---:|---:|
| Latins, including 5,000 cavalry | 85,000 | |
| Samnites, including 7,000 cavalry | 77,000 | |
| Iapygians and Messapians, including 16,000 cavalry | 66,000 | |
| Lucanians, including 3,000 cavalry | 33,000 | |
| Marsi, Marrucini, Frentani and Vestini, with 4,000 cavalry | <u>24,000</u> | 285,000 |

5. Romans and Campanians, with 23,000 cavalry          <u>273,000</u>

      TOTAL, incl 68,500 cavalry                              768,300

assume that the figure, if it be accurate, takes account of the losses Hannibal sustained at that time and at subsequent encounters prior to opening his invasion proper in the spring of 217 BC (but see also Chapter IV). However that may be, the scale of the defensive arrangements which now confronted Hannibal's invading force was daunting, to put it no more strongly.

Nevertheless, Rome also had her weaknesses. Of these, probably the greatest, paradoxically, was the ever increasing size of her population, with the consequent logistical and military pressures which this imposed upon her as a

Table 2: Population of Rome.

| Serial No. | Year BC | Event | Census Total (a) | Reference |
|---|---|---|---|---|
| 1. | c. 550 | Reign of Servius Tullius | c. 80,000 | Livy, i, 44 |
| 2. | 393/392 | Census Year | 152,573 | Pliny, NH |
| 3. | 386 | Brennus' Gallic Invasion | – | Livy, v, 38–44 |
| 4. | 234/233 | War – Cisalpine Ligurians | 270,212 | Livy, Ep, xx |
| 5. | 225/224 | Census Year | 273,000 | Polybius, ii, 24, 16 |
| 6. | 218 | Hannibal crosses the Alps | – | Livy, xxi, 28–37 |
| 7. | 216 | Roman defeat at Cannae | – | Livy, xxii,44–52 |
| 8. | 209/208 | Census Year | (b) 137,108 | Livy, xxvii, 36 |
| 9. | 204/203 | Census Year | 214,000 | Livy, xxix, 37 |
| 10. | 201 | End of Second Punic War | – | – |

(a)   The census figures broadly represent numbers of able-bodied adult men qualified by property assessment to serve in the land forces as *iuniores* (age 17–45) and *seniores* (46–60). Very few men would surely have been excluded in the five crucial years between the Cannae disaster and the capitulaion of Capua.

(b)   The fluctuation of this figure is generally considered incorrect. It is remotely conceivable it may have arisen through war casualties.


city state. It is not easy to put an accurate figure on the size of the Roman citizen population at this moment, mainly because, as we have seen, her periodical census returns were conducted for the military purpose of discovering the numbers of able-bodied men in the various civic categories and age groups. Toynbee,[15] when discussing a census total of 270,212 for the year 234/233 BC, considered that the overall total might have registered as many as one million people, when families, resident aliens and slaves were all taken to account. Further, when examining these numbers, there is yet another influential factor to be remembered. During the years of the Hannibalic War, Rome became a vast supply depot, equipping not only the armies on her land frontiers in Italy but ultimately also those campaigning elsewhere, in Spain, Sicily, Sardinia and on naval operations in African coastal waters. The number of the city's inhabitants would have been swollen not only by refugees but also by technicians engaged in this work. Thus, a population of one million may be considered a not exceptional basis upon which to demonstrate Rome's ration requirements during this period, never forgetting that the problems of supplying her armies in the field were yet another matter.

It has been calculated[16] that a reasonable ration of wheat per head of the population of Rome would have averaged about 40 *modii* of wheat a year, that is to say, an annual total of some 600 lbs per head (1.66 lbs per day) or a daily population requirement of some 750 tons. A wagon of standard size, drawn by two oxen at a speed of about 2 miles per hour, is estimated to have carried a half ton, thus posing a need for 1,500 wagons for a daily lift of this size. This is not an extravagant number. In 212 BC, Hanno, under Hannibal's instructions,[17] was accumulating grain for distribution to the inhabitants of Capua. He instructed them to come to the supply depot he had set up with every sort of vehicle and draught animal they could muster: but, Livy relates, 'with characteristic feebleness and negligence', they turned up with only 400 vehicles, prompting Hanno to exclaim that 'they were worse than dumb brutes, for not even hunger could stir them to take a little trouble'. However, he named another day and, on this occasion, they arrived with 2,000 wagons.

The scale of the wagon requirement to feed Rome would also have been considerable and may be expected to have multiplied with every day on the road. Thus, as an example, assuming it were necessary to travel 100 miles from Rome to obtain a continuous source of supply, this would have meant a fourteen-day return journey by road, requiring an astronomic 21,000 carts and 42,000 oxen. Clearly, these would have been unworkable numbers. It follows that Rome would perforce have become largely dependent upon supplies from such nearby corn producing areas as Etruria, Latium and Campania, from where deliveries could be made by boat, down the Tiber, for example, and thence directly into the heart of the city; or, alternatively, by coastal shipping, in the north travelling from the Arno estuary and the Etruscan ports of Pisa and Caere; and, in the south, from the rich farming lands of Campania.

Ultimately, the growing affect of the war of attrition into which Hannibal's prolonged campaign steadily developed, combined with the logistical and economic demands of road transport, rendered it necessary for Rome to abandon many Italian supply sources such as these and look overseas for bulk grain deliveries. In this manner, many lesser known supply sources developed and flourished. Livy[18] relates that, by the year 203 BC, at the moment when Hannibal was being recalled by Carthage from Italy to defend his African homeland, the Roman general Scipio Africanus was being provided with clothing and grain from Sardinia and Spain, as well as Sicily, which was also contributing weaponry as well. Sicily had played an important role as an exporter of corn from the earliest days of the Greek colonisation of the island.[19] By the end of the third century BC, Rome had gained control of all of Sicily with the exception of the Kingdom of Hiero II of Syracuse but this was a matter of little significance, since the king, as we have seen, by that time had perceptively switched his alliance to Rome from Carthage. When upon Hiero's death, Rome annexed the island, she stimulated wheat production and Sicily's produce was thenceforward reserved entirely for her needs.

Sardinia, the annexation of which, with Corsica, was one of the root causes of the Hannibalic War, also produced a valuable corn surplus for the Roman market. The island was considered unhealthy, particularly the river estuaries feeding the Tyrrhenian Sea, and was troubled by unruly tribesmen. It was not therefore so popularly productive as Sicily but, nevertheless, it played an important logistical role, certainly as an alternative source of supply for Rome

The remains of the Capitol in old Ostia, a 'coastguard colony' and transhipment port for Rome, located at the mouth of the Tiber. (By courtesy of the Italian State Tourist Board (E.N.I.T.) London)

and, additionally, as a provider for west coast operations. Livy,[20] in this respect, recounts how, during the siege of Capua in 212 BC, 'grain which had recently been sent from Sardinia, together with what the praetor Marcus Junius had purchased in Etruria', was brought from Ostia to provide for the army during the coming winter months.

The importance to Rome of retaining these supply bases and, to this end, of maintaining maritime supremacy, will at once be recognised. Evidence[21] reveals that the additional provisions of imported corn from such overseas places, and later from Egypt and Africa, did little more than keep pace with the expanding requirements of the city state and those of her army garrisons with access to the sea. Inland, however, her problems were not so easy to resolve, for Hannibal's operational strategy ensured that the task of feeding her field armies, together with the populations of local conurbations, became progressively difficult.

Finally, in this glimpse of some of the major physical and logistical strengths and weaknesses of Rome which confronted Hannibal upon his arrival in Italy, we must also briefly consider the state of the Roman army at this time of national crisis. Prior to his invasion, the latest intelligence received by the Senate of the whereabouts of the Carthaginians had been the news of their capture of Saguntum. Then, suddenly, alarmed reports were received that Hannibal was already in their country, 'at hand with an army and actually besieging cities in Italy'.[22] The Romans were unprepared: there were no more than four, widely dispersed legions on the Italian mainland, including the island of Sicily, with which to confront him. If we accurately interpret Polybius's meaning, the minds of the Roman authorities were concentrated wonderfully: in his words, the incident produced 'a single-minded concern for the future which is most dangerous for an adversary'.

Immediate steps were taken for the expansion of the armed forces and, when the campaigning season opened in 217 BC, the total legions under arms were now some twelve in number (see Table 4, p. 122), with two in Cisalpine Gaul, two in Etruria, two in Rome, two in Sicily, one in Sardinia and two in Spain. If such an instanteous increase in strength were to work successfully, it would be normal to expect a considerable redistribution of trained manpower within formations with, in particular, a substantial interchange of junior commanders. Inevitably, training standards would have been affected until operational experience had been gained and newly promoted commanders, senior officers especially, had been 'blooded': but the need for an interchange of commanders with operational experience would have been paramount.

This is a matter to which we will return when we come to discuss Hannibal's strategy, but at this stage we should note that the severe discipline observed by the Roman army, together with its high standard of training, more particularly in set-piece battles where accustomed battle drills counted for so much, was contrarily sometimes a weakness as much as a strength. Livy[23] recounts the horrific example set of his son by Titus Manlius, in 340 BC. Orders had been issued by him, together with his fellow consul, that no one was to leave his position to fight the enemy. Young Titus, who bore the same name as his father and had accompanied a cavalry patrol to reconnoitre an enemy outpost, allowed himself to be taunted into personal combat by the opposing commander. He killed the man, a distinguished nobleman with many gallant exploits to his credit and, upon return to camp, reported at once to his father's headquarters 'not knowing what fate and future awaited him, or whether praise or punishment would be his desert'. His father, the consul, received him coldly and at once turned away from the young man, whilst instructing his trumpeter to sound the assembly. When the soldiery thus summoned had come together, Livy records that he spoke as follows:

> Titus Manlius, you have respected neither consular authority nor your father's dignity; you have left your position to fight the enemy in defiance of my order, and, as far as was in your power, have subverted military discipline, on which

Ivory plaque from Praeneste, showing Latin soldier (third century BC). (The Mansell Collection)

the fortune of Rome has rested to this day; you have made it necessary for me to forget either the republic or myself. We would therefore rather be punished for our own wrongdoing than allow our country to expiate our sins at so great a cost to itself; it is a harsh example we shall set, but a salutary one for the young men of the future . . .

The consul then summoned a lictor, who bound his son to a stake and beheaded him, to the horror of all who witnessed the act. Livy's comment on this sorry tale is that 'the commands of Manlius' provided a grim warning for the future; in his restrained judgement 'the brutality of the punishment made the soldiers more obedient to their commander, and not only was better attention given everywhere to guard-duties, night watches and picket stationing, but in the final struggle too, when the army went into battle, that stern act of discipline did them good'.

It is clear that such rigid standards of discipline left little room for personal initiative, a quality which would already have been drastically curtailed by the employment of the set-piece style of battle drill handed down from the days of the phalanx formation. By the time of the Punic Wars, this technique had, of course, already been relaxed in favour of the maniple which, by its size and elasticity, permitted greater manoeuvrability of massed infantry, particularly over broken ground. Even so, as Hannibal, with his inferior numbers, was quick to appreciate, and the Roman army occasionally found to its heavy cost, it was a style of fighting totally unsuited to a fast-moving, thoughtful enemy or unconventional warfare of a guerrilla pattern.[24]

Hannibal, for his times, was to prove a master of original tactical thought.

## CHAPTER IV

# INTO ITALY

Surprise is a Principle of War . . . [It] should primarily be directed at the mind of an enemy commander rather than at his force. The aim should be to paralyse the commander's will.

*The British Military Doctrine*[1]

All War supposes human weakness, and against that it is directed.

General Carl von Clausewitz[2]

Hannibal's invasion of northern Italy had been totally unexpected by Rome. Cornelius Scipio, who, with a small command group, had turned back from the Rhône when he learnt of Hannibal's intention to cross the Alps and link with the tribes of Cisalpine Gaul, had, notwithstanding, ordered his army to hold tight to its original instructions and continue onwards to Spain. It was a bold decision, for the legions of the republic, at this delicate moment, were overstretched and inexperienced to a degree which threatened Rome's ability to defend herself. The legions she could put in the field were only six in number; two were operational in Sicily under Tiberius Sempronius Longus, safeguarding the island against Carthaginian attack and providing support to their ally, Hiero of Syracuse; two were on the Trebbia, soon to be collected by Scipio on his way northward to confront Hannibal; and two were shortly to disembark in Spain, to secure Roman interests and undertake operations against Hannibal's brother, Hasdrubal. Rome itself was without a formal legionary garrison but had the ability to call up reserves from amongst her able-bodied male citizens. However, two new legions were now to be quickly raised and, for the remaining years of the war in the peninsula, she was not left again in such a state of naked defence (see Table 4, p. 122). Indeed, within twelve months, the number of legions fielded by Rome had doubled to roughly twelve and, from the year 214 BC, for the duration of the war, she rarely had less than twenty legions operationally deployed.

In the meantime, the Senate, in their alarm at Hannibal's descent into the Po valley, at once sent orders to Longus at Lilybaeum to abandon his present role and to march north with all speed to reinforce Scipio on the now breached northern frontier. Longus himself,[3] having first ordered his military tribunes[4] to 'administer an oath to the soldiers, binding them to present themselves (after

View of the ancient naval harbour at Carthage, looking across the central island, which accommodated the Admiralty, to the high ground beyond, upon which stood ancient Carthage. (Ian Atkinson)

40 days) at Ariminum before the hour of rest', sailed northwards with his fleet to arrange for their arrival. The action which he took was probably motivated by two factors. Firstly, the need for urgency, for if the army had marched as a formed body it would have required to take heavy baggage and animals with it, thus encumbering the rate of its advance. In this instance, it appears likely that the baggage and animals went by sea with their commander, Longus. Secondly, and ominously significant for the future, a spontaneous, unprepared military overland move of this nature, over such a lengthy distance, would almost certainly have provoked an immediate ration supply and transport problem. The decision by Longus for his soldiery to make their way to Ariminum individually thus lessened the impact on local transport and stocks of grain, as the men scattered over the countryside and foraged for themselves.

Even from this distance in time, it is possible to sense a note of panic in the atmosphere which now prevailed. Hannibal's unorthodox choice of route into Italy, and his ruthless acceptance of a casualty rate which Scipio had imagined the Carthaginian would be unable to sustain if he were to take that angle of advance, had achieved total surprise. The Romans had prepared for an enemy assault on Sicily; indeed, and perhaps significantly in the light of coming events, their navy had just repelled a Carthaginian attempt, with thirty-five quinquiremes, to land a force at Lilybaeum.[5] They had planned that their intervention in Spain would preoccupy Hannibal at home and divert him from any threatening move against Roman territory; and they looked to their two unpractised, almost unblooded legions, north of Rome, to keep a watchful eye on their troublesome Celtic neighbours. Hannibal's sudden arrival in the Po valley had outflanked these precautionary measures. The heart of Italy, including Rome, was exposed until Longus could arrive to help stem the onslaught: but it would take at least six weeks, probably longer, before his men were once again assembled, marshalled, equipped and ready for operations.

In the meantime, Hannibal, following up his success on the Ticinus, had pursued Scipio across the Po, delaying only two days to find a suitable crossing place. Then, in front of Placentia, he formed up his army in battle order, in the manner of the day, and challenged Scipio to come out and fight. When it was obvious that the Roman had no intention of doing so, he withdrew to an encampment some 6 miles distant, to watch and wait for events to develop. The wounded Scipio was by now aware that Longus was hastening to join him: he was also conscious of the raw ability of the soldiers of whom he had taken command. He had no desire to become involved in combat at this stage: he was keen to spend the coming winter months training them for battle before taking them to war. Moreover, he felt insecure in Placentia, with Hannibal encamped on his doorstep. For this reason, he now crossed the Trebbia, and entrenched himself on high ground overlooking the river. Hannibal once more followed in his footsteps, again encamping close by. Initially, the Carthaginians received 'abundant supplies' from neighbouring tribes and many promises of support. It soon became clear to Hannibal, however, that the Gauls between the Trebbia and the Po were avoiding any outright commitment to either contestant until they could be certain of supporting the winning side.

It was an attitude which Scipio was content to accept, since it ensured the neutrality of this potential source of trouble until the arrival of his fellow consul. Hannibal, however, was deeply incensed by the behaviour of the Celts and despatched a mixed force of 2,000 infantry and 1,000 horse, selected from amongst his toughest Numidian soldiery, to raid the neighbouring countryside as far as the Po, as well as to requisition provisions for his men and to remind the Celts that it was they, themselves, who had invited him to northern Italy and to emphasise that he expected their help. This robust action by Hannibal at least persuaded the tribal leaders to make up their minds: they promptly sent a delegation to Scipio's headquarters, seeking aid for their unfortunate peoples, suffering, so they claimed, because of their excessive loyalty to Rome. He received them with considerable distrust. Sempronius Longus, on the other hand, having by this time arrived with his army, expressed the view that the wisest way of gaining Celtic support was to offer them the practical assistance they sought. He despatched a detachment of 1,000 cavalry to the area, supported by a similar number of javelin throwers, with orders to protect the tribal territories from Hannibal.

This large fighting patrol encountered Hannibal's men, scattered on a raid and laden with plunder. The Carthaginians were thrown into complete confusion by the unexpected contact and fled, allowing themselves to be pursued right up to the gates of their camp. Sempronius, understandably in the circumstances, claimed to Scipio, who was still on his sick-bed, that he had gained a famous victory and that the time was now ripe to go on the offensive. Despite Scipio's protests that this was not the moment, he issued orders for the whole army to prepare for action without delay. It was to prove yet another example of disaster springing from the mistaken Roman policy of joint consular command.

Hannibal was anxious to maintain the momentum of his initial successes: he had created a good impression with his new found allies for his success on the Ticinus and he wished to retain their enthusiasm. He was gifted with an extraordinary ability to recognise and exploit any temperamental weaknesses of character in the commanders who opposed him. He had immediately identified the natural impetuosity of Longus. His plan was thus directed at breaking down the methodical battle drills which made the Roman army such powerful opponents. He had selected for his battlefield an area of ground on his side of the river, opposite the Roman camp. It was flat and treeless and upon one flank it possessed an area of sunken ground in which he proposed to conceal an ambush force. For this purpose, on the previous evening, he had carefully hand-picked, and placed in position during the night, a party of 1,000 cavalry and 1,000 infantry, under his younger brother Mago. For the remainder, he issued general instructions that, in the morning, after all men had enjoyed a good breakfast, they were to prepare their arms and horses for action. The weather was bleak, it was commencing to snow and, due to the rain which had been falling heavily, the waters of the Trebbia were in spate.

Nonetheless, Hannibal issued order for his Numidian cavalry to cross the river at dawn and harry the Roman guard-posts around their camp. If they were attacked they were to give ground and lure the enemy across the river into his baited trap – and this was precisely the way in which the engagement developed. Longus, flushed with his recent cavalry victory and tempted by the reappearance of the enemy cavalry on his doorstep, led out his entire cavalry wing against them, followed at first by 6,000 infantry and finally by the remainder of his army, in all numbering 18,000 legionaries, with 20,000 allied troops and some Celtic infantry from the Cenomani tribe amongst others. Then, as the Numidians pulled back across the river, towards their own lines, the Roman horse plunged in after them. Livy[6] leaves us in no doubt about the state in which their army quickly found itself:

> There, between Alps and Apennines, it was a snowy winter's day, and the cold was increased by the proximity of rivers and marsh; men and horses had left the shelter of camp without a moment's warning – they had eaten nothing, taken no sort of precautions against the cold. There was not a spark of warmth in their bodies . . . but worse was to come, for when in pursuit of the Numidians they actually entered the river, it had rained in the night and the water was up to their breasts – the cold so numbed them they could hardly hold their weapons.

Whilst this preliminary action had been progressing, Hannibal's men, having already eaten breakfast, were warming themselves by great fires, lit in front of

War elephant on a coin
from New Carthage. (©
British Museum)

their tents, and massaging themselves against the cold with a special issue of oil.
When news was received that the Romans were across the Trebbia, they ran to
take up their positions in the line. The outcome was inevitable. The Roman line
held its own against the Carthaginian infantry but was broken down by
Hannibal's use of his elephants, firstly, in a frontal attack against the Roman
heavy infantry and then, in a left-flank attack against Rome's Gallic allies. At this
moment, Hannibal released Mago, with his ambush party, who fell upon the rear
of the Roman line, sowing utter confusion and causing the Roman auxiliaries to
break and flee. Rain was by now drenching down, causing the river to rise yet
more and increasing the difficulty of recrossing it. In order to avoid this new
hazard, a formed body of 10,000 Romans fought their way through to seek
shelter in Placentia. There, they were joined by a number of other groups; but
Longus's army had been roughly handled and Hannibal could claim a resounding
victory.

The Carthaginians, numb with cold, abandoned any thoughts of pursuit and
returned to camp. Polybius relates that most of the Carthaginian battle casualties
were suffered by their Celts. He adds, however,[7] that the whole army was
affected by the pouring rain and the snowfall that followed after the battle, 'with
the result that all the elephants died, except for one, and large numbers of men
and horses perished from the cold'.

Hannibal now withdrew to 'winter' amongst his allies in Cisalpine Gaul.
His great march from New Carthage to his victory on the Trebbia had been a
military feat of extraordinary proportions. He and his army had earned the
opportunity for a rest and the chance to reorganise for the campaigns which

lay ahead. Even so, despite his successes and the reputation which he had now earned for himself, particularly in Rome, the next few months were not to prove entirely free of troubles. Plainly, his declared allies were only now beginning to appreciate the practical implications of the conflict they had wished upon themselves by inviting Carthage to join them in a war against Roman expansionism. Hannibal, above all else in the task that lay ahead, needed manpower: but events were soon to show that he was not going to get it in the numbers he required. Livy,[8] commenting on the feelings of the Cisalpine Gauls at this time, whilst Hannibal was staying amongst them, leaves no doubt of the resentment created amongst many of them by his presence:

> . . . the attitude of the Gauls was making it very dangerous to stay where he was; these peoples had expected to enrich themselves by plunder, but now, when their hopes of plundering other men's territory were gone and they realised that their own lands were to be the scene of operations, with the additional burden of having the armies of both sides quartered there for the winter, they forgot their hatred of Rome and turned all the force of their resentment against Hannibal. Gallic chieftains frequently plotted against his life but it was their own mutual treachery that saved him; for they would inform against each other as frivolously as they would themselves conspire.

In whatever way we may read these words, we may at least judge that, for many in Cisalpine Gaul, their enthusiasm for the venture had cooled. Thus, Cornelius Scipio, with his newly recruited legions, may have lost the battles of the Ticinus and the Trebbia but his presence there had gained two far more important and rarely recognised successes, swamped as they were by the evidence of Hannibal's victories. He had fended off instant national defeat and won for Rome invaluable time in which to regain her military posture. Rome was also fortunate that the end of the campaigning season was now at hand, thus enabling her, during the coming winter months, to train and redeploy new forces. There was another factor of importance, which would vitally affect the conduct of the operations which lay ahead: namely, the timing of the coming harvest.

The weather experienced in Italy, in Roman times as much as today, dictates that the peninsula be divided into three climatic regions. The northern plain, watered by the Po and its many tributaries, suffers severe winters and enjoys long, hot summers. The nature of its climate is demonstrated today by the quantity of rice it produces: the area is categorised as belonging to Central Europe.[9] Strabo,[10] in his *Geography*, wrote glowingly of the fertility of this region, with its well-watered soil, lush acorn forests and exceptional crops of millet, 'the greatest preventive of famine, since it withstands every unfavourable weather'.

The central and southern regions of the peninsula, where four-fifths of the area is classified as mountainous, has a climate of a truly Mediterranean type, with most of the rain, here again, arriving in the winter months. Nevertheless, the precipitation received by the southern half of the country is considerably less

Hannibal on horseback.
(From a painting by Ferris.
The Mansell Collection)

than in the north, and, even so, varies in quantity as the prevailing wind carries it from north-west to south-east across the mountains. Because of these conditions, ancient farmers customarily sowed their crops in the autumn, having carefully assessed the temperature of the soil and the likelihood of rain, so that their seed might not wither in the parched earth. Likewise, when possible and in order to maximise crop yield, they continued cultivation deep into the following spring, taking the fullest advantage of the rainy season, so long as it lasted.

For these reasons, depending upon regional weather conditions, the annual harvest generally took place in a broad six- to seven-week period between early April and late May. On this basis, if Hannibal arrived in Italy in November, a six months' supply of grain for winter consumption would still have been available in district granaries. On the other hand, when he opened his campaigning season 'at the first doubtful signs of spring', if that moment is correctly recorded by Livy, it is probable that crops would still have been standing in the fields, as yet ungarnered, and stores of grain, as far as Rome and her armed forces were concerned, would have been perilously low. This, therefore, was a shrewd piece of timing by Hannibal, for it produced a situation greatly to his military advantage. Polybius[11] relates that, when the Carthaginian was planning the resumption of his campaign, 'he made no provision for pack animals, since he reckoned that once within the enemy's territory he would have no need for them if he were defeated, but that if he gained control of the open country, he would have no problems of supply'. Moreover, by the destruction of unharvested, standing crops, he could, if successful, provide himself with an awesome weapon of attrition. In the meantime, the Romans made arrangements for his reception.

Their first and most immediate task was to outguess Hannibal and determine the route by which he would advance into Italy. In order to appreciate this, they would have required to possess a clear idea of his intention; for our part, we are at this point entering a realm of considerable uncertainty, for nowhere has Hannibal's purpose been categorically stated by either of our leading annalists, Polybius or Livy, although Polybius, writing of these early days of his invasion, at one place[12] does speak of Hannibal's 'advance towards Rome', and in another[13] of his decision against 'approaching Rome for the present'. It is thus a complicated matter to which we will return in a later chapter, when the pattern of his campaign has more clearly emerged and we have sufficient data from which to make a judgement of our own. In the meantime, it may not be unreasonable to suggest that the Romans would justifiably have been primarily concerned for the safety of their capital city.

Hannibal had the option of three routes by which to advance into Italy. The first and most apparent of these 'turned' the Apennines to reach the east coast at Ariminum, a Latin colony and seaport, which had been especially sited for two purposes: to watch over the strategically important estuary of the river Po and to safeguard the roadhead, as it then was, of the *Via Flaminia*. This highway would have carried Hannibal to the walls of Rome itself. The second route, commencing from Felsina (Bologna) crossed the Apennines to reach the Etruscan town of Faesulae, a richly fertile area. It was linked by tribal routeways, in one

The river Po, the longest river in Italy, rises at the foot of the Col de la Traversette. (By courtesy of the Italian State Tourist Board (E.N.I.T.) London)

direction with Pisa, at the mouth of the Arno, and in the other with nearby Arretium (Arezzo), lying to its south-east. This central route offered two alternatives, with the same beginning and the same end. The more easterly of these, and the more direct, followed the valley of the Savena River to cross the Apennine range by the Futa Pass. The more westerly followed the River Reno to cross the mountains by the Collina Pass and thence descend to Pistoria. The third option, which Hannibal might have picked up only to discard immediately because of its difficult terrain, would have been to cross the Ligurian range and thence to march down the Tyrrhenian coastline. It would not have been an easy option, nevertheless, at some time in 217 BC,[14] possibly even when the Carthaginians invasion force had reached Faesulae, a Carthaginian fleet of some seventy ships touched at Pisa, the commander seemingly believing they would meet there with Hannibal. The fact that there was a road link between the two places suggests that this was a planned rendezvous.

Cornelius Scipio and Sempronius Longus had wintered with their armies at Cremona and Placentia respectively. The past few months had not been easy, for they had been continually molested by Numidian raiders and all supply routes to them had been closed, apart from such stores as could be brought by boat up the Po. In the meantime, two new consuls, Gaius Flaminius and Gnaeus Servilius, had been designated to succeed them, with orders to absorb the remaining manpower of their legions. Flaminius, ignoring the niceties of his induction, required his reinforcing detachment from Placentia to reach him at Arretium by mid-March. Servilius delayed his move to join his new army in order to fulfil the ceremonial of his appointment. He then took up position at Ariminum from where, according to Strabo,[15] he moved a strong task force forward to defend the pass and defiles which covered access to the town. It was these defences, the latter tells us, that compelled Hannibal to choose the more difficult, central pass for his invasion route but it is more likely, from the way matters resolved themselves, that his final choice, from Bologna to Faesulae, would have suited the Carthaginian's plans more aptly. Hannibal, according to Polybius,[16] had fully briefed himself on the options open to him,

> . . . and had discovered that the other routes for invading Roman territory were not only long but were thoroughly familiar to the enemy, whereas the road which led through the marshes to Etruria was both short and likely to take Flaminius by surprise. Hannibal was always inclined by temperament to favour the unexpected solution and so this was the line of march he chose.

He ignored the fact that the Arno had recently overflowed its banks and that the area had been 'flooded to a greater extent than usual'.[17] The troops were greatly disenchanted at the thought that he would be leading them 'through deep swamps and quagmires' but Hannibal impressed upon them that he had made painstaking enquiries as to the nature of the terrain, the depth of the water and the solidity of the bottom through which they would be wading; moreover, he had been successful in obtaining guides. He then broke camp and began his march:[18]

> He placed the Africans, the Spaniards and all the best fighting troops in the forward part of his column and interspersed the baggage train among them, so as to make sure that all the army's necessities would be available for the immediate future . . . the Celts were stationed behind the troops just mentioned, and the cavalry brought up the rear of the army, the command of the rearguard being entrusted to his brother Mago.

We are not told the strength of the army Hannibal had accumulated for this opening phase of his campaign; it probably numbered some 60,000 men or more.[19]

Patently, he had recruited a sizeable contingent of Celts of whom both Livy and Polybius write disparagingly, criticising, in the main, their lack of enthusiasm, their dislike of hard work and their lack of fitness. The Celts were unfortunate, however, in the position they had been allotted in the column of march, for the ground over which they were advancing had been severely churned up by the men and animals marching with the vanguard. The Gauls, writes Livy[20] in a typically vivid description of the scene, were quite incapable of keeping their feet or of extricating themselves once they had been sucked down into the mud; 'without spirit to spur them on or hope to give them courage, some dragged themselves along in a state of wretched exhaustion, while others simply lay helpless and hopeless and died where they had fallen, amongst the bodies of the drowned and drowning animals'. The tortured journey lasted for four days and three nights. Lack of sleep contributed to the agonies suffered by all, for the conditions rendered it impossible to lie down, except where the carcass of some unfortunate pack animal, in its last service to its human masters, offered itself as a bed.

Again, neither Polybius nor Livy provide us with the casualty figures arising from this disaster. Livy[21] simply states that 'many men and many beasts found a miserable death in the swamps' and Polybius[22] records that whilst the Celts suffered the bulk of the losses, the majority of pack animals perished and many horses became lame because of the prolonged march through the mud. Hannibal, riding on the one surviving elephant, also became a casualty for he suffered intense pain from a severe attack of ophthalmia, which Livy attributed to the severe variations of temperature in the early spring weather. Finally, the affliction caused him to lose the sight of an eye, the condition rendering it impossible for him to stop for treatment, if indeed the medical expertise had been available for the purpose.

The implications of the situation in which the Carthaginian army at this moment found itself are interesting to consider. Hannibal's men, who had commenced their march through the flooded marsh with some considerable uncertainty, not to say unwillingness, had now reached the far edge of the swamp area which had confronted them. Here, they were encamped and resting. They had just experienced several, almost certainly costly, losses both in men and material. Of the latter, the most significant would have been the supplies of grain which we must presume they had carried with them.[23] Many horses had been lamed as a result of the adventure, a factor which must have had an impact on the efficiency of Hannibal's cavalry, the most effective of the supporting arms under his command. Inevitably, morale would have suffered as a consequence of all this and would not have been improved by the news of Hannibal's ailment.

For his part, Hannibal cannot have remained entirely unshaken by the outcome of these events. He had committed himself to a major military operation and was now afflicted with partial blindness. There was a genuine possibility that the infection would also spread to his uninjured eye, thus bringing about his total loss of sight. Equally, his affliction must have sown doubts in the minds of his staff. On top of this, by a supreme physical effort, he had achieved surprise against Flaminius, the advantages of which he would soon lose if he failed to move quickly from his rest area on the edge of the swamp. He

had despatched scouts in advance of his column and these now reported that they had located the Roman forces under Flaminius 'encamped before the city of Arretium'.[24] It was thus only a matter of time before his hide-out was discovered.

Hannibal had at least two courses open to him: he could continue with his march on Rome, if the destruction or seizure of that city were his intention, or he could confront Flaminius and bring him to battle. But if he adopted the first option, he would have been only too aware that he would be leaving an army of four Roman legions to follow in his wake, unscathed and an instant threat to any movement he might choose to make. On the face of it, his most sensible option would have been to confront and defeat Flaminius in isolation before the armies of the two consuls had the opportunity to combine; but his impaired vision and the condition of his cavalry horses probably ruled against this. Yet again, it may even have been that he had a third and pre-planned task within his overall intention, namely, to meet with the Carthaginian naval squadron at Pisa. There can be little doubt of their resolution to meet with him for within a few weeks of abandoning hope of finding Hannibal at that port, they were again to be discovered off the coast at Cosa, some 75 miles north of the Tiber estuary. Here, just about the time that Hannibal was laying siege to Spoletium, Livy[25] records them intercepting Roman merchant vessels laden with supplies for Scipio's army in Spain.

There are a host of reasons why the rendezvous may have been important. Hannibal's army was seriously handicapped by the lack of siege machinery left behind in Spain; they may have been bringing this to him. Hannibal's elephant squadron had been almost totally destroyed: they could have carried replacements to make good his losses. During his operations in the Pyrenees, the Alps and, subsequently, in the Po valley, Hannibal would inevitably have suffered casualties amongst his senior ranks; they may have carried reinforcements for him. Or they may simply have carried gold to finance his campaign.

For whatever reason, Hannibal chose to ignore their presence. He now turned away from Arretium and marched upon Faesulae, which he subjected 'to as much damage as fire and sword could produce'. He then turned and marched southwards, harrying and laying waste the Etruscan countryside as he did so. In Livy's words,[26] he reduced to a desert the whole stretch of countryside between Cortona and Lake Trasimene, the sky blackened by burning farmhouses and standing fields of corn. Livy and Polybius both suggest that he did this with the purpose of enraging Flaminius into following him: and that, in the words of Polybius,[27] the Roman would be so provoked by what he saw that he would follow wherever he was led. Hannibal's reasoning, Polybius expounds

. . . was both far sighted and strategically sound. The truth is that there is no more precious asset for a general than a knowledge of his opponent's guiding principles and character, and anyone who thinks the opposite is at once blind and foolish. When individuals or ranks of soldiers are marched against one another, the one who means to conquer must search out relentlessly how best to achieve his object, and, in particular, the point at which his enemy appears most vulnerable or least protected. In the same way, the commander must

*Opposite:*
The Glandasse mountains, photographed from Die in the Drome valley, arguably one of the routes taken by Hannibal on his march across the Alps. (Roger Day)

train his eye upon the weak spots of his opponent's defence, not in his body but in his mind.

In the event, matters worked out as Hannibal desired. Flaminius, inflamed by the destruction he saw being created by his enemy, gave orders that the standards of his legions be immediately raised and that his army should be marshalled with all speed, ready to march. Such was his own haste and impetuosity that, as he sprang into his saddle, his horse stumbled and threw him. The superstitious Roman soldiery saw this as a bad omen, and their mood was not further improved when news was brought to their general that one of the legionary standards, despite every effort of the standard-bearer, refused to be lifted from the ground. Flaminius sarcastically enquired of the messenger whether, in addition to this affrontery, he had also brought with him a letter from the Senate forbidding him to engage. 'Be off with you!' he cried irately, 'Tell them to *dig* it out, if they are too weak with fright to pull it up.' He then instructed his trumpeters to sound the advance and set off in pursuit of the Carthaginians who, by now, had comfortably eluded his grasp. It was to be a distance of 30 miles, two days' march or more, before he made contact with them again.

Hannibal, meantime, was in no hurry; his arrival across the swamp in the high Arno valley had caught Flaminius off balance. He took full advantage of the time this had created for him. His cavalry ranged far and wide, systematically devastating and plundering the countryside. His army, together with his Celtic allies, had endured much danger and discomfort since they left Cisalpine Gaul and had received little to show for their effort. We may be certain they now took every opportunity to reward themselves from the stored wealth of this most fertile area of Italy, with its prosperous towns.

Whether or not Hannibal was then aware of it, this north-western region of Italy was one to which he was not to return in the sixteen years of war which lay ahead. Favoured by geography, it lay tucked away out of danger, only occasionally disturbed by a whiff of conflict, such as, for example, the arrival of Hasdrubal on the Adriatic coast in 207 BC and his defeat on the Metaurus. As a result of this immunity,[28] the cities of Etruria were encouraged to develop and farming was allowed to continue uninterrupted by events in central and southern Italy. All of them, within their regions, produced grain and food in generous supply, some of it destined for Rome, other of it being despatched to the armies in the field, in one instance as far as Tarentum, when under siege. Equally, they all played their part in essential war production. Arretium specialised in metalwork such as hardware for ships, as well as the manufacture of arms and armour. Volaterrae supplied ships' fittings and Tarquini provided linen for sailmaking. Populonia on the coast, fed by supplies of ore from Elba and elsewhere, became a centre for iron production.

None of Hannibal's actions at this moment provide us with any clear-cut indication of his intentions for the future. Polybius[29] states that Hannibal, when he left his rest area in the Arno floodlands, continued his advance towards Rome. It is difficult to believe, in all the circumstances which now prevailed, with his comparatively small army, the potential military might of his opponent, and his

The battlefield at
Trasimene. (Author)

personal uncertain fitness, that the Carthaginian still contemplated either assailing
the walls of Rome, for which he possessed no equipment, or laying siege to the
city, for which he surely had neither time nor the numerical strength. Indeed, the
'scorched' earth destruction of farms and standing crops upon which he now
embarked, and which included a systematic massacre of all males of military age
found in his path, would seem to suggest a change in operational direction. It was
in this frame that he continued to march southward, passing west of Cortona and
then, leaving behind him a wide area of devastated agriculture in particular, he
swung eastwards to penetrate the hill country fringing the northern shores of Lake
Trasimene. Here, where the hills crowded down to the lake, narrowing the
passage through the defile thus created, he set an ambush to receive an infuriated
Flaminius, who had been travelling fast and was now pursuing him closely.

The descriptions by both Polybius and Livy[30] of the road where Hannibal laid
his ambush and along which Flaminius advanced to the battlefield at Trasimene,
vary in detail. It is thus probably wiser to accept the version provided by
Polybius, whose writing of events is less removed in time than that of Livy.[31] He
relates that Flaminius

> . . . passed through a narrow and level valley enclosed on both sides by an
> unbroken line of lofty hills. At the eastern end of this defile rose a steep

Monument at Lake
Trasimene (see Appendix C,
p. 217). (Author)

eminence with sheer slopes that were difficult to climb; at the western end lay the lake, from which the only access to the valley was a narrow passage which ran across the foot of the hillside. Hannibal led his troops along the edge of the lake and then through the valley. He himself occupied the hill at the eastern end with his African and Spanish troops. His slingers and pikemen were ordered to make a detour and march round from the front under cover of the hills, and were then posted in extended order to the right (south) of the valley. The Celts and the cavalry were moved round to the left (north) of the valley and likewise stationed in a continuous line under the hills, the last of them being posted at the entrance to the defile between the hillside and the lake.

If we are to believe Polybius, all these dispositions were effected during the night, after which Hannibal waited for dawn and for Flaminius to enter the trap. We must look askance at the claim that Hannibal deployed his army in the dark, over what must have been an elongated area of broken and unknown countryside, unless he undertook considerable prior preparation and reconnaissance. The area he chose, according to all accounts, was of a scale large enough to encompass the entire Roman force, which numbered roughly 25,000 men. An army of this strength, in column of march, with men, animals and baggage, a formation forced upon Flaminius by the nature of the ground, would probably have extended over a distance of at least 4 miles, and possibly more. It is thus likely that Hannibal halted his army in daylight at the entrance to his ambush area and that, after all had been reconnoitred, commanders had been carefully briefed and units placed in their correct order of march, he then led his column into the defile, dropping off formations at their allotted positions as he progressed through the length of the position. In order to have allowed him time in which to do this, it would appear that Flaminius must have been moving a day's march to the rear of Hannibal.

On the night that Hannibal completed all these arrangements, Flaminius arrived at sunset and pitched camp nearby along the edge of the lake. Next morning, at first light and whilst the early mist of dawn still clung to the hillsides, he set off once again, first, leading his army along the shoreline of the lake and thence into the valley where, to what we can only judge to have been his total ignorance, an army of twice his strength lay waiting to destroy him. Hannibal, with his Spanish and African veterans, had taken up a position in full view at the eastern end of the valley, where it opened out and offered opportunity for a conventional set-piece battle. Flaminius hastened forward to combat him and, as soon as Hannibal was assured that he had his enemy 'penned in by the lake and the mountains and surrounded, front, rear and flank, he gave the signal for a simultaneous attack'.[32] Men rose from the ground and poured from the hills, emerging from the thick mist which covered everything, to sweep down upon the totally unprepared Romans, denying them the opportunity to manoeuvre into battle formation. Hannibal's commanders, controlling the operation from nearby high ground, were able to see above the fog and 'were able, in consequence, the better to coordinate their attack'. Livy's colourful writing aptly catches the desperate sense of the occasion and the gallantry with which Flaminius responded to it. It is worthy of repeating at some length:

Wherever he could make his voice heard, or force a way through the press, he encouraged his men and urged them to stand firm, crying out that no prayers would save them now, but only their own strength and their own valour. They must cut their way through with the sword, and the greater their courage the less would be their peril. But the din of the mêlée was so great that not a word either of exhortation or command could be heard . . . In that enveloping mist ears were a better guide than eyes: it was sounds, not sights, they turned to face – the groans of wounded men, the thud or ring of blows on body or shield, the shout of onslaught, the cry of fear. Some, flying for their lives, found themselves caught in a jam of their own men still standing their ground; others, trying to return to the fight, were forced back by a crowd of refugees. In every direction attempts to break out failed. The mountains on the one side, the lake on the other, hemmed them in, while in front of them and behind stood the formations of the enemy . . . So great was the fury of the struggle, so totally absorbed was every man in its grim immediacy, that no one even noticed the earthquake which ruined large parts of many Italian towns, altered the course of swift rivers, brought the sea flooding into estuaries and started avalanches in the mountains.

The battle lasted 'three long and bloody hours' and unfailingly at the centre of it was to be found Flaminius, his commanding figure conspicuous by his dress and presence, as he moved from one disaster area to another, striving to hold back the tide of overwhelming defeat. In the melancholy words of Polybius, death took his legions unawares whilst they were wondering what to do. Their general was an obvious target for the enemy and many attacks upon him were beaten off until an Insubrian cavalryman, forcing his way through the confused and desperate fighting, cut down his personal bodyguard and drove his lance through Flaminius's body.[33] This ultimate disaster was the signal for the end. The Roman soldiery threw their arms away and sought every means of escape, many hundreds striving unsuccessfully to swim for it across the lake, either being drowned by the weight of their equipment or cut down by Hannibal's mounted troops who mercilessly patrolled the shallow waters of the shore, awaiting their exhausted return. Many, in their despair, took their own lives.

The Roman dead amounted to 15,000, whilst a further 10,000 escaped 'to find their way back to Rome by various ways'. Carthaginian losses amounted to some 2,500, mainly Celts. Additionally, there were many wounded on both sides and Hannibal took numerous prisoners. Of these, significantly, he released without ransom all those bearing Latin names, a clear indication of his desire to subvert Rome's allies from her side, whilst the Roman captives he detained in chains against the time that their release could be negotiated for cash.

Flaminius has frequently been castigated by historians, both ancient and modern, for his part in this disaster but he had a difficult role to play. Both armies, that of Servilius at Ariminum and of Flaminius at Arretium, had been located, as we have seen, to cover Hannibal's possible lines of advance into Italy. They were also sited, although some 60 miles apart, so as to be mutually supportive of each other once Hannibal had declared his hand. Each commander, dependent upon what transpired, had the responsibility of alerting the other as

soon as the line of Hannibal's advance became clear. Flaminius undoubtedly played his part in this, for Polybius[34] relates that, upon learning of Hannibal's incursion into Etruria, it had initially been the intention of Servilius to march 'with his whole force' to join his brother general but, 'since the size of his army made this impossible, he at once despatched Gaius Centennius with a force of 4,000 cavalry'. We must read from these words that Servilius planned for his infantry to march out encumbered with the heavy baggage and other paraphernalia of his army. If this were so, it was an act which did not display the sense of urgency demanded by the occasion, for Flaminius lay distant at least three days' forced march for foot soldiery marching in column, and at least two days' march for cavalry, depending in each case on good circumstances.

As soon as he heard of Hannibal's arrival, Flaminius prepared to confront the Carthaginian but found himself not only by-passed by Hannibal but also watching the spring corn harvest, yet standing in the fields of northern Etruria, being devastated before his eyes. We may be sure he was not unaware of both the economic and strategic implications of this act. For this reason, he could not afford to wait, immobile, for the arrival of Servilius: time did not permit it. Nor could he rightly allow Hannibal, numerically stronger than him by two to one, to escape southwards, getting increasingly out of the discouraging touch of the only Roman armies in the field, whilst at the same time moving threateningly in the direction of Rome. Even with his best efforts (for armies tend to be awkward, slow-moving animals as Servilius had already demonstrated) it is likely that when Flaminius set forth in pursuit of Hannibal he would have been at least one, probably two days' march behind his enemy. In other words, apart from the occasional sighting on the skyline of Hannibal's Numidian cavalry, he would have been out of physical touch with him.

In this manner Flaminius came to Lake Trasimene. By now, the ever watchful Carthaginian cavalry would have been withdrawn from view in order to add to his uncertainty; and the thought that Hannibal lay in the valley ahead, waiting to entrap him, cannot have escaped him. Flaminius had three options. He could chance that the defile was unoccupied, and march through it. He could push his cavalry through it to 'test the temperature', at one extreme risking their loss if the valley were occupied and, at the other, wasting what he might well consider to be valuable time. On the other hand, in the misty conditions which then prevailed, their presence need not have sprung the ambush. Alternatively, he could withdraw and march around the obstacle, making a rendezvous with Servilius at its eastern end. This latter choice would almost certainly have resulted in Hannibal getting cleanly away but, equally, it was probably the most cautiously sensible of all the options considered by Flaminius. In the event, he chose to gamble that the valley was empty of the enemy. It was to prove a brave, very human but disastrous mistake and he paid a heavy cost.

After the battle, there would have been much for Hannibal to do: wounded to be tended; armour and weaponry to be salvaged; cavalry horses and transport animals to be recovered; captured baggage to be scrutinised and looted; and, importantly, the Roman ration train to be reorganised under Carthaginian control. Hannibal then gave his troops time to rest and buried those of the dead, a total about thirty, who were of the highest rank. The remainder were incinerated (see Appendix C). He also sent a search party to look for Flaminius, but the Roman general's body was not discovered, somewhere lying concealed amidst the horrendous litter of the battlefield.

Whilst this work was progressing, news was received by Hannibal of the approach of the 4,000 strong cavalry contingent which Servilius had sent as reinforcements for Flaminius. He despatched a mixed body of cavalry and pikemen to deal with it, under the command of his Master of Horse, Maharbal. This experienced cavalry commander sought out his enemy with little trouble and made short work of the opposition, destroying half of their number in his first onslaught. The remainder he pursued to a nearby hill, from where they surrendered on the following day, substantially inflating Hannibal's already handsome haul of captured weaponry. It must be doubtful, had he waited for them, whether the arrival of such a comparatively small contingent of cavalrymen would have greatly helped Flaminius's cause, when set against the total of the Carthaginian numbers. Servilius's infantry body, on the other hand, seems still to have been at least two or three days distant, almost out of tactical reckoning for the unfortunate Flaminius.

Greatly encouraged by this decisive victory, Hannibal now continued on his way southwards. He had, according to Polybius, by now decided against the idea of approaching Rome and headed for the Adriatic, plundering and ravaging his way through Umbria and Picenum and killing a number of inhabitants on his route, 'which is customary when a city is taken by storm'. Livy provides us with a slightly varied story but the same outcome. He relates that Hannibal marched through Umbria directly to Spoletium, a Roman colony strategically sited on a spur at the southern extremity of the Umbrian plain. It was a militarily important township because of its situation overlooking the *Via Flaminia* and the command it exercised over the pass leading to Norcia, north of Rome. He was repulsed with heavy loss and Livy[35] judged that, 'discouraged by the strength of one small settlement he had failed to take', he turned away into Picenum and thence to a rest area on the Adriatic. Either way, it appears to have been a profitable operation, for 'during his advance he amassed so much plunder, that his army could neither drive it nor carry it with them'.

Servilius, meantime, headed directly for Rome, probably down the Tiber valley. The walls of the capital were in danger, Livy explained, and he did not wish to be absent at this moment of crisis.

# CHAPTER V

# CRISIS FOR ROME

The provisioning of troops is a necessary condition of warfare and thus has a great influence on the operations, especially since it permits only a limited concentration of troops and since it helps to determine the theatre of war through the choice of a line of operations.

General Carl von Clausewitz[1]

When, some three days after the events at Lake Trasimene, reports reached Rome of the disastrous defeat which had been inflicted upon Flaminius, the population of the city was stunned, almost to a point of disbelief; but worse was to come. Even whilst they were seeking to recover from this initial shock, yet further bad tidings were received which brought the people out on to the streets, demonstrating their alarm and discontent. News had reached them that a contingent of 4,000 mounted troops under the propraetor Gaius Centennius, belatedly hastening from Servilius to reinforce Flaminius, had also been destroyed. Servilius himself, cutting behind Hannibal's line of advance, was said to be returning to Rome with the remnants of his army. Crowds, mainly composed of women, assembled at the city gates, questioning chance comers about the calamity, searching the faces of the dishevelled soldiery as they straggled homewards, above all praying that they might identify a loved one, friend or relative, husband or son. The scale of the catastrophe was magnified by the fact that, for many a long time, defeat had been an unknown experience for the Roman people. Now, the defence of Italy had failed, wrote Livy; henceforward the single purpose of the nation's war effort would be at home, to save the city.

The Senate, in the face of this crisis, remained calm and resolute. They determined that the situation called for the revival of the magisterial appointment of dictator, a rank from time to time created for periods of six month to deal with emergency military situations. It incorporated sweeping powers, including supreme command of the armed forces and the right to set any measures in hand which were considered necessary for national security. The man they selected for this essentially vital role, upon which indeed the future of Rome depended, was Quintus Fabius Maximus, a senior member of the Senate. Fabius, it will be recalled, had led a delegation[2] to Carthage in the previous year to demand the surrender of Hannibal, following the latter's assault upon

Fabius Maximus offers war to the Carthaginians. (The Mansell Collection)

Saguntum. The rejection of the ultimatum which Fabius had then dramatically delivered to the Carthaginians had resulted in a mutual declaration of the war which now beset the Italian mainland. Strangely, and despite their appointment of Fabius to dictator, the Senate denied him the opportunity of selecting his own Master of Horse, a rank which also bore the duties of second-in-command, together with authority to act for him in his absence. Instead, they nominated a political opponent for the task, Marcus Minucius Rufus. It was a decision which was to have initial complications.

One of the first acts of Fabius, in the task which had been delegated to him, was to make a shrewd assessment of the dangerous and unexpected war situation which now confronted the Roman people.[3] His opponents, recruited largely from Spanish, African and Celtic tribesmen, were hardy, well-trained soldiers, many of them mercenaries, accustomed to war almost from childhood. They were educated in its arts. Moreover, they were particularly mobile, being adept at irregular campaigning. Their well-mounted cavalry arm, effective in all aspects of its supporting role, was well commanded by Maharbal, a distinguished Master of Horse. Their young general, Hannibal, a superb commander of men, was also a thoughtful campaigner, unrestrained by the set-piece practices of war then favoured by ancient armies. On the other hand, despite the sharp teeth the Carthaginian had already displayed on the Trebbia and at Lake Trasimene, he was operating in a foreign field and possessed limited resources. When it came to the unavoidable problem of resupply, he was condemned to living off the land and, in the matter of replacing weaponry and equipment, he was entirely dependent upon what could be either salvaged from the battlefield, cajoled from the enemies of Rome, or prised from her allied states. We have already seen how a naval squadron, fresh from Carthage and perhaps laden with military stores, failed to make contact with him at Pisa. Supply by sea was not an easy option to consider.

Rome, on the other hand, was fighting on home ground, with the advantage of a greater local knowledge of terrain than that possessed by her enemy. Her resources of manpower were, in the words of Polybius,[4] inexhaustible, and particularly plentiful amongst her allies, if she could sustain their loyalty. She also possessed a mechanism for speedy recruitment. Her armed forces were even now being rapidly enlarged but the creation of young units on such a scale inevitably meant a dilution, within their command structure, of the training skills and campaign experience essential to battlefield success. Her military supply workshops and granaries, mainly securely located behind the walls of Rome or in the sheltered countryside occupied by the northern Etrurian towns, were equally vast. Rome had the means of survival but required a breathing space to allow for the expansion and training of her armed forces, and the manufacture of hardware with which to equip them.

Hannibal's ultimately crucial problem, well recognised by both protagonists, for wars cannot be fought without casualties, either in battle or through sickness or desertion, resided in his ability or otherwise to replace his inevitably diminishing fighting strength. There were four sources to which he might have looked for a solution. In the immediate term, Hannibal had already received reinforcements from the Celtic nations inhabiting the environs of the Po valley. The precise details of the tribes which subscribed men for this purpose are not clearly stated. We may, however, judge with some certainty that the majority had been contributed by the Insubres and the Boii peoples, together with an element from the Ligurians and some others. Cisalpine Gaul thus represented to Hannibal the most speedy and obvious source of reinforcements, if they could be got to him. Next, as Rome was keenly aware, for she had hastened to conclude her troubles with Illyria at the threat of outbreak of the Hannibalic War, there was always the possibility of partnership with Rome's enemies in the eastern Adriatic and, more immediately and closer to hand, with disaffected tribes in central and southern Italy. Fourthly, there was the central consideration, and surely a vital one for Hannibal, of replacements for the tough, hard core of African and Spanish soldiery who had marched with him from the Ebro. They formed the framework upon which his army was built and provided much of its experience.

Hannibal had planned for more of these tribesmen to join him[5] but their source of recruitment lay at the end of a lengthy, tenuous line of communication where his home base was increasingly beset with many difficulties. Cornelius Scipio, who had hastened back to Italy after his near encounter with Hannibal in the Rhône estuary, only to be defeated by him on the Trebbia, had not been allowed by his masters to deflect from his operational task in Spain. He had been returned there at the earliest possible moment, after recovery from his wounds, to maintain pressure against New Carthage. The Roman Senate, soon also to start harrying the north African coast in the vicinity of Carthage, were seemingly early disciples of the strategy of indirect approach in war, as opposed to direct confrontation, preached by Liddell Hart prior to the Second World War.[6] Hannibal's manpower difficulties rendered him particularly vulnerable to this tactic.

The detailed attention paid by Fabius to military planning at this juncture is noteworthy for its care and precision. Indeed, if only because of the time scale required to bring them to fruition, it is fair to say that many of the important defensive precautions adopted by Rome in the year following his dictatorship were almost certainly set in hand during his months in office. This applies as much to the legions raised by him for the field army in Italy as to the two others also formed for service in Cisalpine Gaul, under Lucius Postumius.[7] Their task, patently, was the far-sighted one of containing the Insubres and the Boii at this juncture and thus preventing them from sending further reinforcements to Hannibal. In addition, arrangements were made for a delegation from the Senate[8] to be simultaneously sent to Liguria to question their politicians about reports of their assistance to Hannibal and, whilst about it, to monitor the sympathies of other Celtic tribes.

The plan for counter operations, which emerged from this assessment by Fabius, was controversial when set against contemporary military standards. It was not immediately popular but it was, nevertheless, a sensible response. He determined to maintain contact with Hannibal but to avoid pitched battle with him, choosing rather to harrass and ambush enemy stragglers and foraging parties upon every occasion which offered itself, and generally to keep to the hill country, thus negating the effectiveness of the Carthaginian cavalry. His purpose was threefold: to reduce his enemy's already limited numbers; to disrupt his ability to feed himself; and, at the same time and by this means, to restore the morale of his own troops, 'whose confidence had been shattered by their earlier defeats'.

Simultaneously, so as to tighten further the screw upon Hannibal's difficulties, he issued a decree destined to shape future Roman tactics, as well as those of the Carthaginians. He gave orders for all local communities to move into safety behind the walls of fortified towns or forts, and to take with them as much foodstuff and supplies as they could manage. Any balance remaining was to be ruthlessly destroyed, so as not to be allowed to fall into the hands of the enemy. Finally, under threat of drastic punishment should they fail to comply with the edict, inhabitants living in open countryside were ordered to burn their homes and destroy their standing crops.

Once the detail of these matters had been attended to, Fabius set out along the *Via Flaminia* to meet Servilius, accompanied by his second-in-command, Minucius, and the four legions which had been conscripted for the emergency. He sighted the returning column near Ocriculum, on the Tiber, towards the end of its 200-mile march from Ariminum. He then took up a position in the path of

Quintus Fabuis Maximus; a seventeenth-century engraving.

the advancing army and, surrounded by his staff, standard bearers and trumpeters and with all the pomp that his newly acquired rank demanded, he summoned the consul to his presence, instructing him to leave behind his lictors.[9] Then, once the trappings of dictatorial handover had been satisfied, he announced himself as the new commander of Servilius's army. It was, recounts Livy proudly, a splendid exhibition of ceremonial, rarely seen in recent years. The two men were soon reminded of the dangerous reality which surrounded them. The exchange of command had barely been concluded when news was received that a Carthaginian naval squadron operating off Cosa, north of the Tiber estuary, had seized a flotilla of merchant ships carrying supplies to the Roman army in Spain. Servilius was at once given the task of responding to the threat.[10] According to Livy, he was ordered

> . . . to go to Ostia at once, to man with fighting troops and allied seamen all ships either there or up river near Rome, and to use them for the pursuit of the enemy squadron and the defence of the Italian coast. In Rome a large force was enlisted; even freedmen, if they had children and were of military age, had taken the oath. Of this force, raised in the capital, all under 35 years of age were sent to serve with the fleet; the remainder were left to guard the city.

Polybius,[11] in his account, gives Servilius a wider remit, namely, 'to hold himself ready to give support wherever necessary if the Carthaginians should attempt any operations from the sea'.

Aerial photograph of
Carthage harbour. (Air
Photo Library, University of
Keele)

It was now approaching mid-July and Hannibal, seizing upon the disarray thrust upon Rome by his sequence of successes on the battlefield, took the opportunity to give his troops a recuperative and administrative break. For this purpose, he headed towards the Adriatic coast, relentlessly pursuing his policy of laying waste the countryside as he proceeded. His men and animals had suffered a severe winter in Cisalpine Gaul and had subsequently been exposed both to the hardship of crossing the swamps of the upper Arno and the fighting at Lake Trasimene. Many were suffering from scurvy and its attendant diseases: others had been wounded and required medical attention. The opportunity now presented itself for these to be dealt with[12] and for the fighting fitness of his force to be restored. Hannibal's successes had made him 'master of a rich countryside' where even old wine was available in such quantity that he applied it to the coats of his horses to revive their condition:

> He also rearmed his African troops with Roman equipment, selecting the best weapons for the purpose, since he was now in possession of huge stores of captured arms. At the same time he sent messengers by sea to give the Carthaginians a full report of what had happened, for this was the first time he had reached the sea since he invaded Italy. The news aroused tremendous rejoicing in Carthage and the authorities lost no time in taking steps to give every possible support to the conduct of the war both in Italy and in Spain.

This last sentence implies that Carthage sent help to Hannibal in Italy at this time, and this would surely have been the moment for him to receive it, but none of the ancient annalists record its arrival. The west coast of central and southern Italy was, by the years of the Hannibalic War, well safeguarded by nine so-called Roman coastguard colonies, carefully located to protect her seaports and to watch over her strategic interests.[13] Their presence, as we have already witnessed in the case of the Carthaginian naval squadron which appeared off Pisa, and then later off Cosa, discouraged enemy aggression. Conversely, as realised by the Allied invasion force which landed at one of them, Anzio (Antium), in the Second World War, their possession had much to offer an invading enemy force.

The Adriatic coast was less well provided. In the mid-summer season, and particularly in the Adriatic Sea, sailing and prevailing wind directions combined to affect the length of time of voyages between Italy and Africa (and, of course, elsewhere, such as Greece, Asia Minor or Egypt). An exceptionally fast run between Ostia and a point off Cape Bon, a distance of 270 nautical miles, was recorded by Pliny as being completed in two days at an overall speed of 6 knots.[14] The ship requisitioned by Hannibal, sailing out of the Adriatic and around Cyprus, may well have taken as many as four or five days to reach Carthage with his despatches. A return voyage to the port of origin on the east coast of the Italian peninsula, in the face of adverse winds, could well have taken twice as long. A journey to the west coast of southern Italy, on the other hand, if a suitable port could have been secured for the purpose, would have had the merit of a faster passage, with less time at sea, vulnerable to possible naval

attack. The early possession of a port on the south-west coast of Italy was, thus, a prime need for Hannibal: but, above all, the question which remains paramount is how much, at this stage of his campaign, did the Carthaginian hierarchy feel obliged to render support to their general fighting in Italy? Appian, albeit writing some three centuries later,[15] suggests a considerable lack of enthusiasm:

> Hannibal, although in his despatches to the Carthaginians he invariably exaggerated his achievements, now, having lost many men and being in want of assistance, asked them to send him soldiers and money. But his enemies, who jeered at all his doings, now too replied that they could not understand how Hannibal should be asking for help when he said he was winning victories, since victorious generals did not ask for money but sent it home to their own people. The Carthaginians followed their suggestion and sent neither soldiers nor money.

One way or another, Hannibal continued to plough a lonely furrow. During his ten-day march to the Adriatic coast from Lake Trasimene, as we have seen, he devastated much of the countryside in his path. He now took the opportunity of his rest period to complete the task, firstly around his present whereabouts, and then scouring the strip of already unproductive agricultural hinterland, found in Apulia and Calabria, lying between the peninsula's south-east coastline and the foothills of the Apennine range. To the north, his raiding parties reached to the territories of Praetutia, Hadriana, Marrucina and Frentana, east of Rome, beyond the Apennines; whilst to the south he ravaged the lands of the Daunii, the Peucettii and the Messapii. The territory of the latter lay between Brundisium (Brindisi) and Tarentum, towards the 'heel' of Italy. Both of the southern provinces, Apulia and Calabria, in which these tribes resided, suffered from a particularly scant rainfall. The situation has little changed. White[16] quotes a modern-day report that settlements and farmhouses are rarely found except where wells have been sunk to provide oases 'in an otherwise waterless country'. Hannibal's raiding parties would therefore have added considerably to the problems of this already inhospitable area of ancient Italy, described by Horace as 'thirsty' Apulia, which had previously suffered great depredation under Pyrrhus some sixty years earlier.

It is arguable that these casual operations by Hannibal, which reached southwards a distance of some 320 miles from the waist of the peninsula, were the first phase of a carefully calculated programme of devastation. Hannibal seemingly now embarked upon the second phase of his plan and set forth marching in a westerly direction, broadly along the axis of the Volturnus river. The Volturnus rises in the Abruzzese Apennines and flows south-east until it joins the Calore river, near Caiazzo. From thence it turns south-west to enter the Tyrrhenian Sea, north-west of Naples, having covered a distance of 109 miles. The river is crossed, north of Capua, by both the Appian and Latin Ways from Rome, situated some 90 miles distant. These two strategic roads join together as they approach the right bank of the Volturnus; they then proceed onwards

*Opposite*: Map showing the campaign area on the Volturnus.

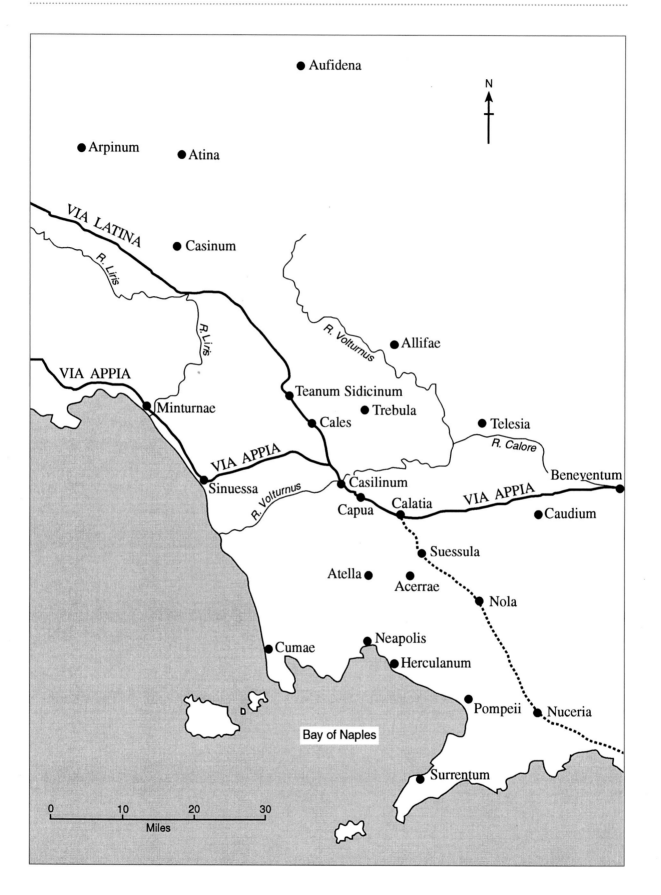

together to Casilinum and Capua before diverging to reassume their respective ways. It is noteworthy that the *Via Appia* had been extended in 244 BC, before Hannibal's arrival, to pass through Beneventum, Venusia, and Tarentum to Brundisium, the latter being always an important seaport but in those years a major military harbour linking with the eastern Mediterranean and the Aegean.

Fabius, whilst all this had been progressing, had received military intelligence that Hannibal was temporarily encamped at Aecae, some 20 miles south of the Latin colony of Luceria and 30 miles inland from the Adriatic coast. The dictator promptly marshalled his army and, together with his Master of Horse, Minucius, he marched to take up a position 6 miles distant from his enemy. As soon as Hannibal heard of his arrival he approached the Roman camp with his whole army and drew up his men in battle order, taunting Fabius to a fight. There, says Polybius,[17] he waited for some time, but as nobody came to meet him he finally retired to his own camp. For his part, Polybius explains,

> Fabius had decided not to take any risk, still less to venture a pitched battle, but to make the safety of his men his first and principal aim and, having chosen such a strategy, he resolutely followed it. At first he was despised for this, and his action gave people the excuse to say it was inspired only by cowardice, and that he was terrified of an engagement. But as time went on he compelled everyone to admit that it would have been impossible for anyone to have acted with more prudence in the existing circumstances. It was not long before events themselves bore witness to the wisdom of his policy . . .

After this incident, Hannibal continued marching westward, passing over the Apennine range and the territory of the Hirpini, to descend on to the fertile agricultural belt of the western coastal plain, devastating the land in a wide swathe as he progressed. The agricultural yields of this area were superlative. Not only did it produce a wheat of rare quality but, the surrounding hills were the source of excellent wines and the highest rated olive oil in Italy. Moreover, from the accounts left to us by contemporary annalists, it does not appear to have been greatly affected by the stern 'scorched earth' order issued by Fabius. Perhaps an explanation is to be found in the proximity to Rome of this abundant larder. Nevertheless, the loss of fruit and grain crops on the scale now inflicted by the Carthaginians must inevitably have delivered a serious blow to the economy and, in the short term, to the Roman war effort.

In one sense, this was quickly made good, particularly industrially, as the population driven from the area resettled northward in a more secure environment. As far as local agriculture was concerned, however, a belt of wasteland had been created which could not be restored to its former fruitfulness until its farming community had returned. In a paradoxical way, the Roman dictator himself would not necessarily have been out of sympathy with the situation thus created, for supplies to satisfy his own needs were beginning to arrive by sea, a facility as yet denied to Hannibal; and the now devastated land, until it were replanted, had nothing to offer the Carthaginians. Instead, it lay barren and unattractive across their path whenever they might decide to march on Rome.

Meantime, as Hannibal busily engaged himself in laying waste the countryside up to the gates of the coastguard colony of Sinuessa itself, he was discreetly followed by Fabius, who closely watched his activities from neighbouring high ground, safe from attack from Maharbal's Numidian cavalry, because of the broken nature of the terrain. He was conscious of the threat to Rome posed by Hannibal's proximity to the Latin and Appian Ways and despatched his Master of Horse, Minucius, to hold the pass, almost overhanging the sea above Terracina, 'to prevent the enemy from entering Roman territory by the Appian Way'. He himself took up a position, on Mount Massicus, north of the Carthaginian army from where, so Livy[18] relates, 'he could see the smoke of conflagrations rising on every hand from the farms in this loveliest region of all Italy'. Minucius, surrounded by officers and his force of cavalrymen, could contain himself no longer at the sight he was witnessing. 'Are we here', he burst out sardonically, but he spoke for the majority of those around him, 'merely to enjoy the pleasant spectacle of our friends being butchered and their houses burned?'

Fabius, however, did not allow himself to be deterred from his resolve. He appreciated that Hannibal would wish to withdraw eastward when his work of destruction was complete, for the winter season would soon be approaching and the Carthaginian would want to get home with, *inter alia*, the plundered foodstuffs, including a vast herd of cattle, seemingly numbered in thousands, which he had accumulated to feed his army throughout the coming months. Fabius also judged, from the pattern of his own dispositions, that Hannibal would either be compelled to return by the way he had come, making use of the pass over Mount Callicula, or 'be forced to winter among the rock of Formiae and the desolate sands and swamps of Liternum'. He therefore despatched a force of 4,000 men to hold the pass, whilst he himself, with the remainder of his army, encamped on a neighbouring hill, overlooking the approach road and within reach of the Latin Way.

It was an ingenious plan, so uncharacteristic of conventional Roman army tactics that Livy felt constrained to tell his readers that Hannibal had been 'hoist by his own petard'. The young Carthaginian was, however, equal to the occasion. His response was swift, efficient and ruthlesly cruel. He sent, first, for Hasdrubal, one of his senior commanders, and instructed him to select 2,000 ploughing oxen from his vast herd of looted cattle. He was then to mass these in front of their encampment, whilst simultaneously preparing as many faggots of wood, twigs and dried grasses as possible. Hannibal then assembled his pioneers and pointed out to them a ridge visible from the camp and the whereabouts of the pass through which he intended to take his army. They were to stand by, ready, upon his command, to drive the animals as fast and furiously as possible, to the summit of that ridge. He allocated his light pikemen to assist them in the drive, with instructions that, upon reaching the top, they were to hold the ridge against Roman attack. His next act, like every prudent commander, was to order his men to have an evening meal and retire to bed, for they were to be called early, ready to march by the end of the third watch of the night.

Appian[19] records that, when his army had been roused, and before marching
out, Hannibal put to death his 5,000 prisoners, 'lest they should turn upon him
in his hour of danger'. It is not an incident mentioned by either Polybius or Livy,
nor are we informed from where these prisoners originated: but, sadly, it is
believable. Then, as the column approached the foothills, the pioneers fastened
the faggots to the horns of the cattle and set them alight. The unfortunate
animals needed little urging as they fled up the mountainside,[20]

> terrified by the glare of the flames, not to mention the pain which soon burned
> down to the root and very quick of their horns. They dashed this way and
> that, and before long all the scrub was burning as if the woods and mountains
> had been set on fire. Tossing their heads in a vain attempt to shake off the
> pain, they succeeded only in fanning the flames to greater violence, till the
> whole scene looked, from the distance, like an army of men, rapidly running
> hither and thither.

The Romans, guarding the gorge through which Hannibal planned to pass,
were suitably confused. They judged, from the torches moving upwards on the
mountainside, that their enemy had discovered a means of outflanking them.
They, therefore, hastily abandoned their position astride the pass and moved
towards the ridge to intercept him. As they approached the cattle in the dark, for
the day had not yet broken, they came into conflict with the pikemen; but, at this
moment, their ranks were broken by a surge of frightened animals and they
parted contact, uncertain as to what was happening, and waited for the dawn.
Whilst this mêlée had been taking place, Hannibal, in a night move which, with
such a large and cosmopolitan force, must have been the outcome of excellent
administrative planning, conducted the main body of his army through the pass,
together with its cavalry, and as much of his baggage train and plunder as had
not been abandoned. He then encamped on its far side. At first light, when he
could see clearly the situation of his pikemen on the ridge, he despatched a
contingent of his Spanish mountain troops to their aid. These fell upon the
Romans, killing about 1,000, and then, extricating themselves with the pikemen
they had been sent to relieve, withdrew to camp 'almost without loss'.

Hannibal now determined that the time had arrived when he should be seeking
a winter base. His scouts had informed him that the region around the Latin
fortress of Luceria and the Apulian city of Gerunium, which lay some 24 miles
further north, possessed abundant supplies of grain and that the latter place was
the better suited, both for its collection and storage. According to Polybius,[21] his
choice fell upon Gerunium and, when its inhabitants refused to surrender to him
upon being summoned to do so, he took the city by storm. Livy provides a
different version, with a more plausible sound.[22] He relates that Hannibal found
Gerunium already deserted by its inhabitants, because its walls had collapsed and
it had become indefensible. Probably as part of Fabius's scorched earth policy, its
buildings had been burnt but, despite this, a few still stood intact, available as
storehouses for grain. Whichever may be the true account of these events,

Hannibal occupied the town, encamped his army in front of it, fortified the whole with a trench and a palisade and despatched foragers to uncover stocks of winter grain: their work was soon to be interrupted.

Fabius, having handed over command of his army to Minucius, now returned to Rome, ostensibly 'to attend to certain religious matters' but more probably to be questioned about his military handling of the situation, about which there was increasing dissatisfaction. Before his departure from his camp, tucked safely away 'high up in the hills', he instructed his volatile Master of Horse to stick rigidly to his strategy of maintaining contact with the enemy but avoiding serious confrontation. As soon as Fabius had departed, however, Minucius moved his army down from its elevated position, seized a Carthaginian outpost which had been located near his new camp to watch his movements and enthusiastically set about Hannibal's foragers scattered over the countryside. He inflicted heavy casualties upon them, forcing Hannibal to fall back behind the entrenchments of the temporary field camp he had established to safeguard his working parties and to cease his corn gathering operations. Minucius then advanced to the walls of Hannibal's defences and found himself so much in control of the situation that his soldiers contemplated dismantling the enemy palisades. This provoked Hannibal to lead a sortie through the gates and some harsh hand-to-hand fighting then ensued, brought to an end by the arrival of Hasdrubal, who had marched to his relief with an accumulated force of some 4,000 foragers.

The encounter left both commanders with differing hopes and fears. Minucius abandoned the field enthusing about the future and the need for a more aggressive policy.[23] He had, Polybius relates, inflicted heavy losses on the Carthaginians, but we are given little indication of the numbers involved. Livy writes of 6,000 Carthaginian dead, with Roman losses amounting to some 5,000. Hannibal, for his part, was shaken by what had happened. Apart from being concerned about such a loss of manpower at this juncture, he was, it would appear, naturally anxious to retain intact his captured herd of several thousand cattle. Its very size made it a vulnerable target, difficult to defend. Likewise, as has already been said, with the onset of winter it was vital his task of foraging for grain should be allowed to continue uninterrupted. It was now urgently required not only for his men, but also, importantly, for 'his horses and pack animals, for the cavalry was the arm upon which he relied above all others'.[24] We cannot share his concern fully, for we are not aware of the quantities with which he returned from his west coast foray; but the gravity of his need is emphasised by the fact that, despite the watchful Roman presence, he was prepared drastically to cut the size of his garrison at Gerunium in order to boost his working parties in the countryside. Hannibal was seemingly right to be disturbed.

The Senate were cheered by the news of this comparatively minor Roman success, which had been well magnified by Minucius in the personal account he sent to Rome. It quickly became the source of much discussion at popular assemblies, adding greatly to the discomfit of Fabius, who refused to believe what he was told. He went further: he declared that even if the whole thing were true, 'he himself was more fearful of success than of failure'.[25] He preached caution but he was listened to, particularly within the Senate, with increasing hostility. Finally, they reached a decision which virtually destroyed his military authority as a dictator, namely that command of his army should be jointly shared between himself and Minucius. Fabius, however, remained adamant in his belief that he was pursuing the correct tactics and, in view of the degree of variation in the thinking of the two men, they agreed, upon his return, to split the army in two halves, with Minucius taking II and III Legions, and Fabius retaining I and IV. In this manner, they both achieved an independent command. The army then separated and the two halves took up positions about a mile and a half apart, each commander pursuing his own policy. Even before this moment, writes Livy,[26] success and popularity had rendered Minucius intolerable enough;

> but now his behaviour went beyond all bounds of moderation and decency, and he bragged about his defeat of Fabius even more than his so-called defeat of Hannibal. That Fabius, sought out in times of stress as the one and only match for the victorious Hannibal, should now, by popular vote, be made equal to a junior officer – he, a dictator, brought to the level of his Master of Horse – and that, too, in a country where mere Masters of Horse had been in the habit of cringing like curs before the dictator's terrible rods and axes: why, the thing was unprecedented in history!

Hannibal, always well informed in intelligence matters, and particularly so about the temperament of his opposing generals, had been watching these events with increasing interest. The terrain between his camp and that of Minucius was flat, bare of woodland, and militarily uninspiring. It was pock-marked with numerous clefts and depressions in the ground, some of them capable of containing as many as 200 men. Towards its centre stood a hill, which overlooked both of their encampments. It was, in any event, an important military feature which he would have wished to occupy. He now decided to use it as a lure to trap Minucius and concealed in the hollows of the plain a carefully selected body of some 5,000 horse and foot. Then, at dawn, he sent a small party to occupy the hill. By its presumptuously overt nature, it was an act carefully calculated to annoy his opponent and Minucius responded predictably. The hill became his sole focus of operations. He at once despatched a contingent of light troops with orders to assault and occupy it. Hannibal, in turn, responded by reinforcing its garrison and Minucius, not to be outdone, now deployed his cavalry, an act which triggered the release of the more powerful Carthaginian horse, followed by their mass of infantry. This was a decisive action which finally drew Minucius from his lines, with his heavy infantry marching in close order, and both sides were now fully committed to battle.

Whilst this build-up of hostilities was being completed, the Roman light troops on the hill broke under pressure and fell back through their infantry, drawn up in array. This was not, in itself, a disastrous happening for Minucius. Indeed, in the normal sequence of such events, it would have opened the way for the two opponents to engage in a set-piece encounter of a kind at which the Roman army excelled. On this occasion, however, it provided the moment of temporary confusion for which Hannibal had been waiting. His signallers sounded their trumpets and the troops lying concealed in ambush emerged from their hiding places to launch 'an attack, with the result that not only the light infantry but the whole of Minucius's force found itself in a critical position': but help was at hand. Fabius, who, according to Polybius,[27] had been an alarmed spectator of the battle, now moved forward to rescue his fellow commander. His approach had a dual effect. It gave heart to Minucius's scattered army, which now rallied to its standards and, despite its losses, made a reasonably orderly withdrawal to the security of his lines: and it caused Hannibal to pull back from contact. He had no wish, at this juncture, when his pressing administrative needs weighed so greatly in his mind, to find himself totally committed to a battle which offered little gain but much to lose. At the same time, Minucius recognised how close he had come to defeat and returned forthwith to Fabius, in front of whom he paraded himself, with his legions, and, formally placing himself once again under his command, avowed his future loyalty.

The six-monthly term of office of Fabius's dictatorship was by now drawing to an end and the Senate elected two men, Lucius Aemilius Paullus and Gaius Terrentius Varro, to assume consular responsibilities when the dictators laid down his powers. Servilius, the erstwhile commander of the army at Rimini and later commander of the fleet, together with Marcus Atilius Regulus, who had earlier been appointed general upon the death of Flaminius, were both invested with proconsular powers[28] and once again assumed field command of the two armies over which they had previously held authority. The Senate laid down clear orders for the future conduct of the campaign, for its members also, as well as Minucius, had by now learnt the wisdom of the Fabian tactics. Pitched battles were to be avoided; every opportunity to improve the confidence and training of the newly recruited armies was to be sought; minor operations were to be encouraged, both with a view to restricting Hannibal's activities and providing active service experience for the young Roman soldiery. At the same time, and undoubtedly with the purpose of restricting supplies and reinforcements reaching Hannibal, the fleet from Lilybaeum was recalled to home waters, overseas operations in Spain were enhanced by the despatch of further supplies and equipment, and, as we have already seen, an army of two legions under command of praetor Lucius Postumius was despatched to Cisalpine Gaul.

We should here pause and, at the risk of some repetition, consider the situation which had now been reached. For Rome, the belief in the infallibility of her armed forces had been shattered by the defeat of her armies on the Trebbia, at Lake Trasimene and at Gerunium. The framework of her defence arrangements had been badly damaged. In Italy, a standstill in operations had been ordered so that the newly raised armies might gain war experience but, patently, Rome itself was to be defended against attack. Fabius had made this clear by his manoeuvring north of the Volturnus, always maintaining a position between the capital city and Hannibal's Carthaginians, whilst keeping a close watch on the Appian and Latin Ways. But, these matters apart, Rome had two invaluable assets. Her manpower resources were vast and her supply lines to the frontier she had established between herself and Hannibal were both short and secure.

Hannibal's military position was almost directly the reverse of that of Rome. Hannibal's great strengths lay in his original thinking; his tough, battle-hardened soldiery; his cavalry, numerous and experienced; his mobility; and the inevitable frailty of some of Rome's alliances which, in times of trouble such as these, lay distant from practical support. Hannibal's weaknesses were to be found in his wasting manpower situation, compared with the vast pool upon which his opponent could draw, and his uncertain supply situation, not only in Italy but also from his home bases. He was dependent for supplies upon whatever he could forage and the friends he could make. He suffered from lack of equipment, particularly at this early stage of his campaign, and was largely reliant upon what he could salvage from the battlefield. He had always recognised his ultimate need for the active support of allies and, to this end, had been circumspect in the handling of those of Rome when they fell into his hands. Clearly, however, their sympathy for his cause depended not only upon their vision of the outcome, but also upon the protection he could offer his allies which, to bring us full cycle, was limited by his lack of manpower.

Clausewitz,[29] in his much quoted work *On War*, argued that the logistical needs of troops help to 'determine the theatre of war through the choice of a line of operations'. He also added, and he wrote in times when modern supply systems did not exist, that the supply situation in any given war zone regulated the scale of concentration of troops. To put it in words more suitable for Hannibal's manpower dilemma, if enemy provisioning could be restricted by devastation, then the deployment of enemy troops, both in scale and scope, would be proportionately limited; and this appears to have become Hannibal's aim. His thrust, from east to west, along the north bank of the Volturnus, together with the booty he had obtained and the accompanying devastation he had wreaked, had added greatly to the scale of this 'barren' area. It will be recalled that Hannibal had previously raided down the east coast of the southern peninsula, reaching as far as the outskirts of Tarentum and Brundisium. The scale and pattern of this devastation, initiated by both contestants, had the affect of creating a frontier area along the axis of the Volturnus, extending eastwards to the Adriatic coast. It became for Rome a defensive frontier, hinged in the east upon the Latin strong point of Luceria, first founded 100 years earlier to watch over the troublesome Samnites.

Further south, in north-west Apulia, across the line of this emerging frontier, Rome had equally firm allies, in particular at Canusium. This town was surrounded by pasture lands capable of sustaining a large cavalry force,[30] and was watched over by a citadel established at Cannae, 'where the Romans had accumulated corn and other supplies from the district'.[31] The military importance of Cannae is not always fully recognised. It was situated on the Aufidus, the only peninsular river which flows from one side of the Apennines to

A view of the Bay of Naples, showing the Castel Nuovo, on Piazza Municipio, facing the harbour. By her system of 'coastguard colonies' Rome denied these waters to Hannibal. (By courtesy of the Italian State Tourist Board (E.N.I.T.) London)

the other, in this manner indirectly linking the fertile Campanian coastal plain with 'thirsty' Apulia. At the same time, its valley, which pointed to the strategically important Gulf of Naples, provided easy access for an army across this southern region of Italy without the need of scaling the mountain range.

Thus Cannae, lying south of the Volturnus line, was more than just another supply base and it was doubtless with these thoughts in mind, in early June (216 BC) when the crops around Gerunium had been gathered in, that Hannibal marched out to remove the threat which its presence posed to his eastern flank.

Polybius expresses the view that the Carthaginian saw an assault upon it as being a simple means to bring the elusive Roman army to battle; but the sensitive Roman reaction to his seizure of the citadel and the stores it was protecting suggests that both sides considered it to be a place of more than ordinary military importance. This is again witnessed by the attitude of the Roman generals in the field, Servilius and Regulus. When Hannibal first seized and occupied the fortress,[32] they relentlessly pursued Rome for instructions on what to do, pointing out that if they approached the enemy it would be impossible to avoid a battle and that this would be contrary to their orders. Meantime, they added, the country was being pillaged and the loyalty of their allies was being severely strained. Significantly, in response to their appeal and, again underlining the strategic value of the citadel in the scheme of Roman defence, the Senate were finally persuaded to grant the consuls the authority they were seeking but stressed that nothing should be done until Paullus had arrived, bringing with him four additional, newly recruited legions.

Fabius was distinctly unhappy at this turn of events and did his utmost to discourage Paullus from undertaking any serious military adventures at this juncture. In the custom of the day, Livy's record of these happenings[33] provides us with an exhortation which Fabius is supposed to have directed at the consul prior to his departure to the war. Whether or not they were the precise words uttered by the former dictator, Paullus would not have found their general purport in the least encouraging. Nevertheless, they bear repetition because they represent a succinct and graphic summary of Fabius's tactical thinking, despite a level of exaggeration in their description of Hannibal's plight:

> Every day that passes makes us better, wiser, firmer. Hannibal, on the contrary, is on foreign and hostile soil, far from home and country, surrounded by every menace, every danger; for him there is no peace on land or sea; no towns receive him, no protecting walls; nothing he sees can he call his own; he has nothing to live on beyond the plunder of a day. He now has hardly a third of the army with which he crossed the Ebro; more of his men have died of hunger than fallen in battle, and the few that remain have not enough to eat. Can you then doubt that *inactivity* is the way to defeat an enemy who is daily growing more decrepit, and has neither adequate supplies, nor reinforcements, nor money?

Paullus, however, equally as Fabius had been during his dictatorship, was saddled with an arrogant, hot-headed fellow consul, Gaius Terrentius Varro, a man who possessed little military experience and yet had been heard to boast upon his appointment that he would bring the war 'to an end on the day he first caught sight of the enemy'. Paullus expressed first caution and then surprise that any army commander, whilst still at Rome and in civilian clothes, before he had yet met his own troops or those of the enemy, and before he had any knowledge of the lie of the land in which he was to operate, should speak in such a manner. Thus the two new generals, who were destined to share

Hannibal's Corn War. After their comprehensive defeat at Cannae the Romans consolidated their position north of line A, running from the mouth of the Volturnus in the west, thence proceeding eastwards, south of Luceria, to the Adriatic coast. Territory lying south of this military frontline was, for the moment, virtually abandoned to Hannibal.

command on alternate days according to the strange Roman custom of the time, held diagonally opposed tactical opinions. Upon arrival in the war zone they were immediately in trouble. Paullus, noting the flat and treeless terrain, recognised it at once as good cavalry country, favourable to Hannibal but not to himself. Inevitably, Varro did not agree with him and an acrimonius exchange of views then took place. The following day being Varro's turn for command, he seized the opportunity to break camp and, despite strenuous protests and 'active opposition' by Paullus, advanced in the direction of the enemy, 'who took him by surprise while he was still on the march'. The confused fighting which then erupted lasted until sunset, without either side being able to claim advantage.

Next, it was the turn of Paullus to command. He felt unable to withdraw safely from the difficult situation handed over to him by his joint commander. He therefore pitched camp on the banks of the Aufidus, and garrisoned it with two-thirds of his force, the remainder of which he sited in a camp on the far side of the river, about 1½ miles equidistant from his main body and that of the enemy. It was his intention, by doing this, to protect his own foraging parties whilst harrassing those of the Carthaginians.

Hannibal allowed the new arrivals no rest. His Numidian cavalry rode right up to the Roman palisades, preventing the water carriers from carrying out their task and infuriating Varro. As a consequence, upon reassuming command and without any prior consultation with his colleague, the latter marched his main body across the river at first light to join with the remainder of his army from the smaller camp. He then marshalled the whole force in battle formation, so that the 'depth of each (maniple) was several times greater than its width'. The object of this grouping in the old-fashioned phalanx style was to provide weight to his centre so that, upon making contact with what he judged to be Hannibal's outnumbered infantry, much of it tribal, he could burst through their lines before the formidable Carthaginian cavalry were deployed. Varro completed his formation by throwing his light infantry forward to cover his front. He then posted his Roman cavalry on his right wing, with their open flank resting on the river and his allied cavalry on his left wing, where he himself took his place, in the overall commanding position. Paullus, deeply offended by his treatment but soon to die gallantly in battle, took command of the right wing and Servilius, the senior of the proconsuls, was granted the task of controlling the centre.

Their opponent was not slow to acknowledge the strangely theatrical formality of the challenge and moved to enter the arena. Hannibal first pushed his light infantry across the river, to cover the passage of his main body. When this had been achieved, and as they arrived, he drew his contingents up in line to confront Varro's army. He had equipped his experienced African heavy infantry with Roman armour, shields and weaponry recovered from the battlefields of Trasimene and elsewhere. He now located them in two divisions, so that they flanked the less formidable Spanish and Celtic foot soldiers stationed in the centre. The Numidian cavalry were posted on his right wing, facing the Roman

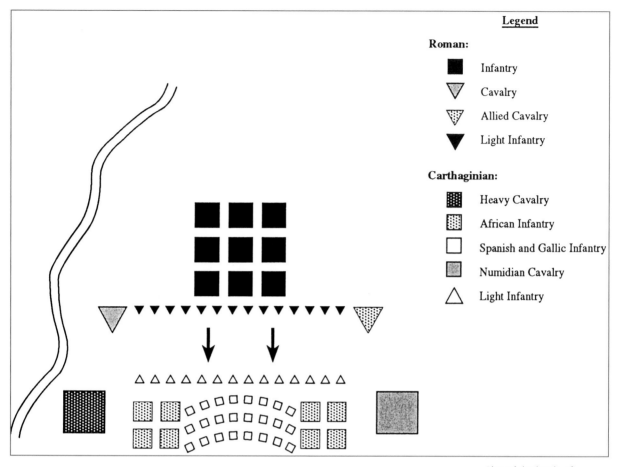

Plan of the battle of Cannae.

allied horse, whilst his Spanish and Celtic cavalry took their place on the opposing wing, with their open flank resting on the river. Polybius comments upon the 'strange and terrifying' spectacle presented by the Hannibalic army, the troops drawn up in alternate companies, the Celts naked, and the Spaniards in their national dress of short linen tunics bordered with purple. Hasdrubal commanded the Carthaginian left, Maharbal, the right,[34] and Hannibal, with his brother Mago, the centre.

The total numbers of the forces involved at Cannae have been much discussed. Both Polybius and Livy are in agreement that Hannibal fielded some 40,000 infantry and 10,000 cavalry, both arms being drawn from Spanish, African and Cisalpine Gallic sources, the latter, in each case, providing about half of the total manpower. In addition, Hannibal possessed some contingents of light troops, probably Balearic slingers. Some historians[35] argue that Hannibal's infantry totalled no more than 35,000. In view of the losses sustained by the Carthaginians arising from their expedition of the previous year to the mouth of the Volturnus, later followed by those collected during their operations around Gerunium during the winter months, there is no reason why this variation should be unacceptable.

The ancient annalists[36] broadly agree on the size of the Roman army brought to the field by Varro. Polybius writes of 80,000 infantry and 'a little over' 6,000 cavalry. Appian records '70,000 foot and 6,000 horse' and Livy writes that 'at the time of the battle of Cannae, Rome had 87,200 men in service'. The eminent historian H.H. Scullard,[37] suggests smaller totals numbering 48,000 infantry and 6,000 cavalry. Toynbee[38] on the other hand, and after detailed consideration, argues that, upon entry into battle, the Roman army comprised '80,000 infantry, and 6,400 or 7,200 or 9,600 cavalry'. The comparative strengths of the armies which lined up against each other at Cannae may thus be judged broadly to have been: Roman, 86,000 (80,000 infantry, 6,000 cavalry) and Carthaginian, probably no more than 50,000, comprised of some 40,000 infantry, with 10,000 cavalry.

Hannibal was the first to advance towards his opponent. As the two armies came together, the cavalry encounter on the river bank, tightly jammed between the water and the mass of infantry, soon compelled the abandonment of the horses and deteriorated into a foot soldiers' battle, overwhelmingly won by the Numidians as they cut and thrust their way remorselessly forward. The infantry battle was decided by Hannibal's decision to move his Spanish and Celtic troops forward of the line as they advanced, so that they assumed a crescent-shaped formation, with its arc bending towards the Roman infantry. As the two sides joined in fighting, the centre of the Carthaginian line fell back, encouraging the Romans to surge forward in their pursuit. Simultaneously, Hannibal's African infantry first stood firm and then turned inwards to attack the now exposed flanks of the Roman phalanx, which, already tightly formed in mass, were afforded no opportunity to make the maximum use of their superior numbers. At this point, Hasdrubal, with his cavalry, fell upon the Roman rear with devastating effect and, 'as their outer ranks were continually cut down and the survivors were forced to pull back and huddle together', the whole force was finally broken and dispersed.

Livy[39] relates the end of the unfortunate Paullus:

Lentulus, the military tribune, as he rode by, saw the consul Paullus sitting on a stone and bleeding profusely. 'Lucius Aemilius' he said, 'you only, in the sight of heaven, are guiltless of this day's disaster; take my horse, while you still have some strength left, and I am here to lift you and protect you. Do not add to the darkness of our calamity by a consul's death. Without that, we have enough cause for tears.' 'God bless your courage,' said Paullus, 'but you have little time to escape; do not waste it in useless pity – get you gone and tell the Senate to look to Rome and fortify it with strong defences before the victorious enemy can come. And take a personal message too: tell Quintus Fabius that while I lived I did not forget his counsel, and that I remember it now in my hour of death'.

The two men were still speaking when a crowd of fugitives swept by, the Numidians close on their heels. Paullus fell under a shower of spears, his killers not even knowing whom they had killed. His death signalled the end of the

The death of Paullus at the
battle of Cannae.

battle. After that, wrote Livy, as dusk descended, nothing was to be seen or
heard but men fleeing for their lives. Dawn, when it came, revealed Romans
'lying dead in their thousands' but even then the killing did not cease. The
Carthaginians returned to the battlefield for their spoils, after a night of
celebration. They cold-bloodedly despatched any of the enemy they found still
clinging to life.

The numbers of Roman dead were never clearly established. Polybius,[40]
records a total of 70,000, Livy a lesser total of 48,000, including 45,500 infantry.
Hannibal, for his part, is thought to have lost between 5,000 to 8,000 men, a
comparatively modest number but even so it was one he could have ill afforded.
It was doubtless this factor, above all, which deflected him from marching on
Rome when encouraged to do so by his Master of Horse, Maharbal. 'I commend
your zeal', he is said to have replied to his senior cavalryman, 'but I need time to
weigh the plan which you propose.' 'Assuredly', Maharbal responded,[41] 'no one
man has been blessed with all God's gifts. You know, Hannibal, how to win a
fight; you do not know how to use your victory.'

In all the circumstances, it was an unprofessional judgement by Maharbal to
suggest a march on Rome: but if he were frustrated, as he should have been, at

the sight of Hannibal pausing whilst allowing his army time to plunder the battlefield, then some comment from him would have been justified. If, at this moment, Hannibal had maintained the momentum of his extraordinary victory and followed up the remnants of the defeated Roman army to crush them utterly, then victory could, indeed, have been his. Truly, victory lay close at hand but not in the direction indicated by Maharbal. In the event, as we shall see, this mistake, coupled with unkind chance and a skilful Roman military recovery, was to deny Hannibal the opportunity of seizing it.

## CHAPTER VI

# HANNIBAL'S OBJECTIVE

The strategical background to a campaign or battle is of great significance. What was the aim? What was the commander trying to achieve? An objective may be very desirable strategically; but that which is strategically desirable must be tactically possible with the forces and means available.

FM Viscount Montgomery of Alamein[1]

It is a good military maxim that in any enterprise, however speedily circumstances may demand its completion, it is invariably wise to take time for reflection, brief though it may be, before embarking upon it, for to be over-hasty is frequently as bad as to be indolent. Truly, speed of action is a recognised principle of war, for it leads to surprise; and, states Clausewitz, without surprise 'superiority at the decisive point is hardly conceivable'. Hannibal was therefore right, after his resounding victory at Cannae, when he responded cautiously to Maharbal's challenge to march immediately on Rome. Whilst he admired his companion's zeal, he 'needed time to weigh the plan' so suddenly sprung upon him by his eager second-in-command. According to Livy,[2] Maharbal's plan was simplicity itself. 'Sir,' the cavalry commander had proposed to his general, 'if you want to know the true significance of this battle, let me tell you that within five days you will take your dinner, in triumph, on the Capitol. I will go first with my horsemen. The first knowledge of our coming will be the sight of us at the gates of Rome. You have but to follow.'

Several questions would have crowded into the mind of any responsible commander at that moment. How alert were the enemy in Rome to the disaster which had just overtaken their forces in the field and what would be their response? How suited was his own army to undertake the commitment proposed for it? What other options were open to him? And, whatever he chose to do, would it be in line with his prime objective?

Bad news always travels fast, and word of the catastrophic destruction of the Roman army at Cannae had reached Rome well before any official communication had been received from Varro, the surviving consul. Appian[3] recounts that the commanding general, for all his brave words before his departure from Rome, had been among the first to flee the battlefield. Livy, commenting that in such circumstances a Carthaginian general would have been punished with the utmost rigour of the law,[4] marvels at the extent of Roman popular acceptance of his behaviour. He relates that men 'of all conditions' came to Varro upon his recall to the City to associate themselves with the gratitude which, remarkably, had been publicly bestowed upon him. Polybius,[5] in his version of the affair, likewise records Varro's early escape to Venusia with a handful of men. He sardonically comments that, in this way, the consul 'matched a tenure of office which had proved disastrous to his country, with an equally disgraceful flight'.

At Venusia, Varro, now joined by some 4,000 other fugitives, received notice that a further group of a similar size had gathered at Canusium under four military tribunes: Fabius Maximus, of the First Legion and son of the dictator; Appius Claudius Pulcher of the Third; and Lucius Publicius Bibulus and Publius Cornelius Scipio, both of the Second. The latter, still only nineteen years of age, was the young man who had ridden to the aid of his wounded father, Scipio, at the battle of the Trebbia. He was later to become known as Scipio Africanus, the conqueror of Hannibal. He was already displaying the strength of character and mind which was later to distinguish him as a soldier. Varro at once moved to join forces with this party and by doing so created a force which at least resembled 'a consular army, so that all now felt that they would be capable of defending themselves within the fortified walls of the town at least, though hardly in the open field'.

In Rome, despite panic on the streets, upon which they immediately moved to restore order, the Senate behaved again with commendable steadfastness, as they had done when, in the previous year, Hannibal had first descended upon Italy. As yet without any official confirmation of the facts, they recognised the urgent need to collect intelligence of the scale of the disaster. To this end, they despatched lightly armed scouts along the Appian and Latin Ways with instructions to question any survivors they might encounter; to gather, from any and every source, tidings of what had happened to the two consuls, with their armies; and to discover what they could of the whereabouts of Hannibal and of his future plans. Whilst all this was going forward, two messages were received. One, at last from Varro, contained the delicately slanted information that 'the consul Paullus had perished with his army and that he himself was at Canusium engaged in salvaging what he could from the wreck'.[6] The other came from Titus Otacilius, the propraetor in Sicily, and conveyed yet more ominous news. A Carthaginian fleet was operating off Syracuse, on the far, eastern, side of the island, and was inflicting serious damage upon the territory of their close ally, Hiero. Otacilius could do nothing to help since a second Carthaginian fleet had also been sighted off the nearby Aegates islands, waiting to attack his home port, Lilybaeum, should he sail from it.

The Senate took such remedial action as they could, within their limited circumstances. Marcus Claudius Marcellus, currently commanding the fleet at Ostia, was to hie himself to Canusium to take command of the troops accumulating there and, when his duties had been handed over, Varro was to return to Rome. Marcellus was an ideal choice: he was a popular hero, a *beau sabreur*, who had been awarded the rare honour of *spolia opima*[7] for personal gallantry during the Insubrian War of 222 BC, when he had slain the Gallic chief Viridomarus in single combat. Marcellus, in turn, and before setting out, was to hand over command of

Marcus Claudius Marcellus.
(The Mansell Collection)

the fleet at Ostia to his colleague Philus. He had earlier contributed a party of 1,500 marines to Rome to reinforce its defences and, even before that, as soon as news of the Cannae calamity had been received, he had despatched a marine legion under its military tribunes to take post at Teanum Sidicinum, an allied colonial citadel lying two days' forced march south of the City. Its position, on the Latin Way and 6 miles north of the Volturnus, covered the bridge which carried the Appian and Latin highways across the river. It thus guarded the southern approach to Rome and its military importance requires no further underlining.

In parallel with these urgently taken counter-measures, Marcus Junius, appointed dictator for the duration of the immediate crisis, set about the task of raising land forces, on a scale never previously experienced. Two city legions had been raised by the consuls at the beginning of the year. Now, from an Italian peasantry already suffering grievous family losses, he proclaimed[8] a further levy of manpower of men from the age of seventeen, and some still younger, 'not yet out of their boys' togas'. From these numbers four legions were raised, together with 1,000 cavalrymen. He invoked the agreements between Rome and her allied communities, together with the Latin Confederacy, for the provision of reinforcements; he took the unusual step of arming 8,000 volunteer slaves, purchased from their owners at public expense; and, 'in a desperate situation where honour must give way to expedience', he released 6,000 prisoners serving sentence for capital punishments and debt, providing they agreed to serve under him. He issued orders for the urgent manufacture of arms, weapons and equipment but, since their production would require time, he instructed that all spoils of arms captured in former wars weere to be removed 'from temples and porticoes' and distributed to the newly formed units. These included the considerable number of Gallic weapons carried in the triumphal procession of Gaius Flaminius, after this victory in the Po valley in 223 BC.

Coincidentally, it was from here, and at this juncture, that yet another piece of bitter news was received. Lucius Postumius, the praetor sent to Cisalpine Gaul to keep a watchful eye on the Celts and restrain them from sending help to Hannibal, had allowed himself to be ambushed and his entire army of two legions had been destroyed.

We are given no inkling of the time-scale within which the defensive measures enacted by Marcus Junius were set in place. Plainly, many would have taken several days, perhaps longer, to bring to fruition. Nevertheless, they are all worthy of mention here since they provide a sense of the defensive capability of Rome, even at this calamitous moment. Nor should we fail to note that some, particularly those involving Marcellus, were effected within a few days of the earliest rumours of the Cannae disaster reaching Rome. Of these, the one carrying the greatest military importance and the earliest to be initiated, was the despatch of a legion of marines to Teanum Sidicinum. We have already discussed the military importance of this location, but the deployment of such a select unit in this direction at such a time bore wider implications. Teanum Sidicinum was a city state and a frontier town of the Latin Confederacy. The Confederacy was, and for some few years yet was to show itself to be, a firm ally of Rome, closely tied to a common defence policy. Rome, at a moment of crisis, had now called upon it to activate its mutual agreements and the movement of the marines to the frontier at this crucial time demonstrated her personal commitment to the defence of the alliance. Moreover it provided a screen behind which prearranged mobilisation plans could urgently be set in train.

Thus, Rome, behind her sturdy walls, with her confederation of Latin allies and with great resilience, was already vigorously anticipating Hannibal's arrival. She drew great strength from the Latin commitment[9] to provide 80,000 infantry

Tortosa stands on the lowest crossing place of the river Ebro and has been strategically significant since the earliest times. During Hannibal's War it would have been well used by both Carthaginian and Roman forces. (The Spanish Tourist Office)

and 5,000 cavalry in the event of such an emergency as this. Nor were her own defences insignificant. Hannibal was thus, at first sight, wise to dampen the well-intentioned zeal of his cavalry commander, for he could well have been riding his squadrons into an aroused hornets' nest. 'I will go first with my horsemen', if we may rehearse again what he is reported by Livy to have said. 'The first knowledge of our coming will be the sight of us at the gates of Rome. You have but to follow.' But would it have been as easy as that?

Hannibal had initially crossed the Ebro with a force of 102,000 men and 37 elephants. For a variety of reasons, which we have already examined, by the time he descended on to the Po plain his fighting strength had been reduced to a total of 20,000 infantry and 6,000 cavalry. We are not told how many of his soldiery were killed in the battles of the Ticinus and the Trebbia, but the information would in any event be irrelevant since his numbers were subsequently enhanced by a contingent of some 30,000 infantry and 4,000 cavalry contributed by his Celtic allies.[10] He is then said by Livy to have lost 'many men and many animals', including his last elephant, whilst crossing the marshes of the upper Arno. Without any other guidance as to the size of these casualties, a figure of 2,500 infantrymen may be fairly conjectured for, according to all accounts, the

Table 3: Hannibal's Fighting Strength as Reduced by Casualties.

| Year BC | Place | | Fighting Strength | | Total | Amended Balance | Reference |
|---|---|---|---|---|---|---|---|
| 1. 218 | Ebro Crossing | | Infantry | 90,000 | | | |
| | | | Cavalry | 12,000 | 102,000 | | Polybius, iii, 35 |
| 2. 218 | a. Pyrenees | (a) | Infantry | 20,000 | | | |
| | | | Cavalry | 2,000 | 22,000 | 80,000 | *ibid.*, 35–9 |
| | b.    " | (b) | Infantry | 20,000 | | | |
| | | | Cavalry | 1,000 | 21,000 | | *ibid.* |
| 3. 218 | Rhone | (b) | Infantry | 50,000 | | | |
| | Crossing | | Cavalry | 9,000 | | 59,000 | *ibid.* |
| 4. 218 | Alps | (b) | Infantry | 30,000 | | | *ibid.* |
| | | | Cavalry | 3,000 | 33,000 | | Livy, xxi, 38 |
| 5. 218 | Arrival | | Infantry | 20,000 | | | |
| | Po Plain | | Cavalry | 6,000 | | 26,000 | Polybius, iii, 33 |
| 6. 218/7 | ADD Celtic | | Infantry | 30,000 | | | |
| | contingent | | Cavalry | 4,000 | | 60,000 (est) | |
| 7. 217 | Arno Swamp | (b) | Infantry | 2,500 | 2,500 (est) | | |
| 8. 217 | a. Lake | | Infantry | 47,500 | | | |
| | Trasimene | | Cavalry | 10,000 | | 57,500 | |
| | b.    " | (b) | Infantry | 1,500 | | | Polybius iii, 85 |
| 9. 216 | Gerunium | (b) | Infantry | 6,000 | 7,500 | | Livy, xxii, 24 |
| 10. 216 | a. Cannae | | Infantry | 40,000 | | | |
| | | | Cavalry | 10,000 | | 50,000 | *ibid.*, xxii, 46 |
| | b.    " | (b) | Infantry | 5,500 | | | |
| | | | Cavalry | 1,700 | 7,200 | 42,800 | Polybius, iii, 117 |

(a)    Deducted: forces allocated by Hannibal to Hasdrubal for the prosecution of the Spanish as well as those returned to their homes before Hannibal's army entered Gaul.

(b)    Battle and other casualties deducted.

mounted horsemen clearly had an easier passage through the swamp land. Subsequently, Hannibal is shewn by annalists to have lost 1,500 men at Lake Trasimene, 6,000 at Gerunium and 7,200 at Cannae. His fighting strength *post-Cannae* was therefore reduced to roughly 42,800.

None of these figures can be confidently stated. When considering them, one is very conscious that many, if not most, of the totals provided to us are rounded up to the nearest 1,000 or, at best, 500; that the wounded, their care, condition, recovery or evacuation are seldom, if ever, mentioned; that casualties incurred or inflicted in local engagements (for example, Hannibal's adventure to the east coast prior to wintering at Gerunium) are rarely quoted and their numbers are imponderable. In modern warfare, the proportion of wounded to killed may be roughly categorised as 3:1.[11] In ancient times, due to the savage nature of the hand-to-hand fighting and frequently merciless treatment of the wounded, we may judge the proportion to have been considerably less. Nevertheless, Hannibal was the clear victor at Cannae and we may conclude that his wounded, perhaps numbering as many as 4,000 to 5,000 men or even more, were retrieved from the battlefield and nursed to recovery. Shortage of manpower was, after all, one of his prime concerns. In this case, it must also be granted that the wounded would have required attendants and protection. The fugitive Roman soldiery gathering at Canusium might not yet have recovered their morale but their numbers and presence posed a threat which Hannibal could not easily have ignored.

Thus, Hannibal's effective fighting strength at this moment, making allowance for a garrison for his firm base and his severely wounded, was probably nearer to 35,000 men, comprising 8,000 cavalry and 27,000 infantrymen. Moreover, he would have been very conscious that any further adventure, unless soundly based, would have had the affect of reducing these totals still further, unless he could find some means of increasing his numbers.

Before we turn from Hannibal's manpower problems, there is another connected aspect which should not be overlooked, for it was soon to be reflected in his army's battlefield performance. Appian[12] records that, immediately after the battle at Cannae, Hannibal went to view the dead and that 'when he saw the bravest of his friends lying amongst the slain, he burst into tears and said that he did not want another such victory'. We may be sure that the friends about whom Appian writes were some of his most senior and experienced commanders. The young general must have felt, as the annalist suggests, that, despite the scale of his success, the combination of their loss, in many ways irreplaceable, combined with his army's reasonably modest but nevertheless steady manpower drain through casualties, had provided him with something of a Pyrrhic victory. A period of consolidation was now required. Further, and importantly to both sides, the battlefield upon which he stood, apart from the dead and dying, was covered with vast quantities of booty and abandoned military equipment, waiting to be salvaged. The presence of this booty bore very real implications. His soldiery were mercenaries: they had served him vigorously and loyally, persuaded as much by his compelling leadership as by the prospect of loot. They now deserved their moment of reward and it would be difficult to refuse it to them.

The salvage of such a vast quantity of weaponry would also have been a matter of prime concern to both sides. If it lay within Hannibal's possession, its denial to the enemy would have been much more than a mere irritant, for not only would their military expansion programme have been obstructed, but they would have been put to the financial and material cost of replacing it. Rome was already facing serious economic and supply problems due to the war. Livy[13] records that, in the weeks after Cannae, the Roman Senate received urgent despatches from their propraetors in both Sicily and Sardinia, complaining that 'neither the soldiers nor the ships' crews were being punctually paid; nor were supplies arriving on time'. Furthermore, there was nowhere they could turn for help. Their pleas understandably received short shrift, for Rome herself was experiencing sharp difficulty in feeding her citizens. Both generals were told curtly that there was nothing available to send and that the responsibility rested with them to do the best they could for the forces under their command.

Plainly, all these considerations, Hannibal's vulnerability should he suffer further manpower losses, his army's need for a period of consolidation, together with the depth and strength of the Roman defences, point to the fact that the Carthaginian general was correct to have no truck with Maharbal's suggestion to march on Rome. Indeed, it is arguable that the structure of the army with which he had earlier crossed the Pyrenees suggests that he had never contemplated such a move for, at that time, he brought with him a contingent of elephants, a specialised arm used for the support of infantry in battle but of no value in siege warfare, and he left behind the siege engines, battering rams and other equipment he had earlier deployed so successfully against the walls of Saguntum. Whilst wintering in the Po valley he seemingly made no effort to replace this equipment. Indeed, his campaign in southern Italy was soon to suffer greatly from its lack. Nevertheless, the fact that he is sometimes accused of losing the war by failing, at that moment, to take advantage of the city of Rome's frailty, poses the question of how such an action, had he carried it through, would have conformed with his overall objective, for, in the conduct of war, whilst it is admitted that within his strategic directive a commander may have several courses of action open to him, it is a recognised principle that its aim should be clearly defined and its achievement relentlessly pursued.

Hannibal's true purpose in invading Italy has never been clearly defined by the ancients although they expound at some length upon the causes which brought it about. Polybius[14] relates that the young Carthaginian, in his handling of the events leading up to the outbreak of the war, was in a mood of unreasoning and violent anger with Rome. He suggests that matters might have turned out differently if Hannibal 'had demanded that the Romans should hand back Sardinia and at the same time remit the indemnity which they had unjustly extorted' from Carthage. He points out, and this was confirmed by their state of unpreparedness, that Rome had never expected the war, when it occurred, to take place in Italy but had assumed that it would be fought in Spain. Livy[15] argues that, from the outset, Hannibal 'had acted as if he had definite instructions to take Italy as his sphere of operations and to make war on Rome'. Appian[16] writes that Hannibal,

> believing, as was a fact, that a war between the Romans and the Carthaginians, once begun, would last a very long time, and that the undertaking in itself would bring great glory to himself, even if he should fail, (it was said, also, that he had been sworn on the altar by his father, while yet a boy, that he would be an eternal enemy of Rome) he resolved to cross the Ebro in defiance of his treaty.

In view of this lack of clarity, with no positive statement of his war aims, we are left to judge by Hannibal's actions, and the Roman response to them, what his ultimate objective may have been. In all these circumstances, it seems

Remains of the Roman
amphitheatre at Capua. (By
courtesy of the Italian State
Tourist Board (E.N.I.T.)
London)

improbable that the siege and capture of Rome formed any part of his plan. On
the other hand, his careful handling of the Roman allies, particularly his
generous treatment of their prisoners of war, clearly suggests a plan of conquest
aimed at their defection from Rome and their cooperation with him, leading to
the ultimate disintegration of the republic to the advantage of Carthage.
Without this sort of outcome his manpower problems would continue to persist,
unless he could establish sea communication with Carthage or reactivate the
land route from Spain: but the latter was to prove fatally vulnerable, largely
because Spain had not been properly secured as a base, and the sea route from
Carthage could not be reliably maintained whilst Sicily was held in hostile
hands.

Despite the harshly severe punishments they might expect to receive should
their decision prove to be mistaken, the defections of Rome's allies began to
reveal themselves immediately after Cannae, when the full scale of the Roman
losses was revealed. A number of states amongst the southern tribes, including
the Apulia, Hirpini, Lucani and Bruttium, their territories cutting a swathe across
southern Italy from the east coast to the toe of the peninsula, together with three

Roman municipalities in Campania, began a process of secession in favour of Hannibal: but, it must be said, their decisions were frequently painfully reached, for opinions were sharply divided on the merits of doing so and many stood staunchly loyal to Rome. The three *municipia* to hand themselves over were the prosperous and strategically sited city of Capua, with her associates Calatia and Atelia. The secessionist Bruttian states, the most southerly of all, ultimately included all of those city states located along the extreme south of the Tyrrhenian coastline.

Capua, strategically well sited south of the Volturnus and long known as a prosperous commercial centre, was the first to move. Its Senate sent representatives to Varro, after Cannae and whilst he was still at Venusia, ostensibly to offer help and reinforcements but in fact to assess the situation as it affected them. The Roman consul's personal demeanour, combined with the low morale of the poorly equipped refugee troops they saw gathering there, did nothing to sustain their confidence. At Cannae we lost everything, Varro told them[17] and then asked, in an outburst which well revealed the amount of booty gathered by Hannibal from the battle-field:

> Do you expect us to ask you for a reinforcement of foot soldiers – as if we were, of course, well off for cavalry? Or to say we are short of money – just *money*, as if it were all? Allies reinforce – but fortune has left us nothing which can *be* reinforced. Our legions, our cavalry, our arms, standards, horses, men, money, supplies – everything went in the battle or in the loss of the two camps next day . . .

The envoys, says Livy, were filled with contempt at his manner and the conditions they had witnessed, and returned home to open, with Hannibal, negotiations for the terms of their secession to his cause.

Another state to make early overtures to Hannibal was that of Compsa in Hirpini territory, lying in the western foothills of the Apennine range and overlooking the tactically useful valley of the Aufidus, the value of which we have already noted. Hannibal promptly recognised that its capital town, with its secure and central position, situated on a useful routeway through the mountains, which in its turn linked in either direction with two discreetly distant Roman highways, provided him with an ideal location for the administrative base he was now seeking. He moved at once (according to the inventory of losses quoted by Varro to the Capuan envoys it must have presented a logistical challenge of considerable size) and deposited there all his stores, baggage and captured material. He then divided his army, yet further weakening his strike force, and appointed his brother, Mago, to command the base, giving him instructions 'to take over all the towns of that part of Italy as they seceded from Rome and to compel the secession of any which showed signs of resistance'.

As soon as these arrangements had been completed, Hannibal set forth to the southern Tyrrhenian coast with the aim of launching an attack on Naples and acquiring the vital seaport so important for his survival. Upon approaching its gates, he immediately recognised the formidable nature of the city walls and the impossibility of his army carrying them by assault. He therefore strove unsuccessfully to gain access to the city by subterfuge but was defeated by the alertness of its defenders. This persuaded him to abandon the idea for the present and, without further waste of time, he turned away to Capua where, at ceremonies arranged by the city elders in his honour, he put his seal to a treaty of alliance.

This document contained important military provisions for both signatories. It was agreed that no Campanian should be required to serve in the army against his will and that no Carthaginian military or civil officer should have any jurisdiction over a Campanian citizen. The creation of a Campanian military force loyal to Hannibal was therefore implicit in the agreement. Authority was also granted for the Carthaginians to provide a garrison for the city of Capua. The signing of the document was, for both parties, a move of outstanding significance,[18] for Capua, following upon the crippling defeat of Rome at Cannae, now claimed to be not only the capital city of Campania but the capital of all Italy. The pact represented to the Campanians a release from Roman shackles, which they quickly compounded by the unpleasant murder of several Roman officials and citizens. To Hannibal, it provided a political alliance of considerable stature which also provided sinew to his frontier defensive position, with the promise of added manpower and resources, albeit within a flimsy command structure.

Mago's sudden appearance in Carthage so soon after being given the task of base commander at Compsa and, indeed, before he personally could have tackled it, leaves little doubt that Hannibal had undergone a sudden change of mind about his priorities. It was perhaps brought about by his evident military weakness before the walls of Naples. In a further, unsuccessful, and it might be said unnecessary, attempt to persuade the city to secede or, alternatively, to frighten it into submission, he returned there again after completing the treaty signing ceremonies at Capua. He appears to have wasted little time in this renewed effort to bring about its surrender and it seems likely that his second visit provided a cover for the acquisition of a vessel and the despatch of Mago to Carthage to plead for reinforcements and resources.

The list of successes the latter had to report to the senators was formidable. His brother had fought six major engagements; he had slain over 200,000 of the enemy and had taken more than 50,000 prisoners; his opposing generals had either been utterly defeated or killed or both and as a result of these victories many of Rome's southern allies had defected and joined the Carthaginian cause. As evidence of his words, Mago had carried with him a mass of captured gold rings – 'of that sort worn only by knights, and only by the most distinguished in that Order'. In order to illustrate the scale of these victories, he poured these trophies out of their container and on to the courtyard floor of the Senate House in which he was making his address. Livy narrates that the thrust of Mago's speech was this:

> . . . that the nearer that Hannibal came to his hope of bringing the war to a successful conclusion,[19] the more necessary it was to give him every possible assistance and support. He was fighting in enemy country, far from home; money and grain were being consumed in large quantities; the numerous engagements,

besides destroying the enemy forces, had also to some extent diminished the power of the victor. Accordingly money must be sent; grain must be supplied, and money for the pay of the troops who had served Carthage so well.

After considerable discussion the Senate expressed the view that at the present rate of progress the war would soon be over: the provision of reinforcements was therefore agreed, although not entirely unanimously, on the grounds that their arrival would hasten Hannibal's victory. If it truly were their opinion that success in Italy could be so easily reached, then it seems likely that Mago, in his efforts to persuade the home politicians to release resources, had painted an excessively glowing picture of his brother's military situation. In the outcome, it was decided to provide him with 4,000 Numidian cavalry and 40 elephants, together with a large sum of money in silver. His requirement for foot soldiers was also recognised and an officer was sent with Mago to Spain for the purpose of enlisting 20,000 infantry, with a further 4,000 horse. In view of what we have been told of Hannibal's circumstances at this moment, these hardly seem to have been influential numbers: but, despite this, it was also resolved that, of these totals, a proportion was to be allocated to reinforce the army based in Spain.

Livy relates that the decision to muster these extra men, 'as so often happens when things are going well', was executed in 'a slow and dilatory manner'. It may also be that the opposition faction delayed matters by their intrigues. In due course, a task force, now reduced to a modest 12,000 foot, 1,500 horse and 20 elephants, together with 1,000 talents of silver,[20] was raised for Mago to take to Italy. He was on the point of setting sail from Carthage, under an escort of sixty warships, when his orders were suddenly cancelled and, after much debate as to which operational theatre to send him, Mago, together with these limited but valuable reinforcements, was diverted to Spain instead. As a result of this last minute change of plan, he was destined never to see his brother again.

Whilst Mago was engaged in these matters overseas, Hannibal, by diplomacy, by threat or simply by brute military force, concentrated on persuading Rome's allies to secede to his cause. He directed his effort particularly at such states as Nola, Acerrae Casilinum and Nuceria, the territories of which lay clustered in the Neapolitan hinterland, south of the line of the Volturnus river and astride the highway to southern Bruttium and Rhegium, a southern seaport overlooking the Straits of Messina. The reason for this is clear. Reinforcements reaching Hannibal from Carthage could only have arrived with him in one of three ways: they could have made landfall somewhere along the stretch of Tyrrhenian coastline, south of Naples; they could have entered the Straits of Messina and come ashore at one of the old Greek colonial ports; or, alternatively, they could have landed in Sicily and thence crossed over to Bruttium, in the toe of the Italian mainland. It was, doubtless, in anticipation of Hannibal's arrival in this area that, only a few weeks earlier and immediately following his victory at Cannae, a Carthaginian fleet entered these waters and lay off the Aegates Islands 'fully equipped and ready for action', whilst another attacked the Syracusan kingdom of Hiero, Rome's staunch ally.[21]

Warship slipway in the Carthaginian naval base, uncovered by a team of British archaeologists. The Carthaginian naval fleet was a force to be reckoned with, at times hundreds of ships were available to be put at its disposal. (Ian Atkinson)

After taking over Capua and again being rebuffed at Naples, Hannibal now marched on Nola, which occupied a position commanding one of the main routes from Samnium territory in the north-east. The inhabitants prevaricated when he approached them and alerted the Roman general Marcellus, who, with his army, was at that moment at Casilinum. Marcellus marched at once to their relief but, as he drew near, Hannibal pulled away and, yet again (one senses a touch of desperation) marched down the coast to confront Naples. Upon arrival, he discovered, and it must have been to his considerable frustration, that it was now held by a Roman prefect, Marcus Junius Silanus, who had been called to their aid by the Neapolitans. He therefore withdrew and moved on to lay siege to Nuceria. Here again, his efforts peacefully to win over the inhabitants were rejected. On this occasion, he laid siege to the city and the townspeople were ultimately forced by starvation to surrender. When, upon doing so, they refused his inducements to join his army, their town was sacked and burnt.

From Nuceria, Hannibal turned again north-west and marched towards Casilinum, having learnt that Rome's dictator, Marcus Junius Pera, was in the vicinity, probably at Teanum Sidicinum, with an army of considerable strength.[22] In view of the town's proximity to Capua and the size of the Roman army, he feared for the security of his new found ally. Yet once again, however, he was thwarted on approaching the walls of his objective, for he found them stoutly defended by Latin troops, recently reinforced by a cohort from Perusia. They rejected his attempts at a peaceful overture but, more seriously, they ambushed his party by bursting suddenly through the gates. Hannibal responded by laying siege to the city, an operation which his men tackled half-heartedly, earning a rebuke from their commander as a consequence.

Livy's account of this operation is intriguing because it hints that Hannibal may, by some means not recorded, have received at least a few reinforcements.[23] He relates that, in one encounter at Casilinum, elephants had been sent 'to cut off the enemy's retreat', and his record of the siege operations themselves suggests that presence of new equipment and techniques, with mantlets brought up and saps being dug. These methods are not generally recorded as practised by Hannibal during this phase of his Italian campaign; and, as far as the use of elephants was concerned, it was not until the following year, probably some nine months after this event, that the Carthaginian general Bomilcar landed in southern Italy with twenty elephants and the long expected reinforcements to replace those which had disappeared with Mago to Spain. It is, perhaps, weakly conceivable that the Carthaginian fleet, reported lying off the Aegates Isles by Otacilius and 'ready for action', may, at some time, have put troops ashore to bolster Hannibal's numbers before sailing for home: but the presence of elephants as part of such a task force must surely be considered doubtful.

Ultimately, in face of determined opposition by the besieged citizens of Casilinum, Hannibal left a holding garrison in place and withdrew into quarters in Capua for the winter of 216/215 BC.

At this point it is appropriate to return to the matter of the objective Hannibal had been striving to achieve at this stage of his campaign. Clearly, during the phase reviewed in this chapter his thoughts and efforts were initially directed at the conquest of southern Italy, hopefully aided by the defection of Rome's allies to his side. His lack of success in achieving this objective had overridingly been due to his losses in manpower, coupled with his lack of ready reinforcements and the steady wastage of junior commanders, the lack of whose skills was beginning to affect his battlefield performance at all levels. Thus, confronted with a classic example of Field Marshal Viscount Montgomery's *dictum* that 'that which is strategically desirable must be tactically possible with the forces and means available', he found himself compelled to modify his immediate aim by restricting his operational activities to securing his eastern flank and tightening his grip on the zones of Campania and Bruttium he had already occupied.

In the following year (215 BC), two significant developments occurred which

Coin showing Philip V of
Macedonia, 238–179 BC.
(© British Museum)

gave him further hope. Firstly, the Carthaginian admiral Bomilcar arrived at Locri, on the south coast, bringing with him the much-needed and long-awaited elephant, logistical and troop reinforcements from Carthage.[24] Locri, where they came ashore, was one of a group of Italiot Greek trading centres on the southern coastline of the toe of Italy, which had succumbed to Carthaginian pressure and seceded from its alliance with Rome. Another of these centres, Croton, a town which had suffered greatly in the Pyrrhic War and lay largely half-occupied as a result, was now also destined to play a minor role in a second incident which, at first sight, foreshadowed a sharply favourable change in Hannibal's fortunes. It was not, however, to be.

Philip V of Macedonia, from the security of his position across the Adriatic Sea, had been watching events in Italy with increasing interest. It may be that his attention had already been invited to them, either by Carthage or by Hannibal himself. In any event, he found himself well impressed by the dramatic scale of the latter's three victories over the Romans at Trebbia, Lake Trasimene and Cannae and saw opportunities for his own ambitions in the war which the Carthaginians were so successfully conducting. To this end, he despatched envoys to liaise with Hannibal and negotiate an alliance. These ambassadors landed at the temple of Lacinian Juno, near Croton. From there, they made their way through Apulian territory towards Capua, carefully avoiding the Roman held towns of Tarentum and Brundisium. For what reason they followed such a circuitous route, instead of proceeding directly north through the occupied and largely friendly province of the Bruttii, is not clear. As it happened, they were intercepted by Roman patrols and taken to the praetor Laevinus at Luceria. Here, under questioning, they carefully adapted their story to say that 'they had been sent by King Philip to arrange a pact of friendship between their master and Rome' and that they were the bearers of messages of goodwill to the Senate and to the Roman people. Their arrival at such a time, when Rome was seeking friends from any and every quarter, assured them of a warm welcome. Laevinus provided them with all assistance and then, after carefully briefing them on the whereabouts of hostile and friendly troops and the most trouble-free routes to be followed, he set them on their road with a military escort.

The envoys disposed of the latter as quickly as possible and then made their way by the shortest route, through Roman lines, to Capua, where their leader signed a detailed treaty of friendship with Hannibal. The terms, recorded by Livy, are noteworthy since the two parties, by defining their joint intentions so clearly, simultaneously defined what we may judge to have been Hannibal's operational objective. King Philip, Livy[25] tells us

> was to cross to Italy with the largest fleet he could raise (perhaps 200 ships), harry the coast, and carry on offensive operations by land and sea to the best of his ability; at the end of the war, *Rome and all Italy were to pass into the hands of Hannibal and the Carthaginians, and all captured material was to be ceded to Hannibal* [author's italics]. Italy once crushed, the Carthaginians were to sail for Greece and make war upon any states the king might choose. The mainland states and offshore islands should become the property of Philip and be incorporated in his kingdom.

Sadly for Hannibal, this vital alliance, so important for the outright success of his campaign, failed to materialise. It happened in this wise. As soon as the content of the treaty had been agreed, the envoys returned to the anchorage at Juno Lacinia, where they had concealed their ship and, from there, they sailed for home, taking with them three of Hannibal's men, representatives empowered to discuss and finalise the document with Philip before jointly signing it on behalf of Carthage. Their ship, however, was intercepted off the Calabrian coast by a vigilant Roman naval patrol and then, under questioning, the truth soon emerged and the treaty document prepared for signature between Hannibal and the king of Macedonia was discovered. The entire party was now taken by sea to Rome, where they were placed in chains and their servants sold, and the Senate, 'far from sinking under this initiative, promptly initiated discussions on how best to keep the enemy out of Italy by themselves taking the offensive'.

The collapse of this enterprise clearly dealt Hannibal's operation a grievous blow. The shock waves which would have been created by the arrival of a Macedonian army to join the Carthaginians in southern Italy at this critical juncture, supported by a fleet of 200 ships, would almost certainly have been of sufficient force to bring about a mass desertion of Rome by her allies, certainly those inhabiting southern Italy. Indeed, it would have been such a fortunate happening that one is led to question whether Hannibal had not canvassed and agreed some such intervention by Philip, in the manner that he had enlisted the cooperation of the tribes of Cisalpine Gaul, before setting forth from Spain. The young king of Macedonia, newly ascended to the throne in 221 BC, was already looking to expand his territories and was no friend of Rome: but the capture of the Macedonian and Carthaginian envoys had now destroyed this tantalising possibility, leaving Hannibal, with inadequate resources, the difficult task of realigning his planned route to his objective.

## CHAPTER VII

# ROME'S INDIRECT RESPONSE

In history, the indirect approach has normally consisted of a logistical military move directed against an economic target – the source of supply of either the opposing state or army.

Liddell Hart[1]

As the winter season of 216/215 came to an end, the armed forces of the republic, including the large but mainly unskilled numbers which had been building up in Teanum Sidicinum under the dictator Pera, were redeployed in differing roles, according to their experience and standards of training. Many also received new general officers. Tiberius Sempronius Gracchus was given command of the slave volunteers, together with 25,000 allies, with orders to report to Sinuessa, a 'coastguard' colony north of the Volturnus estuary but also situated in such a position as to safeguard the southern approach to Rome along the *Via Appia*. Fabius took command of the forces which remained at Teanum after the departure of Gracchus. These initially appear to have been held as a tactical reserve.

The doughty Marcellus, with two city legions, moved from Cales, south of Teanum on the *Via Latina*, and crossed the Volturnus to Suessula, where he occupied the Claudian Camp on Monte Cancello. This overlooked the vital routeway to and from Campania and covered the northern approach to the already contested city of Nola. His arrival displaced the survivors from the army at Cannae who, in their turn, were despatched to Sicily. This latter force comprised two legions, the unfortunate *legiones Cannenses*, raised from the men brought back by Marcellus from Canusium, *post* Cannae, to help hold the line of the Volturnus.[2] Their arrival in Sicily enabled the two legions they relieved there to be recalled to Rome, together with the praetor M. Valerius Laevinus. Laevinus, upon his return, was ordered, with his legions, to Apulia. Here he replaced Varro, whose disgrace seems by this time to have been at least partially recognised, for, upon hand-over, he was pointedly posted to Picenum, at that moment a backwater unlikely to feature as a war zone, with instructions to arrange the defence of the area whilst energetically recruiting for the army. It was a necessary if not outstanding role but, nevertheless, one which, according to Livy, he achieved with some success.

All in all, it was a sound defensive deployment of forces which, despite in many cases their lack of skills and battle experience, Hannibal would have found wellnigh impossible to penetrate should he have chosen to march on Rome. Fabius, at Teanum, added another shrewd touch, with the authority of the Senate. He issued an order, the scope of which we will later be able to see in greater detail, for all grain to be harvested before 1 June and stored within fortified towns. Anyone failing to comply with this ruling was to have 'his farmlands ravaged, his slaves sold by auction and his farmhouse burned down'.[3]

The campaigning season of 215 BC opened without great flourish. Gracchus appears to have been the first to move. He crossed the Volturnus to encamp at Liternum, now Patria, a few miles north of Cumae, the seaport which Hannibal had in mind as his link with Carthage. As there was little for his men to do, and because of their lack of experience, he spent much of his time on manoeuvres and engaged on military training. These skills were soon to be needed, for it was not long before he was alerted by the townspeople to a forthcoming ceremony to be held by the Campanian senate at nearby Hamae, to which the Cumaean senate had also been invited, ostensibly for consultation about the war situation. They had been told that the meeting place was to be heavily guarded so as to prevent outside interference and they suspected trickery. Their doubts had been confirmed when they learnt that a force of 14,000 armed men, under a Campanian magistrate, was lying concealed nearby and they came to Gracchus for help and advice. He counselled them to remove all property from their farms into the town, to seek shelter behind its walls and to remain there until the situation had been clarified.

The ceremony at Hamae was timed to take place after dark and was designed to be over by midnight, by which hour, it was judged by his Cumaean informers, those attending would have returned to their lines. Gracchus, therefore, waited within his camp until the end of the first watch and then set out with his army to march, 'without a sound', the intervening 3 miles to Hamae. Upon arrival, he stationed raiding parties outside each one of the enemy's gates and, upon a given signal, they burst in upon the sleeping garrison. In the ensuing mêlée, 34 military standards were captured and some 2,000 Campanian soldiers were slain, including their leader, Marius Alfius. The ability of several thousand men to move into such a position in the dark 'without a sound' must surely be questionable, particularly since we are reminded by Livy that Gracchus was 'far from confident of the men under his command'.[4] However the operation may have been achieved, an outstanding success was scored and news of the disastrous losses inflicted upon his Campanian allies quickly reached Hannibal on Mount Tifata, near Capua. Without delay, he marched to bring them help but arrived 'only to find the enemy camp deserted and the dead bodies of his allies lying all over the place'. Gracchus, probably anticipating his arrival, had sensibly withdrawn within the town.

Hannibal, in his urgency to get to Cumae, had left behind his supplies, heavy baggage and equipment so that he might travel light and fast. He had no option now but to return to his Mount Tafata base to collect these stores. On the day after having done so, he returned to Cumae again, this time to lay siege to the

Head of Hannibal on a coin. (© British Museum)

city but with no better success. Perhaps through over-confidence, perhaps, as is sometimes alleged, because of a general decline in morale and military competence within the Carthaginian army due to an over-relaxed winter in Capua, he allowed his troops surrounding the walls to be surprised by sally parties which burst simultaneously through the two town gates. This created such panic amongst his men that they were driven to their camp in confusion at the cost of some 1,300 killed. Next day, after a display of force in front of the town, a gesture which Gracchus ignored but which was designed to draw him into battle from the security of his walls, Hannibal withdrew yet again, but this time with some loss of face.

Whilst Gracchus had been engaged in this minor, but nevertheless significant, encounter with Hannibal, the other generals had been moving from their winter bases into areas from where they might better conduct operations during the coming campaigning season. Fabius, who might have played a decisive role at Cumae by joining forces with Gracchus, had already moved forward from Teanum to Cales but took no part in the encounter. He made it clear that he had no intention of getting involved, since his sacrificial omens had demonstrated he would be unwise to do so. When he had finished his rites of appeasement, he moved eastwards to seize the towns of Compulteria, Trebula and Austicula. These had all declared for Hannibal and lay within the elbow shaped by the Volturnus as it bent sharply northwards towards Telesia. As soon as this had been done, Fabius crossed the river to take over the camp occupied by Marcellus on Monte Cancello, above Suessula, and despatched Marcellus to provide a garrison for Nola. The positioning of these three armies, at Cumae, Suessula and Nola, clearly illustrates an intent to tighten the squeeze on Hannibal, then still located in his 'winter' camp on Tifata. In the meantime, Laevinus, east of the Volturnus at Luceria, had conducted a similar tidying-up operation against three villages of the Hirpini.

At about this moment, Hannibal's manpower situation was enhanced by the disembarkation of Locri of the long-awaited reinforcements of troops, elephants and supplies from Carthage.[5] They had been brought by Bomilcar and, upon coming ashore, had promptly marched up-country to join Hanno in Bruttium. They thus evaded the Roman forces which, alerted to the fact that the enemy fleet was entering the Straits of Messina, had pursued them across the water from Sicily in a vain attempt to intercept them. The reinforcements reached Hanno roughly at the time the siege of Cumae was being lifted and, upon their arrival, he set out at once to join Hannibal at Tifata. The journey was not without incident. Livy relates that on his way northwards, near Grumentum in central Lucania, Hanno encountered a force led by Sempronius Longus, possibly on or near the ancient highway from Rhegium to Rome, later to be replaced by the *Via Popillia*. This inevitably would have been the route followed northwards by the Carthaginians. It will be recalled that Longus was the Roman general who, some three years earlier, had marched to the aid of Scipio on the Trebbia. In the battle which now ensued,[6] he captured 41 standards and caused Hanno to return to Bruttium with a loss of some 2,000 killed.

This episode is sometimes queried on the grounds that it is not easy, at first sight, to understand how Sempronius Longus, so suddenly, could have penetrated so deeply into the largely hostile territory of Lucania. It is quite conceivable, however, that Longus had been detached from a larger force, perhaps that of Valerius Laevinus, who was due shortly to be moved south from northern Apulia to assume newly allotted command duties at Brundisium. If Longus had crossed from southern Apulia, Grumentum would have been a logical place for the encounter to have occurred. The incident, however, is worthy of note for two reasons: firstly, the heavy casualties allegedly inflicted on Hanno,[7] and the improvement in Roman military morale which gave rise to the whole affair. Even more important is the implied suggestion that the Romans in their operational handling of Hannibal were improving in confidence, were learning greater flexibility, and were willing, at last, to 'fight fire with fire' in terms of tactics. In the outcome, Hanno was not delayed unduly, for he was soon to be discovered joining Hannibal, who, once again, was preparing to besiege Marcellus at Nola.

The events which followed were very similar to those which had recently occurred at Cumae. Hannibal opened the proceedings by sending Hanno forward to parley with two senators of the town, who emerged through the gates having gained the permission of Marcellus to speak with his enemy. We may expect that their master had great confidence in their performance, for in the previous year he had put to death seventy members of the local anti-Roman party for lack of loyalty and had confiscated their property for the benefit of the Roman Treasury.[8]

When it became clear from Hanno's discussions that he would get little help from the inhabitants, Hannibal surrounded the town and commenced preparations for an assault upon it. Marcellus, studying his enemy's every movement, recognised an opportunity in the manner in which this was being done. He formed his men up inside the town gate and, seizing the right moment, 'out they came with a rush and a roar'. A savage struggle ensued, until both sides were forced apart by a downfall of rain and hail of extraordinary ferocity. Heartened by the performance of his troops in this newest skirmish, Marcellus marched out of Nola on the following day and, about a mile from the town, formed his army up for battle, taunting his enemy to fight. Hannibal accepted the challenge but the courage of his men soon ebbed away and he withdrew to seek refuge within the defences of the Carthaginian camp. He had suffered 5,000 killed, together with 600 men and 19 standards lost to the enemy. In addition, he had lost six elephants, including four killed. Again, the numbers of the Carthaginian casualties would have been magnified by an uncertain number of wounded. This constant problem bears repeating here because of the increasing burden of the reinforcement requirement, in terms of both quality and number, which was now confronting the Carthaginian general.

Hannibal, with these multiplying losses, now wisely decided to declare the close of his summer campaigning season on the western Volturnus. He marched eastwards to winter camp near Arpi, in northern Apulia. Valerius Laevinus, it must be assumed, had already vacated the area for Brundisium, with orders 'to defend the Sallentine coast and to take any necessary measure for a war with Philip and the Macedonians'.[9] Hannibal, when he heard of this tactically significant deployment, undoubtedly would have been concerned about its effect upon the morale of his southern allies and the security of his seaport at Locri. We may therefore judge that it was for this reason he ordered Hanno to return to Bruttium, with the army he had brought with him.

In order to complete the seasonal sequence of Roman operational deployment, Gracchus was now moved eastwards from Cumae to replace Laevinus at Luceria, thus strengthening the south-east coastal area both against the presence of Hannibal and the threat of Macedonian intervention. In the meantime, Fabius reorganised Roman forces south of the Volturnus. He ordered Marcellus to leave 'in Nola a garrison adequate for its defence and to dismiss the rest of his troops to Rome, to save the country expense and the allies the burden of their maintenance'. He next replenished and strengthened the garrison on Monte Cancello and then moved his own camp nearer to Capua. Once there, and content that his supplies of grain from Nola and Naples were both ample and secure, he set about the systematic devastation of the Campanian farmlands around the city. This pressure compelled the Capuan citizens to turn out an army of some 6,000 men to safeguard their vital grain-growing lands – 'infantrymen, and poor stuff at that!' writes Livy. Their cavalry, however, were of better material, and cavalry skirmishes continued well into the winter season.

As both sides consolidate their positions at the end of the campaigning season of 215 BC and deploy to their winter stations, this is a suitable moment to pause and assess their individual accomplishments.

Each protagonist appears mutually to have accepted the obstacle provided by the Volturnus as a broad dividing line. Rome, after her initial losses, was now seeking to build up her forces and was determined to concede no more to Hannibal. Hannibal, on the other hand, must have been well satisfied with the groundswell of support he received, *post* Cannae, from Rome's erstwhile allies of Apulia, Bruttium and Campania, as well as others in southern Italy, such as the Hirpini peoples; but he had received a mixed reception in northern Campania. This had enabled and encouraged Roman forces, particularly those of Gracchus and Marcellus, to penetrate south of the river and widen their influence. Hannibal's greatest single again, both tactically and politically, had been the city of Capua, a centre of 'great wealth and luxury, which had long prospered as the favourite of fortune'. Militarily, it brought him good value because of its geographical position adjoining two major highways and covering the Volturnus crossing. Politically, it competed with Naples to be the second city of the Roman republic, it was widely known as a financial and trading centre, and its secession in his favour was therefore an outstanding success in public relations, which, as we saw in the previous chapter, had already been registered by King Philip V of Macedonia.

In practical terms, however, both materially and militarily, the acquisition of Capua was muted unless complemented by the possession of Nola, an ancient agricultural centre, lying some 12 miles to its south-east, in the midst of a rich and fertile plain. Cato's widely quoted *post*-war shopping list[10] noted Nola as a distinguished market town where olive pulpers, oil vessels, hooks, water pitchers, wine vessels and bronze containers might be purchased. Agriculture, however, was not its sole asset, for Nola was also strategically important. It adjoined two ancient trackways, the first being the route we have already noted as favoured by Hannibal, namely, along the line of the river Aufidus and thence through the Apennines, thus linking the western and eastern coasts of the southern peninsula; and the second, the old highway to Rhegium, which we have already witnessed as used by Hanno and which, in its passage, carried its path, south of Nola, through the nearby towns of Nuceria and to the north, Suessula and Calatia.

The importance attached by both sides to the possession of Nola may be gauged by their military attitudes to it. Hannibal, with the intent of either capturing it or persuading its inhabitants to secede to his cause, presented himself before its walls on three separate occasions, albeit fruitlessly, during the campaigning seasons of 216/215 BC. He needed its food stores even more importantly than the ability to exploit its tactical location. The Romans, for their part, provided the town with their most worthy general, Marcellus, together with his army, to defend it; and they built a camp at Monte Cancello to keep watch over it throughout the year. The steadfastness of Marcellus at Nola thus frustrated Hannibal's intentions and denied him the supplies which might otherwise have sustained him in the area, probably in his base at Monte Tifata, during the coming winter months.

Hannibal's failure at Nola profited Fabius. The latter is significantly noted by Livy, at the end of the campaigning season, as conveying 'grain from Nola and Naples to the camp above Suessula'.[11] With his supply bases thus firmly established with foodstuffs denied to the Carthaginians, Fabius moved his own camp nearer Capua and commenced a 'systematic devastation of the Campanian farmlands'. It was a ploy which enabled him to tighten his grip on Capua and her satellites, with their Carthaginian garrisons, and to add to the complicated feeding problems of their inhabitants. Their difficulties had already been compounded during the summer months by Rome's strengthened political and military ties with the adjoining seaports of Cumae, Naples and, ultimately, Puteoli.[12]

It is clear that Hannibal's inability at this moment to gain access either to the Nolan or Neapolitan supply depots was the prime reason for his withdrawal eastwards across the Apennines to a winter camp at Arpi. Thus, Rome had, by a variety of indirect means, regained the initiative: she exploited her success even further by initiating the surprise thrust by Longus into mid-Lucania, which we have already witnessed, where he intercepted Hanno at Grumentum. Its effect could only have been, from that moment forward, to pose in Hannibal's mind a constant concern for the security of his lines of communication with the southern coast and Locri. By this means, as well, doubtless, as the newly arrived presence of Laevinus at Brundisium, she compelled the return of Hanno to Bruttium after the siege at Nola had been lifted.

Rome's crucial tactics, in this third, longest phase of Hannibal's campaign, which in essence already reflected his fading struggle for Italy, conformed with those explored, under the label of 'the indirect approach', by that eminent modern military critic Sir Basil Liddell Hart. He had learnt his lessons in the bloodstained trenches of Flanders in the First World War, and saw this philosophy as a means of paralysing the enemy's action as an alternative to enduring massive manpower losses in confrontational warfare. The Romans pursued this same thinking during Hannibal's War, as an option to indulging in the eyeball-to-eyeball, phalanx style battle drills they had inherited from the Greeks. Instead, they aimed to destroy Hannibal by striking at his lifelines. They concentrated upon containing the spread of the war he had brought upon them by closing down his supplies and denying him access to the major resources he needed for the efficient prosecution of his war, including, importantly, food supplies and war experienced reinforcements from Carthage or Carthaginian Spain.

Liddell Hart awarded the palm for 'logistical strategy amongst the ancients' to Scipio Africanus, whom we have already met at Trebbia and Cannae. Scipio's enthusiastic pursuit of the policy of the indirect approach led him to victory on the final battlefield of the war at Zama. An earlier supporter of the doctrine, however, was Quintus Fabius Maximus, for it was he who introduced a similar tactic, the militarily controversial *Fabian Strategy*, the doctrine of watch, wait, and harry, when he was army commander in the darkest days of 216 BC. By this means, he provided Rome with the time and space she needed to recover her balance and restore her defences. Another who, in that same year, had advocated a similar policy of less confrontational involvement was King Hiero of Syracuse. As soon as he received news of the Cannae catastrophe, he had despatched gold and shiploads of wheat and barley to Rome, together with a contingent of 1,000 bowmen as a gesture of support for a friend at a calamitous moment. He backed up the gifts with advice for his allies to pursue a more indirect tactical approach, namely, 'that the praetor who was serving in Sicily should invade Africa, for, if he did, Hannibal

Coin showing Hiero II of
Syracuse, c. 306–215 BC.
(© British Museum)

too would have a war on his hands at home, and Carthage would be less free to send him reinforcements'.[13] A classic example of the indirect approach.

Whether or not it was in response to this advice is unclear but, at about the time of the year when these welcome gifts from Hiero arrived on the Tiber, Gnaeus Servilius Geminus, who after Trasimene had been despatched by Fabius to Ostia as commander-in-chief of the navy,[14]

sailed round Sardinia and Corsica and, after taking hostages from both islands, crossed to Africa . . . and then made for the African coast, where he disembarked his troops. Plundering raids began at once, the ships' crews roaming the countryside as free and easy as if they were out to strip some uninhabited island. Their recklessness soon led them into a trap and they found themselves surrounded: unlike themselves their enemies were familiar with the country, compact bands easily rounded up the scattered parties of invaders, with the result that they were driven back to their ships badly beaten up, and leaving many dead on the field.

Geminus, having lost 'something like a thousand men' as a result of this African adventure, returned to Sicily, where, at Lilybaeum, the Roman trading port and naval base on the island's western extremity, it was handed over to the praetor Titus Otacilius. Then, under orders from the Senate, it was returned to Rome. Geminus himself was instructed to return home immediately to reassume army duties. A similar raid upon Africa occurred a few months later, so Livy relates, when a fleet again arrived at Lilybaeum, upon this occasion carrying praetor Publius Furius, who had been badly wounded and was in grave danger of his life. The soldiers and crew had not been paid and there were no rations to feed them. Otacilius sent a mission to Hiero, Rome's 'solitary standby in her hour of need, and received from him the money he required, with six months' supply of grain'. When Geminus returned home, the appointment of commander-in-chief, navy, was granted to Otacilius. The terms of his duties are detailed by Livy[15] and, in the context of the indirect approach we are discussing, they are noteworthy. His responsibilities were to raid the African coast, to protect the coast of Italy, and, most particularly, to prevent reinforcements, together with money and provisions, from reaching Hannibal from Carthage.

Otacilius, almost at once, appears to have undertaken a further raid on the North African coastline, where he inflicted severe damage on the countryside around Carthage. He then sailed for Sardinia, having heard that Hasdrubal was in the vicinity, and found the rumour to be correct. He encountered the enemy fleet during his passage and dispersed them, after capturing seven Carthaginian ships, with their crews. It was, at first sight, a successful foray but, within the parameters of his operational guidelines it was an ill-considered venture, for Bomilcar's fleet, destined to meet up with Hanno in Bruttium and laden with reinforcements, supplies and elephants, appears to have taken advantage of his absence from Lilybaeum to slip into the Straits of Messina. For whatever reason, but probably because of this, Otacilius was publicly rebuked by Fabius when the Senate was assembled to consider its operational appointments for the coming year, 214 BC, and the admiral was bidding to be appointed consul. 'Men of Rome', said Fabius, in his address to the assembly,

> if Otacilius has rendered his country I will not say all, but any single one of these services,[16] then elect him consul; but if, Otacilius, during your command even such things as Hannibal did not need reached him as safe and sound as if he had cleared the sea of his enemies; if the Italian coast has had more dangers for us this year than the coast of Africa; can you then give any reason why we should choose you, of all men, to lead us against such a foe as Hannibal?

Thus, the military picture viewed from Rome, as Hannibal's War entered its fifth year, was one of containment and minor success. Roman armies, whilst generally avoiding direct confrontation with Hannibal, had penetrated across the Volturnus and were breaking up his northern Campanian territories by destroying local food production and controlling supplies. Seaports on the south-western coast were being denied to him. On both eastern and western coasts, naval patrols had been enhanced. Despite the military troubles of the operational army at home, a programme of nagging, containing raids on the Carthaginian African coastline had been commenced. As a similar exercise of containment, the war in Spain continued unabated and well resourced. The Senate could have been tolerably satisfied. If so their pleasure was destined to be shortlived, for news now reached Rome from Sicily of the death of their old ally, Hiero. It was to bring a chain reaction of events which demanded a reassessment of priorities.

Hiero II reigned as absolute ruler of Syracuse for a period of some fifty-five years until his death in 215 BC. Upon the withdrawal from Sicily of Pyrrhus of Epirus, c. 276 BC, Hiero was appointed commander of the Syracusan army. Within a few years he had distinguished himself in a war with the Mamertini, a body of Campanian mercenaries who had occupied the fortified seaport of Messana (Messina) on the north-eastern promontory of the island. He soundly defeated them in battle near Mylae but, in a probable desire to keep such a peculiarly strategic location from entering into such powerful hands, the Carthaginians intervened to prevent the Syracusans from assuming occupation of the city. Nevertheless, Hiero's grateful countrymen, in recognition of his services to them during those troubled years, now appointed him king. Within a few years, he found himself once more at war with the Mamertini but, on this occasion, his enemy called upon Rome to come to their aid. Hiero could see threatening, long-term implications in the alliance which now confronted him, and joined forces with the Carthaginian leader, Hanno, who had but recently landed in Sicily and was equally reluctant to see this vital seaport in Roman hands. The two allies were unsuccessful in their efforts to prevent this happening, and their combined armies were defeated in battle by a Roman force commanded by Appius Claudius.

Table 4: Expansion of the Roman Army.

| Serial No. | Deployment Area | Year BC | | | |
|---|---|---|---|---|---|
| | | 218 (a) | 217 (b) | 216 (c) | 211 (d) |
| 1. | Cisalpine Gaul | 2 | 2 | 2 (f) | 2 |
| 2. | Sicily | 2 (e) | 2 | 2 | 4 |
| 3. | Spain | 2 | 2 | 2 | 2 (f) |
| 4. | Etruria | | 2 (f) | | 2 |
| 5. | Sardinia | | 1 | 1 | 2 |
| 6. | Rome | | 2 | 2 | 4 |
| 7. | Campania | | | | 6 |
| 8. | Apulia | | | 8 (f) | 2 (f) |
| 9. | Macedonia | | | | 1 |
| | Total Legions | 6 | 11 | 17 | 25 |

(a)    Hannibal crossed the Alps into northern Italy.

(b)    Hannibal crossed the Apennines and defeated Flaminius in battle at Lake Trasimene.

(c)    Romans comprehensively defeated at Cannae (Apulia).

(d)    The year of Hannibal's march on Rome and the surrender of Capua.

(e)    These two legions moved north under Longus to reinforce Scipio.

(f)    Destroyed by enemy action.

Hiero, after this experience of witnessing first hand the quality of the Roman fighting forces, quickly recognised the advantages of allying himself to such a powerful neighbour. He thus abandoned his ties with Carthage and concluded a treaty with Rome, gaining thereby her acceptance of the territorial bounds of the Syracusan kingdom in south-east Sicily, including a reach of the island's eastern coast as far as Tauromanium (Taormina). A glance at the map reveals the strategic importance of this concession, for the town lies roughly 30 miles from Messina, just west of the southern entrance to the straits and ideally situated for use by coastal shipping moving between Syracuse and the Italian mainland. In other words, with Syracuse allied to Rome, and the remainder of the island under Roman influence, the Straits of Messina, the southern seaports of Italy, together with Sicily itself, would be denied to Carthage. Conversely, if Syracuse were to ally herself to Carthage, the latter would gain access to these waters; and, moreover, vital ports such as Tarentum and Brundisium, on the 'heel' of Italy and essentially of military interest to Rome, would become vulnerable to attack by her.

Thus, in the context of the containment of Hannibal's War, an alliance with Syracuse or, failing that, the occupation of Syracusan territory, would have been a matter of overriding importance to Rome, particularly when framing any strategy of indirect approach which featured a policy of denial of mainland seaports to the enemy.

*Opposite*: Detail from a map of Syracuse by de la Rochette dating from 1793 and published by William Faden in 1799. (BL. Press mark K Top II.59)

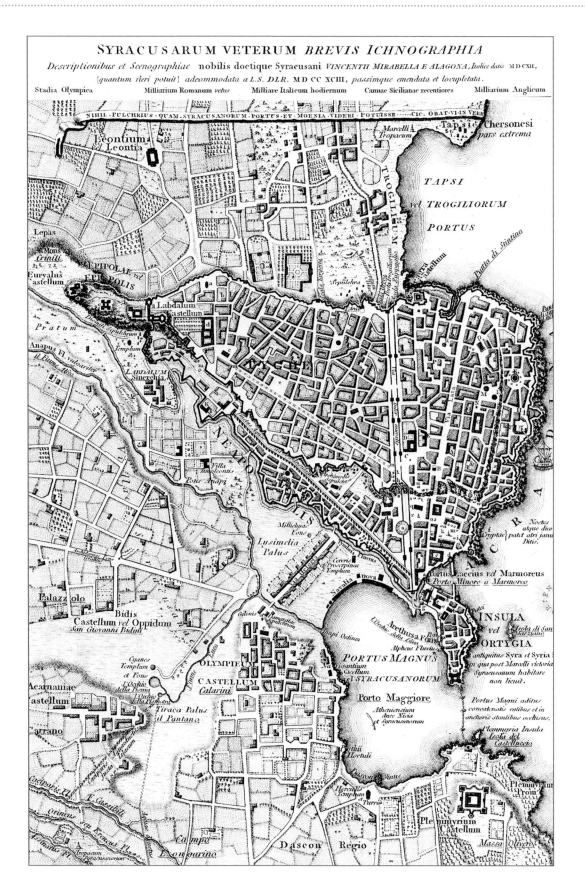

SYRACUSARUM VETERUM *BREVIS ICHNOGRAPHIA*

*Descriptionibus et Scenographiae* nobilis doctique Syracusani *VINCENTII MIRABELLA E ALAGONA, Italice datis* MDCXII, *[quantum fieri potuit]* adcommodata a L.S. DLR. MDCCXCIII, *passimque emendata et locupletata.*

Stadia Olympica     Milliarium Romanum *vetus*     Milliare Italicum hodiernum     Cannae Sicilianae recentiores     Milliarium Anglicum

Throughout his reign, Hiero II strictly observed the terms of his agreement with Rome and frequently exceeded it. Upon at least three occasions, he despatched unsolicited supplies and reinforcements to her when she was in particularly dire need. In this manner, he proved himself a worthy friend and, with his experienced army, powerful defensive fleet and immensely strong fortified city base designed by the renowned Archimedes, he contributed greatly to the political stability of Sicily during his lifetime and, consequently, to mainland Italy and Rome itself.

The island of Sicily, by its geographical location, lying in the central Mediterranean at the foot of the Italian peninsula, has always been considered a place of great strategic importance. In our own times, the allies of the Second World War used it as a stepping stone from which, in Winston Churchill's famous words, to strike at 'the soft underbelly of Europe'. Pliny the Elder, writing some two centuries after Hannibal's War, opined that the island outshone all others in fame,[17] and that

> It coastline is 528 miles long, according to Agrippa. Formerly it was joined to Bruttium, but subsequently the sea encroached upon the land and it became separated from the mainland by a strait next to the Royal Pillar, 14 miles long and 1½ miles wide. Because of Sicily's 'breaking away', the Greeks named the town situated on the Italian side of the strait, Rhegium. In those straits are the rock of Scylla and the whirlpool of Charybdis, both well known for their treacherousness. Sicily is triangular in shape: the promontory of Palorum points towards Italy, opposite Scylla, Pachynum towards Greece – the Peloponnese is 440 miles distant – and Lilybaeum towards Africa, some 180 miles from the promontory of Mercury and 190 miles from Caralia in Sardinia.

He paints a picture of a maritime crossroads. Lilybaeum, initially founded in 396 BC by Carthage to replace Motya, after it had been overrun by Dionysius, was a long-established and important trading port which, under siege both by Pyrrhus and the Romans,[18] had on each occasion displayed its worth as a formidable and impregnable military stronghold. It was now no longer Carthaginian territory. In accordance with the terms of the treaty she had signed on the conclusion of the First Punic War, Carthage had ceded her interest in Sicily in favour of Rome, together with her rights in the adjoining Aegates and Liparean groups of islands. Both of these clusters of islands were strategically valuable. The Lipareans covered, and thus controlled, the western approaches to the Straits of Messina; and the Aegates had the ability to threaten Lilybaeum, with its trade routes to North Africa and the western Mediterranean. It was the fact that Otacilius had left these natural gateways unguarded, and carelessly permitted Bomilcar to land at Locri with Hannibal's reinforcements, which had caused Fabius publicly to castigate him in the forum for neglect of duty. The importance of Lilybaeum to the Roman cause cannot be overstated.

Hiero was succeeded on the throne by his grandson, Hieronymus. According to Livy, the young man had been brought up by his father to distrust their

Coin showing Hieronymus
of Syracuse, 215–214 BC.
(© British Museum)

Roman allies. His fears in this regard were sharpened shortly after his accession, when he was warned of an alleged Roman plot against his life in which, he was informed, the leader of the pro-Roman faction in Syracuse had been implicated. Hieronymus was, if Livy is to be believed, an unlikeable young man. 'It would not have been easy for any king', so he tells us,[19]

> even for one who ruled well and justly, to find favour with the Syracusans after Hiero, who had been so well beloved. But Hieronymus, on his very first appearance, showed how sadly things had changed. It was as if he were being deliberately vicious in order to make people wish his grandfather back again.

The tales of his behaviour, left to us by ancient historians, particularly Polybius and Livy, reveal Hieronymus as tactless, arrogant, conceited and provocative. When Rome sent envoys to encourage him to renew his grandfather's treaty of alliance, he mocked them with the ironic question 'of how they had fared at the battle of Cannae'. In another instance, when his envoys, as a result of negotiations he had opened with Hannibal, had agreed with Carthage the terms of their alliance at this dangerous moment, to the effect that the isle of Sicily would be divided between them at the conclusion of the war, he later repudiated the arrangement, declaring that Sicily should be his. Carthage should acquire her own empire within Italy itself. The Carthaginians refrained from being critical of his overweening manner, their main interest being in persuading the young king to break with Rome.

As a result of these and other irresponsibilities, the political stability which Hiero had left as a legacy to the Syracusan people was quickly shattered, riven into diametrically opposed groupings of peoples supportive of, or opposed to, the Romans, the Carthaginians or, indeed the monarchy itself. In this sort of atmosphere, it is unsurprising to learn that Hieronymus was assassinated, stabbed to death in a back alley of Leontini by his own soldiery. In the outcome, a confused situation cleverly and ruthlessly exploited by Carthaginian agents, the pro-Carthaginian lobby gained a difficult upper hand and Syracuse closed its gates to the Romans.

Whilst these events had been developing in Sicily, Rome, heartened by the evident improvement in the battlefield performance and morale of her armed forces during the previous year, had continued with the expansion and development of her army and navy. As a result, by the spring of 214 BC, she was well equipped to commence the new campaigning season and had eighteen legions to put in the field, including two city legions for the defence of Rome.[20] Additionally, work was about to be set in hand to bring the fleet to a total of 150 ships, including those stationed at Brundisium and elsewhere, for the defence of Calabrian coastal waters.

The Senate announced the arrangements for the deployment of these formations on the day that the two newly appointed consuls, once again Fabius and Marcellus, assumed office. Wisely, it had been agreed to make no changes amongst the army commanders: their experience was thus retained. Fabius was posted to Apulia and Marcellus was to remain at Cales. Three other generals, Gracchus at Luceria, with his slave volunteers, Varro in Picenum, and Pomponius in Cisalpine Gaul, were to remain for the moment in their present locations. The praetors for the previous year, now pro-praetors, were deployed, Quintus Mucius to Sardinia and Marcus Valerius Laevinus to Brundisium. All of these commanders were allotted two legions apiece, with the exception of Varro, who was granted one legion, and an additional legion was allocated to Valerius Laevinus for service at Brundisium with the fleet, where he had the specific task of patrolling the waters between Tarentum and Brundisium. Finally, in response to growing rumours of unrest in Sicily, following the death of Hiero II, the praetors Lentulus and Otacilius were ordered to the island, the former to take command of its army of two legions and the latter to assume responsibility for the defence of the coast and to direct naval operations.

The Campanians, particularly the inhabitants of Capua, had been watching Rome's growing might with considerable dismay. They saw themselves, not unreasonably, as the prime target of the great enemy force now accumulating in central Italy and despatched a delegation to Hannibal, still in his Apulian winter camp, near Arpi, to voice their deep concern. Their worries, says Livy, were expressed 'in such a flurry of excitement and alarm that Hannibal felt that no time was to be lost'. He marched westwards at once, having alerted Hanno to join him from Bruttium, and within a few days had reoccupied his old camp at Monte Tifata, above Capua. Then, leaving his Numidian and Spanish contingents to guard the city, he resumed his pattern of operations of the previous year. He made a sudden thrust at Puteoli, in the hope of finding the seaport unprepared for sudden assault, but discovered it to be well defended by a Roman garrison of 6,000. He thus wasted no further time upon it but turned away towards Naples, systematically devastating the surrounding farms and fields of the countryside as he progressed.

Campania was soon in turmoil. Fabius, learning of the return of Hannibal to Capua, ordered Gracchus westward to Beneventum, a rich grain-growing centre on the *Via Latina*, and appointed his son, who bore an identical name to his father, to move with his army to fill the vacuum thus created at Luceria. Gracchus, upon reaching Beneventum, found himself face to face with Hanno, freshly arrived from southern Italy, in response to Hannibal's call, with an army of 17,000 foot, mostly Bruttians and Lucanians, and 1,200 horse.

Whilst these events were in train, the commons of Nola, conscious of Hannibal's return, had sent representatives to the Carthaginian general, offering to surrender their town. The senatorial party in Nola, however, learning of this treachery, despatched a messenger to Marcellus, informing him of what was happening and seeking help. He reacted with typical urgency and dash. He covered the distance from Cales to Suessula in one day, and from there put 6,000 foot and 300 horse into the town that very night. The vigour and promptness which enabled Marcellus to be first into the town, Livy tells us, 'was as marked as the dilatoriness of Hannibal, whose two previous failures had made him less ready to believe what the people of Nola told him'. For whatever reason, Hannibal arrived to find Nola already occupied and, after a brief skirmish in which Livy claims the Carthaginian lost 2,000 men, he turned away and marched towards Tarentum, 'spreading destruction in his path'.

If we assume, as we are entitled to do, that Hannibal was working towards a clear campaign objective, then it is not always easy to discern, from the information provided to us, the full purpose of this marching and counter-marching. Without doubt, much of it was flag-showing, to sustain the morale of his detached garrisons; some of it was exploratory, probing for a weak spot; some of it, such as his march to Cumae, to the aid of the Campanians, was predictable; but, increasingly, it appears that the Roman 'scorched earth policy', together with their oppressive handling of the recovered allied territories which had seceded to Hannibal or had assisted him in any way, was beginning to influence his choice of a sphere of operations. The tidying-up exercise conducted by Fabius in the wake of the Carthaginian leader's march on Tarentum provides a case in point. The two consuls had joined forces for the successful recapture of Casilinum, which had been held by 2,000 Campanians and 700 of Hannibal's soldiers. Fabius now turned his eyes towards Samnium[21] and proceeded to

> . . . devastate the countryside and to recover the towns which had seceded from the Roman alliance. The country around Caudium received the severest treatment: farmlands were burnt over a wide area, cattle were driven off and men taken prisoner, and the settlements of Compulteria, Telesia, Compsa,[22] Fugifulae and Orbitanium were attacked and captured. The Lucanian settlement of Blandae was also taken, and the Apulian town of Accae. In these places a total of 25,000 men were either captured or killed, and 370 deserters were caught.

The Roman army was providing supplies and recruiting for itself on internal lines. Hannibal had to be dependent either on the uncertain resources of the allies he could persuade to join him or on whatever he could forage or whoever he could recruit to his cause, whilst either on operations or whilst occupying his chosen winter base. He had constantly to search for a dependable source of supply. He might have resolved his problems by capturing one of the seaports in the Bay of Naples; but Roman military planners had astutely anticipated his need and these towns had been strengthened politically and reinforced militarily against attack. His manpower difficulties were being exacerbated by casualties inflicted by Fabius upon Carthaginian sympathisers in Sansium, now being carried forward proportionately into the wider field of operations. Roman devastation of the land, combined with the destruction which Hannibal was inflicting upon it, was by now creating seriously restrictive logistical problems for the armies operating upon it, particularly Carthaginian.

Amongst the courses open to him at this stage, however, there was an important consideration of which he must have been aware. A Carthaginian task force was about to be ordered to Sicily in support of Syracuse. Hannibal's intelligence agents, Hippocrates and Epicydes,[23] were already active, both in that city and in Leontini, and would have been keeping him well plied with information. In addition to this, he himself had written a letter to the Carthaginian senate, recommending 'that the time had come to win back Sicily as the national honour demands'.[24] By now it must have been received and considered by the senate at Carthage, even if action upon it had not yet been initiated. In essence, Hannibal could not have been unaware of the events developing in Sicily, and could not have ignored them. It was, for example, only a matter of weeks before Himilco was to land at Hericlea Minoa, south-east of Lilybaeum, with 20,000 foot, 3,000 horse and 12 elephants.

More than this, the expressed willingness of Philip of Macedonia to intervene in Italy on his behalf should a suitable opportunity arise, could not have been something he could have entirely set aside, despite the misfortunes which had overtaken the proposed alliance. Equally, Hannibal must surely have been aware of the events now developing on the eastern shores of the Adriatic, where the king had begun an assault upon Apollonia, with the purpose, so it was alleged,[25] of occupying coastal towns whose position made them a likely base for an attack on Italy. One of these was Oricum, an ally of Rome, whose elders hastily despatched envoys to Valerius Laevinus at Brundisium begging his help.

Laevinus promptly responded to the appeal and, leaving his second-in-command, Publius Valerius, in charge of a garrison of 2,000 men at Brundisium he sailed without delay for Oricum, where, finding the town held only by a weak garrison, he recaptured it almost immediately. He then put ashore a landing party of 2,000 men to march to the relief of Apollonia. They successfully entered the allied town unperceived by the Macedonians and then, after joining forces with the population, they fell upon the carelessly guarded enemy camp, capturing or killing 3,000 men and driving the remainder, including the king himself, to seek refuge on their ships. Livy records that Philip, thus rudely made aware of the limitations of his army, now beached and burned his boats and 'returned overland to Macedonia, with an army for the most part disarmed and despoiled'. Laevinus, with the Roman fleet from Brundisium, decided to winter at Oricum.

It will be recalled that Hannibal, after his rebuff at Nola, had set out to march to Tarentum. It is quite conceivable that this place, a prosperous and strategically well-sited seaport, had already been his intended destination before he allowed himself to be distracted by the cry for help from Capua. If so, the delay this would have imposed upon him would have been crucial, for when he arrived before the gates of the town, it was already too late. They were closed against him: he had been forestalled by the alertness of Valerius Laevinus, who had learnt of his approach, and 'three days before his coming', had sent an officer, Marcus Livius, to organise the town's defences.[26]

Livius enrolled all men of military age, posted guards at every gate and, wherever necessary, around the walls, and by exercising the greatest vigilance day and night left no loophole for a hostile move either by the enemy or by the possible treachery of friends. Hannibal, in consequence, was merely wasting his time, and after a few days during which not one of the men who had visited him at Lake Avernus either came to him in person or communicated with him by messenger or letter, he left the neighbourhood, realising that he had been led, all too easily, to follow a mere empty promise.

It is revealing to notice the inter-relationship of the events, which occurred in the later part of the campaigning season of 214 BC. It would appear that when Hannibal reached Tarentum, Laevinus was still at Brundisium with his army, or was possibly about to sail to bring aid to Rome's allies in Greece, for, as we have seen, he had only 'three days earlier' sent Marcus Livius to reinforce the city. At the same time, Philip of Macedonia was successfully engaged in collecting coastal towns on the eastern shores of the Adriatic, 'because their position made them a likely base for an attack on Italy'. In Sicily, Hannibal's personal intelligence agents were successfully bringing about the vital defection of Syracuse from their Roman alliance, and a fleet of fifty-five Carthaginian warships, under their famous admiral, Bomilcar, had entered the Grand Harbour. The Carthaginian general, Himilco, with an army of 25,000 foot, 3,000 cavalry and 12 elephants, had arrived at Heraclea Minoa, in the south of the island. From there he had marched to take up a position on the river Anapus, 8 miles from Syracuse.

In all these circumstances, it might well have seemed, wrote Livy,[27] that the seat of war had shifted from Italy altogether, 'so intent were both antagonists upon Sicily'. Roman naval forces, already located at Lilybaeum, commanded the Straits of Messina and neighbouring waters, whilst her fleet based at Ostia patrolled the south-west coastline of the peninsula. Rome now despatched her *beau sabreur*, Marcus Claudius Marcellus, to bolster her land forces on the island. Carthage, by the reinforcements she was making available from North Africa, left no doubt that she was determined to oppose her. Hannibal, however, other than sending his personal representatives to Syracuse, chose to remain strangely aloof, whilst conducting a mainland campaign which was already showing signs of 'withering on the vine' in the face of Rome's strategy of containment.

## CHAPTER VIII

# THE BATTLE FOR THE SEAPORTS

Time and again their pilots had tried to persuade them not to sail along the southern coast of Sicily where it faces the Libyan Sea, as it is a rocky shore which faces few safe anchorages.

Polybius[1]

It is tempting to refer to the next phase of Hannibal's War as the battle for Sicily, for it was here, as Livy sensibly remarked, that both opponents had now so keenly concentrated their attention and resources that it seemed 'the seat of war had shifted from Italy altogether'. Truly, the final outcome was to leave the victor in total control of Sicily but, for the Carthaginians, their campaign at this moment was primarily directed towards the occupation and use of the seaports along the island's southern and eastern coastlines. These offered the first friendly landfalls for ships plying from North Africa to Syracuse and, thence, to the east coast of Italy. To this end, the acquisition of Syracuse, or an alliance with her rulers, was now their prime objective.

As a result of the First Punic War (264–241 BC), Sicily, with the territorial exception of Syracuse, which remained independent under the control of Hiero II, had emerged as the first Roman province outside Italy. The kingdom of Syracuse extended from Taormina, on the east coast, to Cape Pachynum, today the Capo Passero, on its extreme south-east corner. One of the island's richest seaports, initially founded by the Carthaginians, lay on the opposite, western extremity of the south coast, on Capo Boeo. This was Lilybaeum, the lively and prosperous fortress town we have already noted,[2] lying within easy range of North Africa. In its history, it had withstood lengthy attacks by each of Dionysius, Pyrrhus and ultimately the Romans,[3] but fell to none, until, by the terms of a peace agreement after the First Punic War, it passed into the possession of Rome. Between Lilybaeum, along the rugged shoreline reaching to Cape Pachynum, stood four other ancient trading ports, all of them founded upon natural, estuary harbours. Each of them were of varying degrees of importance and had been physical and economic casualties of the First Punic War: they were, in turn,

The ruins of the Temple of Juno at Agrigentum; the buildings were burned by the Carthaginians in 400 BC but were later restored by the Romans, only to be subsequently destroyed by an earthquake. Agrigentum provided the main Carthaginian military base in Sicily during Hannibal's War. (By courtesy of the Italian State Tourist Board (E.N.I.T.) London)

- **Selinus**, which, during the fighting of those years, had been razed to the ground by the Carthaginians, as punishment for its stubborn resistance during the war, when some 15,000 of its inhabitants had been killed. Those remaining were subsequently moved to and enslaved in nearby Lilybaeum. The harbour area of Selinus lay in the estuaries of two nearby rivers, the Selinus and the Hypsas.

- **Heraclea Minoa,** situated on the Capo Banco, directly east of the present-day river Platani.

- **Agrigentum,**[4] a large and ancient town, 'encircled by natural and artificial defences of unusual strength', was first sacked by the Romans in 261 BC, and then by the Carthaginians, 256 BC but survived as a powerful, well-populated centre during Hannibal's War. Two rivers, doubtless used for commerce in their lower reaches, ran either side of the town and came together before entering the sea some 4 miles distant. Its citadel, almost entirely surrounded by a ravine, save for an approach road, was virtually impregnable.

- **Camarina,**[5] a one-time prosperous seaport, whose influence had extended deep into the hinterland, was destroyed by Rome in the First Punic War and its people enslaved. In ancient times it lay on a terrace between the river Hipparis and the Cava di Randello.

In addition to all of these, there was a natural, sheltered anchorage at Cape Pachynum, where shipping was accustomed to lie up before tackling the contrary winds regularly met when rounding the cape from either direction, but, in particular, the seasonal northerlies blowing from the Adriatic.

The dangerous nature of these Sicilian waters may be measured by a Roman experience at the outset of the First Punic War, when a fleet commanded by Lucius Junius Pullus set sail from Syracuse for Lilybaeum. In those days of simple navigation, he was probably hugging the line of the shore and, as he progressed southwards, he observed the Carthaginians lying in wait for him. In order to avoid them, he altered course and put in on 'a rock-bound and altogether dangerous part of the coast'. The pilots of the Carthaginian fleet, presumably local men, at this moment noted a change in the weather conditions, and ran to take cover in the lee of Cape Pachynum until the coming storm had subsided. The Romans, on the other hand, had no such choice and were caught in the open, on a stretch of rocky coastline: their fleet was totally destroyed. The incident was particularly disastrous as it arrived hard on the heels of a similar occurrence in the previous year, when a convoy was trapped on the high seas in a storm which, in the words of Polybius, beggared description.[6] As a result, vessels returning to Sicily from Africa, heavily laden with troops, were driven on to the Sicilian coast near Camarina, with a loss of 284 ships and many dead.

North of Cape Pachynum, roughly 35 miles distant, lay Syracuse, a trading centre and fortress which, in ancient times and for many centuries, had been the largest and the most prosperous in Sicily. The heart of the city, and today the most attractive part, was the island of Ortygia, where the original Grecian settlers had first landed. On its southern edge lay the Grand Harbour, a deep and natural basin with a narrow entrance, capable of accepting large numbers of vessels and ideally shaped for it purpose; to its north was to be found another, smaller, harbour, the Porto Piccolo. Ortygia was linked to the mainland by a bridge which gave access to the four remaining districts. These were Achradina, bounded to its southern border by the Grand Harbour and, on its eastern, open flank, overlooking the Ionian Sea, by a section of the great city wall; the two central districts of Tyche and Neapolis, both of which, the former to the north and the latter to the south, were bounded by the city wall; and, finally, in the extreme west, on high ground, the district of Epipolae, which provided the heart of the city defence system. This district was contained by the city wall defences on its three exposed flanks, and included in its far west, the citadel of Eurysius, and, at Hexapylon, on the eastern end of its northern flank, the City Gate. The sturdy city wall, commenced by Dionysius the Elder in 401 BC, surrounded the entire city and extended a distance of more than 20 miles. In the west it was further strengthened, as it skirted the citadel, by three external defensive ditches.

North-east of Syracuse, on the 'instep' of mainland Italy and some 200 miles distant if heading directly across the sea, was Tarentum, the seaport which, at this stage of his campaign, was fast becoming the centre of Hannibal's attention. It was situated at the base of the Salentine peninsula and on a northern inlet of the Gulf of Tarentum. It was already in commercial decline at the time of the Second Punic War but it was still a major port, with an inner and outer harbour, and its untrammelled possession would have made an invaluable and positive contribution towards resolving the steadily increasing logistical difficulties of Hannibal's campaign in southern Italy. For this reason, when considering the battle for the Sicilian seaports, the parallel struggle for the control of Tarentum cannot be omitted.

It is thus revealing to notice the crucial inter-relationship of events which occurred in the latter part of the campaigning season of 214 BC. In the above chapter we recorded Hannibal's fruitless arrival at Tarentum and his return to Salapia in northern Apulia. Before he departed, he appointed two agents, Hippocrates and Epicydes, to Sicily, but particularly with Syracuse in mind, to encourage unrest and stimulate dissatisfaction with the Roman presence. We may judge that Laevinus, the appointed guardian of the Salentine coast was, at that moment, still at Brundisium with his army, for only 'three days earlier', just prior to Hannibal's arrival, he had sent Marcus Livius to reinforce Tarentum. In this event, Philip of Macedonia would still have been happily and uninterruptedly engaged in collecting coastal towns on the eastern shores of the Adriatic, as coastal bases from which to launch an attack on Italy; and the Carthaginian general Himilco was about to disembark, or was disembarking, at Heraclea Minoa with an army of 25,000 foot, 3,000 horse and 12 elephants.

In the midst of this surge of events, Marcellus arrived and marched at once, with his entire army, for Syracuse, only diverting to overrun Leontini, which, taking every advantage of the confusion arising after the murder of Hieronymus, had been the first to declare its independence from Rome. It had called upon Syracuse to provide it with military support and the city senate, heavily divided and as yet unable to decide a proper course to adopt, seized the opportunity to rid themselves of what Livy colourfully describes as an explosive and disorderly rabble of 4,000 deserters and mercenary auxiliaries. Upon the surrender of Leontini, Marcellus extracted 2,000 deserters from within this contingent and summarily ordered them to be scourged and beheaded. It was a brutal but contemporarily normal judgement, speedily executed. Nevertheless, it had the effect of stiffening the growing resistance to the Roman alliance, for Hippocrates and Epicydes, who had by this time been elected generals in the Syracusan army, wasted no time in noising it about that Syracusan prisoners of war had been included in this number.

The Roman commanders now resumed their march on Syracuse, where, upon arrival, they took up a position about a mile from the city, near the temple of Olympian Jupiter. From here, despite a rebuff received by some envoys they had earlier sent by sea to negotiate a peaceful settlement, they tried again to open negotiations and, on this occasion, sent a delegation to the city gates at Hexapylon. They were met outside the walls by Hippocrates and Epicydes. The two men were supported by a strongly armed contingent of troops, present to obstruct the envoys from entering the city. Again the Romans found their overtures rejected. 'If you attack us,' said Epicydes, as spokesman for the Syracusans, 'experience will soon show you that an attempt upon Syracuse is by no means the same thing as an attempt upon Leontini.' He then turned and walked away and the city gates were closed behind him.

The Romans had been prepared for a reception of this nature and now, without further delay and having marshalled every piece of artillery for the purpose, they launched a simultaneous attack on Syracuse by land and sea. But the Syracusans were fortunate in possessing a secret weapon they had not yet disclosed, namely, the Greek scientist Archimedes, a renowned mathematician and mechanical genius of ancient Grecian stock. Archimedes, who at the time of these events would have been some seventy-five years of age, was locally born and had resided in the city[7] for the best part of his life. Apart from his mathematical genius, he was also celebrated, but probably less known, for his work as an inventor of 'all types of artillery and military devices', as well as for his scientific handling of these in operation, by which, claimed Livy,[8] 'he was able by one finger as it were, to frustrate the most laborious operations of the enemy'. He was equally famous for his innovational thinking on fortress design and, greatly supported by Hiero II, he had caused much of this to be included in the city fortifications.

The ground over which the city wall had been constructed varied greatly in nature. Mostly, it was high, steep and difficult but elsewhere there were level stretches where it could be approached across low, flat ground. Archimedes had given considerable thought to the differing defence demands posed by these contrasting conditions. He had already drawn up plans for the various sectors which defined, by range capacity, the types of artillery and weight of shot to be employed, together with the fire tables and scale of weapon concentration to be followed. He was, once again, well ahead of his time and this is particularly noticeable when we consider his fire plan covering the sea approaches. It was this flank which Marcellus considered to be the most vulnerable and it was here, with sixty quinquiremes, that he launched his first assault, on the wall at Achradina, where the wall ran through the water. He was due for a surprise. He divided his

Archimedes, c. 287–212 BC. The Greek scholar was born in Syracuse. (From a painting by Jusepe Ribera. Bridgeman Art Library, SCP 036733)

force into two divisions: the first armed with archers and slingers, to stand back and provide covering fire; and the second equipped with assault towers, several storeys high and constructed on ships lashed together in pairs. Archimedes was ready for them; he countered by[9]

. . . moving into position on the wall pieces of artillery of varying size; at the ships offshore he hurled stones of enormous weight, assailing those closer in with missiles which, though lighter, could for that reason be discharged more frequently. Then, to enable his own men to discharge their missiles at the enemy without danger to themselves, he made loopholes, ranging from top to bottom of the wall and some 18 inches wide, through which, themselves unseen, they could shoot at the enemy either with arrows or with smallish catapults. Some of the enemy ships came close inshore, too close for the artillery to touch them; and these he dealt with by using a swing beam and grapnel.

Marcellus quickly appreciated the futility of continuing with such an expensive assault, in terms of both manpower and shipping, on this well-defended flank and the Romans now switched their effort to an overland attack but this proved to be equally difficult. As a consequence, they divided their effort and, whilst one part of their force set up a blockade by land and sea, Marcellus, 'with about a third of the army', marched off to recover the towns of Helorus, Herbesus and Megara which had declared for Carthage. He achieved this with little difficulty.

Whilst the Romans had been engaged in this manner, the Carthaginian general Himilco had landed at Heraclea Minoa and had then advanced to Agrigentum, both of which towns had ceded to him, the latter, particularly, being an important prize. At the same time, within Syracuse, Hippocrates and Epicydes, confident of their ability to hold the city and having become aware of Himilco's arrival, had apportioned their military duties so that the latter assumed responsibility for the defence of the Syracuse, whilst Hippocrates left the city with a force of 10,000 men, somehow finding a way through the Roman lines, to reinforce the Carthaginian arrivals. Unforgivably, whilst engaged in making camp for the night, and with his men totally unprepared for an engagement, he allowed himself to be surprised by Marcellus. In the resulting mêlée, in which he lost the bulk of his infantry, mostly taken unarmed, Hippocrates escaped with his mounted troops and joined Himilco, whom he found marching to Syracuse.

There now occurred one of those increasingly frequent failures of seemingly sensible planning that frustrated the latter part of Hannibal's War. Himilco, intent upon bringing Marcellus to battle before he rejoined the main body of the Roman army, pursued him to the banks of the Anapus, within 8 miles of Syracuse, where Appius Claudius had recently been strengthened by the arrival of yet another legion from Italy. Almost simultaneously, within the city itself, Bomilcar had recently run into the Grand Harbour with fifty-five Carthaginian warships. It is not clear from Livy's account of events whether there was any planned relationship between the movements of Bomilcar and Himilco, or whether, which is not easy to believe, their simultaneous arrivals were purely uncoordinated. Be that as it may, the kettle having been brought to the boil, the Carthaginian generals now decided to extinguish the flame. Himilco, deterred by the size of the enemy army entrenched around the city, pulled away 'to encourage by his presence any of the Sicilian communities who supported the Carthaginian cause'. Bomilcar also decided to withdraw and return to Carthage. His reasons were clear: he found himself outnumbered by the Roman fleet and, because of the shortage of supplies within the city, he felt the presence of his fleet imposed an unwarrantable drain upon its resources.

Livy neither provides us with a full account of their reasoning in reaching these decisions, nor does he mention the purpose, if any existed, for which they came together in the first place. Nevertheless, it is possible, in this feeble outcome, to sense an opportunity which would not have been wasted on Hannibal had he been in such a situation.

The matter of finding billets for the coming winter (214 BC) now became the concern of all field commanders. Himilco, having seized the prosperous city of Murgantia, together with a large Roman supply depot, appointed Hippocrates to command it, and then marched to winter in Agrigentum. Marcellus constructed for himself a winter camp at Leon, 5 miles from Hexapylon, from where he could supervise the blockade of Syracuse. Appius Claudius, as a candidate for the consulship, returned to Rome for the elections, leaving his army under command of Marcellus. Hannibal, on the mainland, determined to march north to winter in Spalatia.

Two imperatives beckoned Hannibal northwards. Patently, one of these was the need to impress upon his enemy the fact that he had not relinquished his interest in Campania and northern Apulia, together with the threat this implied for the city of Rome itself. His periodic return to the frontier war zone thus had the effect of tying down a number of formations and resources which might otherwise have been employed against him further south; furthermore, his sudden sweep northwards denied the Romans the opportunity of exercising against him that most vital of military principles – concentration of force. In order to retain his acquisitions there, however, during his absences in the south, it had been necessary for him to provide Carthaginian garrisons of varying size to strengthen the defences of the towns which had seceded to him. We have no indication of the numbers involved, either in terms of manpower or locations. Casilinum, which had fallen earlier in 214 BC to Marcellus and Fabius, had been provided with a garrison of 2,000 Campanians and 700 of Hannibal's soldiers. Arpi, which had seceded to Hannibal and now, contrarily, was about to return to the Roman fold, housed a garrison of 5,000 Carthaginians. There were doubtless many others, such as the old Hannibalic base at Compsa, recently recaptured by Fabius, and Salapia, where he was now heading.

Hannibal was, in fact, already in the midst of a dilemma which Polybius[10] denied eloquently on his behalf:

He could not keep guard over all the (secessionist) cities from one single point when when the enemy was putting a number of armies in the field against him. Nor could he break up his own force into a number of separate detachments. If he had done that he would have made himself an easy prey for his adversaries. He would have been inferior in numbers and he could not have taken personal command of all his detachments simultaneously.

But whatever else he did, it was vital that he should use every means to sustain the morale of the cities which had seceded to him, together with that of the garrison troops with which he had provided them, for it was here that he hoped to welcome his brother, Hasdrubal, if and when he arrived from Spain to join him.

The consideration which he attached to this may be measured by the logistical effort this move demanded of him, for his destination, some 50 miles distant, was suffering from a grain shortage. Livy[11] tells us that Hannibal therefore 'had the grain brought in from the country around Metapontum and Heraclea', on the Gulf of Taranto. If we judge Hannibal's strength at this time to be a modest 20,000 men, each of whom would have consumed 3 lb of grain a day, then his ration requirement for a period of six months, taking no account of his animals, would have been a total of approximately 5,000 tons. He would thus have been presented with a considerable haulage problem, calling for some 2,000 wagon loads or more. Such a number would not have been excessive as we have already seen when discussing the problems of feeding the people of Rome.[12]

At the opening of the campaign season in the following spring (213 BC), Hannibal once again directed his attention to Tarentum. This appears from Livy's annals to have been a markedly uneventful year but he does suggest that the fall of Tarentum to Hannibal probably occurred at this moment rather than in 212 BC as he himself records it.[13] The surrender of the town was finally provoked by an unnecessarily savage act by Rome. Some Tarentine hostages, bored by their prolonged detention in the capital, escaped from the city to enjoy a brief spell of freedom from custody. It must be doubtful, according to the code of hostage-taking, whether they would have been made welcome had they returned to Tarentum, but they were not allowed to escape: they were pursued and caught in a day and their punishment was brutally harsh. They were summarily tried by the people, 'taken into the Comitium, scourged and hurled from the Rock'. The severity of the punishment, which was probably intended to quieten any thought of revolt amongst the population of Tarentum, had precisely the opposite effect. It was understandably deeply resented and a party of young aristocrats at once made overtures to Hannibal, who had once again moved south and was encamped, some three days' march distant.

A plan was agreed by which one of the young men, under the guise of a hunting party, would establish a pattern of regular, and obviously successful, night time expeditions, conducted from the same postern gate and employing the same routine on each occasion, so that 'the thing became so much of a habit that the gate was opened for him at any time of the night in answer to his whistle'. Hannibal, as he waited for this situation to develop, let it be publicly known that he was sick, in case the Roman garrison should become concerned about his prolonged stay in the neighbourhood.

When he was satisfied that the right level of relaxation had been achieved, Hannibal carefully selected a force of 10,000 foot and horse, and marched in the direction of the town. He maintained a high level of secrecy and advanced behind a cavalry screen, deployed across a wide front and thrown well forward. Their instructions were to conceal the approach of his main body by pretending to be a raiding party and they were to seize or eliminate any person who might catch a glimpse of his main column and break the security silence he had also rigorously imposed upon his own men. When he reached a point 15 miles from Tarentum, he halted 'on the banks of a river which flowed through a ravine and offered excellent cover'.[14] There, they enjoyed an evening meal and he briefed his offers but, even then,

> . . . he did not explain the details of his plan but dwelt on three points. First of all, he appealed to them to fight bravely, since the prize for success had never been greater; secondly, each of them was to keep the men under his command in close order on the march, and severely punish any who left the ranks on any pretext whatsoever, and lastly, they were to carry out his orders to the letter and not attempt anything on their own initiative.

Hannibal resumed his march immediately after dark, at 'the time of the first sleep' and, led by a guide, found his way to the postern gate where the hunting party, now assured of his presence, whistled for admittance and, upon entering, cut down the unsuspecting guard. A follow-up party of thirty Carthaginians, led personally by Hannibal if Livy is to be properly understood, then forced open the main gate, thus allowing the main column of Carthaginians to pour through in silence, like a subdued torrent. Once inside, they rejoined their commander who, by now, had reached the forum. The town quickly succumbed; a large proportion of the Roman garrison was killed and the remainder, some 5,000 in number according to Appian,[15] together with their commander, Livius, and some Tarentine sympathisers, sought refuge in the citadel.

The citadel at Tarentum had been carefully sited on a rocky promontory, and was approachable by land from one side only, namely, from the northern flank which allowed access to and from the town. To its west it looked out over the Gulf of Taranto, and to its south and east it covered both the outer harbour and the narrow, bridged water passage which controlled the flow of shipping to and from the inner harbour. The Tarentine fleet was anchored in the inner harbour and the hostile Roman occupation of the citadel meant that it was now unable to break out on to the high seas.

Whilst recognising this, Hannibal saw his next immediate task as the isolation of the citadel from the rest of the town by the construction of a palisade along the outside edge of the water-filled moat at the foot of the north wall of the fortress. This provoked an angry response from the garrison, who

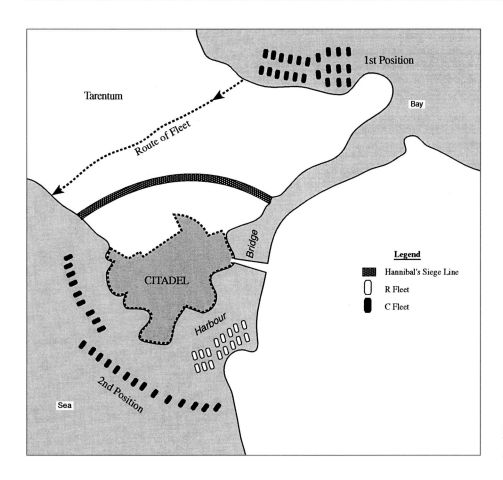

Map showing the citadel at Tarentum.

sallied forth to attack him, but he was prepared for them. In accordance with an agreed plan, the Carthaginian working party allowed itself to be driven back and his main force, which had been held in readiness but out of sight, now emerged from hiding and inflicted severe loss on the enemy attack force. The work on the palisade was then allowed to continue uninterrupted. According to both Appian and Livy, Hannibal, employing 'siege towers, catapults and pent-houses'[16] and 'all sorts of artillery and siege engines',[17] next attempted an assault on the citadel. Polybius, for his part, and probably more believably, for Hannibal is unlikely to have constructed a palisade as an obstacle to his own assault, relates that the Romans, in a night attack, succeeded in destroying 'all of Hannibal's machines and apparatus'[18] and that he then abandoned the idea of taking the citadel by storm, particularly since his enemy had already received reinforcements by sea from the garrison at Metapontum. He continued instead with the improvement of his circumvallatory wall, until it was of such a strength that the Tarentines could man it reliably, without further help from himself.

*The prize for success has never been greater* are the words with which Hannibal briefed his officers, as they supped in the field on the eve of their assault on Tarentum. It is an illuminating statement, reflecting the frame of mind in which Hannibal entered upon the operation. Success was, indeed, a crucial necessity and it could only be measured by the total occupation of the town with its harbour facilities. Tarentum, as we have already seen, was a major seaport, equally as accessible from Greece as from Sicily. If from Sicily, then also from Carthage; and if from Greece, and Brundisium could be subdued, then the way would be open for Philip of Macedonia. The whole future of Hannibal's campaign, beset with its manpower and supply problems, rested upon the capture of this town and its facilities. The harbours of Tarentum, however, were unusable if the citadel were held in hostile hands. Equally, the citadel could not be blockaded, and starved into submission, unless access to it by sea could be severed. This could only be achieved by armed ships, lying off the Taranto passage, preventing the landing of supplies; but, as the townspeople themselves explained to Hannibal, the warships suited for this purpose and ready to hand, their own Tarentine navy, were lying locked up in the inner harbour.

Hannibal was an indomitable soldier. For him there was never a task too difficult nor a problem incapable of solution. In this instance, the key had been turned in the lock: it now remained for the door to be opened. His fertile brain had already discovered a solution. He had noticed that the dockside and the town were well served with roadways. He now proposed that the ships should be lifted from the water and placed upon wagons lashed together, that selected roadways should be repaved to assist their progress, and that the ships should be hauled through the town by men and mules, to the sea on the far side. The exercise was a brilliant success; within a few days, the fleet, to the surprise and frustration of the Romans, we may imagine, 'sailed around the citadel and came to anchor directly in the harbour mouth'. Hannibal then returned to his winter quarters, leaving behind a party to help with work on the circumvallation and strengthen the town's defences.

The minor seaport of Metapontum, encouraged by this victory and the departure of their Roman garrison to reinforce the citadel at Tarentum, now declared for Hannibal. They were quickly followed by Thurii, always doubtfully loyal to Rome, whose people surrendered to the Carthaginian generals Mago and Hanno after contriving their own defeat. These latest acquisitions meant that only one seaport town on this southern coastline, Rhegium, still remained in the Roman domain, but its possession was vital. Together with Messina, it covered the straits between Sicily and the Italian mainland and it watched over traffic moving north and south along the south-western coast of the peninsula.

Rhegium, almost certainly, would have played a part in the decisive blow which, although it warrants only a few lines in Livy's history, Rome was now about to deliver upon Hannibal. Roman planners, as well as the Carthaginians, were well aware not only of the military value of Tarentum but also of the importance to her cause that the town's citadel should continue to remain in Roman hands. By so doing, she not only tied down the Tarentine navy but also denied harbour facilities to Hannibal: but at this moment in Hannibal's campaign, there was a real danger her garrison would be starved into submission. Rome, therefore, despatched one Gaius Servilius to Etruria, in northern Italy (212 BC), to purchase grain and, with a seaborne convoy, 'he succeeded in slipping through the enemy patrols and bringing a number of laden ships into the harbour'. It was a master stroke, which must be considered a turning point in Hannibal's War, for although the Carthaginians were to continue to besiege Tarentum, from this time forward they were denied any hope of real success.

Remains of the Roman amphitheatre in Syracuse. (By courtesy of the Italian State Tourist Board (E.N.I.T.) London)

Nor could Hannibal, wintering in northern Apulia, have found much to inspire him with hope. The Romans were tightening their grip on Capua, around which three armies were now stationed. Each had its own sector and had commenced the construction of a fosse and rampart circumvallation so as to deny movement to and from the city. In view of the state of the Capuan grain supplies, which Hanno in his resupply attempt had been able only partially to relieve, this new tactic signalled the beginning of a tight blockade but, despite these events, Hannibal once again turned towards Tarentum in a renewed but abortive effort to reduce the citadel, 'by fair means or foul'. From there, 'convinced that it would be betrayed into his hands', he marched on Brundisium. His persistence in probing these seaports, whilst himself under such pressure, underlines the very urgency of his commitment; but he was destined to be disappointed, for Brundisium was not interested in his overtures. Whilst he was yet engaged in these operations, he received a delegation from the Capuan senate, which arrived to complain that he had abandoned them. In their address to him they emphasised their plight and entreated his help. He replied that he would come when he could and that, when he did so, as had happened in the past, the Roman consuls, with their armies, would be unable to withstand him. The delegation was then dismissed and had great difficulty getting back into Capua before its surrounding wall was completed.

Meantime, events in Syracuse were proceeding with little better fortune, despite the fact that the Carthaginians were devoting considerably more military and naval effort to Sicily than to the Italian mainland. The Romans, around Syracuse, had settled down to a steady siege, recognising that the defences of the town were too strong for them to overcome. On the eve of the festival of Diana, however, a Roman deserter came to Marcellus, informing him that Epicydes, confident of the strength of the walls, had released quantities of wine for consumption. He suggested that this would provide a rare opportunity for an assault on the city. Marcellus at once convened a conference with his officers, an assault party was hand picked and the walls were surmounted without difficulty. In the outcome, the Romans breached the Hexapylon gate and seized the citadel of Epipolae, from the heights of which Marcellus was enabled to look down on the city below him, 'in those days, perhaps, the most beautiful in all the world'.

At this juncture, the Carthaginian admiral Bomilcar, who had been anchored in the Grand Harbour with a fleet of some ninety ships, was despatched by Epicydes to alert Carthage to the way matters were developing and to seek further reinforcements. Bomilcar took advantage of the distraction offered by a local storm and slipped out of harbour with thirty-five ships, leaving the remainder in Syracuse in support of Epicydes. Upon reaching Carthage he was listened to sympathetically by the senate and provided with additional warships. He then turned around at once and, within a few days, ran once again into the Grand Harbour, bringing with him 100 ships, thus enhancing the strength of the fleet under his command by sixty-five vessels.

During his absence, matters had not improved. Marcellus was now planning an assault upon the principal Syracusan district of Achradina, a section of the town which had been well provided with its own system of defensive walls and would not be easy to overrun. Recognising this and before turning his attention in that direction, he broke into the neighbouring districts of Neapolis and Tyche and looted these two townships systematically. When he eventually turned towards Achradina, his movement coincided with the arrival of the Carthaginian army under command of Hippocrates and Himilco, who had moved up, by forced march, from Agrigentum and Murgantia. In the battle which then followed, largely fought out in the streets, the Romans found themselves under attack from all sides. The outcome was inconclusive but the Carthaginian force, weakened by a broad intake of Sicilian tribes, revealed itself to be sadly lacking in training and experience. The two sides drew apart after their initial clash. Fate then took a hand in the shape of a virulent plague which swept across the battlefield, affecting all in its path. The Carthaginians suffered particularly severely, since, unlike the Romans, they possessed no camp beyond the town walls, in the open countryside, upon which to retire. Hippocrates and Himilco were amongst those who perished and the destruction of the Carthaginian land force was virtually complete.

When the plague was showing signs of abating, Bomilcar sailed once more for Carthage, again to brief the senate on the situation of their allies in Syracuse. Once more, by his powerful presentation of their case,[19]

> he was able to persuade his government not only that effective help could still be sent to them but also that the tables might still be turned upon the Romans, who at the moment virtually held the city. He thus induced the authorities to send with him as many merchant vessels, laden with supplies of all sorts, as they could raise, and to reinforce his fleet. Accordingly, he sailed from Carthage with 130 ships of war and 700 transports.

Upon making landfall on the southern coast of Sicily, Bomilcar left the transport division of his convoy at Heraclea Minoa, whilst he reconnoitred forward with his fleet to Cape Pachynum. Here, he discovered that a foul wind was blowing from the east, which did not allow him to negotiate the Cape. News of his presence, with such a large convoy, was immediately carried to Syracuse, to Roman and Syracusan alike. Both commanders at once recognised the importance of this moment. Marcellus, determined, at all cost, that Bomilcar should be prevented from reaching the city with such quantities of supplies, and despite his smaller numbers, gave order for his fleet to prepare to sail at once. Epicydes, for his part, was concerned that Bomilcar, faced with adverse winds, might return to North Africa. He therefore handed over command to a subordinate general and sailed for Cape Pachynum to ensure that this did not happen.[20] He was quickly followed by Marcellus, who dropped anchor on the opposite, northern, side of the promontory, blocking the coastal sea lane.

Epicydes found Bomilcar unwilling to fight his way past the Roman fleet because, he argued, in the event of a sea battle, Marcellus had the advantage of the strong north-easterlies behind him. Nevertheless, it was Bomilcar, probably under pressure from Epicydes, who took the first initiative: he set forth, and as his oarsmen rounded the promontory, he suddenly veered into deep water and headed directly for Tarentum. Simultaneously, he sent a message to Heraclea Minoa, instructing his transport division to return to Africa. It is difficult to believe that Epicydes was party to this decision, but it meant that the latter had no option but to make his way to Agrigentum until matters had been clarified. The city of Syracuse surrendered soon afterwards and from that moment, with Hannibal contained in the south of the Italian peninsula and the Roman navy supreme in Sicilian waters, it may be thought that the war was lost, although some years of conflict still lay ahead.

The Romans were quick to take full advantage of the respite offered by the departure of the Carthaginian fleet. Titus Otacilius, with eighty quinqueremes, now crossed from Lilybaeum to carry out a raid on Utica, the wealthy trading port lying on the African coast, a few miles west of Carthage. Three days after setting forth, he was back in Sicily with a prize of 130 merchant ships, loaded with grain and other supplies, which he at once despatched onwards to Syracuse. Their timely arrival, writes Livy,[21] 'saved victors and vanquished alike from the very real threat of starvation'. This highly successful raid by Otacilius, the first of a growing number of similar sorties, had a yet further affect. It reminded the Carthaginians of the vulnerability of their own homeland and pinned down resources which otherwise would have been set aside for overseas operations perhaps in Spain but particularly in Sicily or on the Italian mainland: but with the fall of Syracuse, access to Hannibal's forces in the heel of Italy had become wellnigh impossible.

Such enemy opposition as remained in Sicily was now concentrated around Agrigentum, under Epicydes and Hanno, the longstanding commanders of the Carthaginian and allied forces on the island. It was at this juncture that Hannibal sent a new, third, general to replace Hippocrates, who had died in the Syracusan plague. His successor was a man[22]

> . . . known as Muttines in his own country; he was of Libyphoenician blood, a native of Hippacara, and an active soldier who had been thoroughly trained by Hannibal in the whole science of war. He was given command by Epicydes and Hanno of a force of Numidian auxiliaries with which he so successfully overrode the enemy's territory . . . that in a short time he filled Sicily with his name and was the chief hope of all who favoured the Carthaginian cause.

Hippocrates and Epicydes, both men born in Carthage and of Syracusan origin, were intially appointed by Hannibal as his representatives in Syracuse and held high rank, perhaps the highest of the Carthaginians in Sicily. Hannibal had now appointed another of his senior military officers to replace

Hippocrates. It would thus be fair to judge that Hannibal considered himself to be commander-in-chief of Carthaginian and allied forces in Sicily but of this we cannot be certain. The implication of this uncertainty is something we will consider in a later chapter. Suffice it to say, however, that the quality of the man he now despatched to Sicily, 'trained by Hannibal in the whole science of war' and 'the chief hope of all who favoured the Carthaginian cause', depicts a general officer of such experience that his master would not have been averse to see his latest replacement as the senior Carthaginian general on the island.

Unhappily, neither Hanno nor Epicydes were willing to accept Muttines in any such role, not even as a joint commander with themselves. This may have been partly because his military prowess excelled anything they could achieve: it was also, sadly for Hannibal, because racism appears even at that time to have been a human failing. Hanno considered it 'preposterous that he, a commander of the Carthaginian armies, commissioned by the government and the people, should be taught his business by a half-breed African'. It is notable in this statement, quoted by Livy,[23] that Hanno makes no mention of his responsibilities to his own commander-in-chief, Hannibal.

As we have already witnessed in the above pages, the control of Sicily had become increasingly recognised as a crucial issue, by both Rome and Carthage alike, as the battle for the southern seaports developed. Central to the struggle was the Roman occupation of the fortified harbour of Lilybaeum, the most powerful naval base in the Sicilian theatre. It dominated the southern waters of the Tyrrhenian Sea, as well as the strategically important Liparean and Aegates groups of islands; it commanded the vital shipping lane which linked North Africa and the west coast of Italy, and it held joint responsibility, with Rome's Syracusan ally, for the security of the Sicilian coastline. It also exercised control, greatly strengthened since Rome's acquisition of Messina, of the sheltered waters of the straits which, flowing from north to south, provided access between the east and west coasts of the peninsula without the need of negotiating the frequently troubled southern Sicilian waters around Cape Pachynum, on the extreme south-east corner of the island. Thus the defensive strength of Syracuse and its proximity to this demanding promontory, from which it lay some 35 miles northwards, upon its windward side, gave this large fortified seaport particular military importance.

In these circumstances, it has to be considered that Bomilcar's avoidance of Marcellus at Cape Pachynum, with the resulting return to Carthage of his huge convoy of war supplies and the consequent fall of Syracuse into Roman hands, dealt two fatal blows to Carthaginian war aims. With the Straits of Messina already closed to her, it destroyed the efforts by Carthage to establish a firm line of communication with Hannibal's forces in southern Italy; and it released a substantial element of the Roman navy to open a robust sequence of raids against Carthage in North African coastal waters, which, in due course were to lead to the invasion headed by the young Cornelius Scipio. Simultaneously, Hannibal was kept isolated and penned up in southern Italy, whilst the resources of Carthage were poured into a war which had, to all appearances, already been lost.

It is not easy to understand how Hannibal should have allowed this to happen and did not move to Sicily to take personal command of the vital theatre operation now being fought out on the island. He was not so inclined, however, and in 212 BC, despite the events in Sicily, he once again headed for Salapia, between Arpi and Canusium and some 50 miles north-west of Tarentum, where he made plans to spend the coming winter.

## CHAPTER IX

# THE WAR IN SPAIN

A great battle will be fought, which I shall gain; but I must count upon 30,000 men killed, wounded or taken prisoners. If I march on London a second battle will be fought. I shall suppose myself again victorious. But what shall I do in London with an army reduced three/fourths and without hope of reinforcements. It would be madness.

F. de Bourrienne [1]

These words, used by Napoleon to describe the predicament which would have confronted him had he chosen to invade England in 1805, without first securing for himself a channel for reinforcements, could equally well have been applied to the dilemma which faced Hannibal when he carried his war to southern Italy, *post*-Cannae.

Hannibal had anticipated three clear sources of manpower from which to fill his ranks as he delved deep into the Roman peninsula. One of these, the Celtic tribes of Cisalpine Gaul, located in the Po valley, became increasingly unenthusiastic and inaccessible to him as he marched further and further south, and he became unable any longer to offer them the umbrella of his protection. Another, the allies of Rome in central Italy, despite their brave noises, did not secede to his side in the numbers for which he had planned. The third source, the trained and experienced reinforcements he had expected to receive from New Carthage, failed to materialise for two reasons, both directly due to the arrival of Scipio's army in northern Spain. By its very presence, it cut his lines of communication with New Carthage and it created growing unrest amongst the tribes who had previously given their allegiance to Hasdrubal. In Italy, moreover, Hannibal's difficulties were further enhanced by the tight naval and military grip imposed by Rome on the seaports along the western and southern coasts of the peninsula, by this means denying him freedom of access to the sea.

Thus, however great his victories in battle, if Hannibal were 'without hope of reinforcements', to quote Napoleon's vision of the 'madness' of landing on English soil, his campaign was fated not to succeed. The emperor, according to de Bourrienne, declared that he would not risk France on the cast of a dice. Hannibal, if he truly appreciated the difficult decisions which arose after his brief skirmish with Scipio's cavalry on the Rhône, was seemingly willing to gamble on the future of New Carthage, if not Carthage itself. His decision to continue with his thrust across the Alps, whilst leaving his Spanish province temptingly vulnerable to attack in his absence, may have kept alive the hope of victory for the next seventeen years but, in essence, it spelt defeat.

The author of his problems was Publius Cornelius Scipio, who, whilst himself returning home to Italy to intercept Hannibal in Cisalpine Gaul, had instructed his brother, Gnaeus, to continue to Spain as had been originally planned. He was to take with him the main body of their army and, once arrived, he was to begin the business of showing the flag and reinstating Roman influence north of the Ebro. Gnaeus Scipio sailed westward from the Rhône estuary, past the Pyrenees, and brought up at the trading station of Emporiae, where he disembarked his troops. They were wildly welcomed by a populace which was already strongly Roman in its sympathies. He enjoyed an immediate success. Hanno, who, it will be recalled, had been left behind by Hannibal, with a force of 10,000 foot and 1,000 horse, with instructions to keep open the Pyrenean mountain passes into Gaul and safeguard his commander-in-chief's communications with New Carthage, unwisely decided to move immediately against Scipio[2] without awaiting the arrival of Hasdrubal. He was totally destroyed, losing 6,000 men killed, with a further 2,000 taken prisoner, together with the garrison of his nearby encampment, which was overrun. Hanno and his staff were captured, together with the heavy baggage and captured treasure left by Hannibal in his care before his departure.

After one or two border skirmishes with Hasdrubal on the line of the Ebro, Gnaeus garrisoned Tarraco, based his fleet upon Emporiae and generally set about establishing his position in northern Spain before the advent of winter. Hasdrubal chose not to disturb him. He was content to withdraw into southern Spain and to use the winter months to add ten ships to the number left with him by Hannibal. Then, at the opening of the campaigning season of 217 BC, he placed his entire fleet of forty warships under the command of Himilco and marched from New Carthage to seek out the enemy. He followed the line of the coast, closely supported by his warships. Gnaeus, meantime, had received news that Hasdrubal was on the move and, with his thirty-five vessels, adopted the same tactic of parallel movement by land and sea but, since he feared that he would be outnumbered in a land battle, he reinforced his warships with a handpicked force of marines.

On the second day out from Tarraco, he laid up 10 miles from the mouth of the Ebro. From there, he despatched two light reconnaissance craft to the estuary to see what they could find. It was a profitable move, for upon their return they reported that the enemy fleet was lying in the river and that Hasdrubal's army was encamped nearby. Gnaeus set sail at once and, although the Carthaginian army was alerted by watch towers of his approach, the sight and sound of the movement of his ships was denied to their navy by a headland which covered the estuary. The ships' crews, strolling ashore or still in their tents, were totally unaware of the disaster which loomed until they were 'scrambled' by gallopers despatched by Hasdrubal. The arrival of the latter shortly afterwards, with his

A view of the river Ebro at Miravet. (The Spanish Tourist Office)

whole army, did nothing to lessen the confusion. Whilst soldiers and sailors strove to get aboard ships to their action stations, Livy[3] relates, in his typically robust style, 'soldiers and their gear got in the way of the sailors, whilst the sailors in their excitement and confusion prevented the soldiers from preparing their weapons and equipment for the coming action'.

In the end, many of the Carthaginians ran their ships ashore, where they abandoned them to seek sanctuary in the ranks of the army, as it marshalled in battle formation along the bank of the river. The presence of Hasdrubal's land force had no influence on the outcome. He could only watch as his fleet was systematically destroyed. Those of his ships which were moveable were towed by the Romans into deep water and sunk. The remainder, which had been 'stove-in when they ran ashore or were stuck too hard to be moved', were left upon the beach. It had been a minor action but Gnaeus, by this simple but impressive stroke, had achieved naval supremacy in Carthaginian coastal waters, south of the Ebro. He now proceeded to demonstrate the superiority he had gained by sailing along the coast to Onusa, below New Carthage. Here, he landed, and stormed and ransacked the town before returning to the capital itself, where he devastated the surrounding fields and destroyed the settlement lying outside the city walls.

The Spanish peoples in the north had been watching these developing events with deepening interest and, in the late summer, they demonstrated their support for Rome when envoys from more than 120 tribes, at an assembly convened near Emporiae, agreed to subject themselves to the 'authority and dominion of Rome' and to provide hostages to Scipio as a token of their good faith. At about this same moment, Publius Cornelius Scipio, now fully recovered from the wound he received on the Trebbia, returned to Spain to join forces with his brother, Gnaeus. The Senate had wisely recognised the value of his service during his consulship and had extended the period of his military command. They also provided him with a further 8,000 men, 20 warships and a large quantity of provisions and equipment. The fleet which brought him, swollen hugely by the large number of transport vessels he had brought to carry his supplies, put into Tarraco. It was received with considerable excitement by Romans and allies alike and doubtless strengthened yet further their already high morale.

Henceforward, the brothers operated a joint command, Publius accepting responsibility for the navy and Gnaeus for the army.

Hasdrubal was in a most unenviable position. Little more than eighteen months had now elapsed since he had inherited from his absent brother, Hannibal, responsibility for Carthaginian territories in Spain. Since then, the Roman army had arrived under Scipio and Hanno's frontier force had been destroyed. As a consequence, he had been compelled to surrender Carthaginian influence in northern Spain and now had lost naval supremacy in the coastal waters fringing his province. The tribes north of the Ebro had clearly lost sympathy with his cause and there were increasing signs that those in the southern territories of Spain, from whom Carthage had been accustomed to seek loyalty, were also becoming affected by unrest. It is thus not surprising to learn from Livy[4] that Hasdrubal, since his disastrous encounter with Gnaeus, had lost confidence in the adequacy of his armed forces and was deliberately avoiding contact with the Roman armies. He had persistently called upon Carthage for reinforcements and had met with silence, until, in the summer of 216 BC, after a long delay, they sent him a surprisingly scant 4,000 foot and 500 horse. Hannibal, after all, had been enjoying considerable success in Italy throughout this period and it might be thought, in view of the economic and military importance of their Spanish province to Carthage, that they would have availed themselves of this breathing space to consolidate their position there and reopen the land route with Cisalpine Gaul.

The arrival of this contingent at least enabled Hasdrubal to put his fleet in a condition to defend his coastline and offshore islands but his effort was immediately set back by the desertion of his naval captains. Seemingly, they had been recruited from the Tartesi tribe and had been reprimanded by Hasdrubal for their behaviour on the Ebro, when the fleet had been abandoned in panic. They now fled to their homelands, disgruntled men, where they disaffected their fellow tribesmen. As a consequence, the Tartesian people not only discarded their allegiance to Carthage but stormed and captured other neighbouring towns which had remained firm. Clearly, Hasdrubal found this situation both dangerous and intolerable and, without delay, took out a punitive expedition against them. The Tartesi surrendered, after having suffered considerable slaughter.

It was at this moment that the senate in Carthage chose to reveal its total misappreciation of the situation in Spain. They decided that the time had arrived for Hasdrubal to march to Italy to join his brother, Hannibal, and issued orders for him to do so. When Hasdrubal protested that to do this on his present manpower would simply be to hand their Spanish territories to Rome, Himilco was despatched from Carthage, 'with a fully equipped force and an enlarged fleet', to take over his duties. Himilco brought with him the senate's decree, the equivalent of 'orders in writing'.

Inevitably, as soon as rumours of Hasdrubal's departure began to circulate, they had the affect, in Livy's words, of 'diverting the allegiance of nearly all the Spanish tribes to the Roman interest'. The incident is noteworthy because it leaves us in little doubt, despite much that is sometimes argued to the contrary, that the senate appears to have been well aware of Hannibal's campaign plans and of his wish for Hasdrubal, with an army, to join him in Italy at the earliest moment. Hasdrubal paused only to brief Himilco on the uncertain operational situation he was taking over; then, having raised subscriptions from allied tribes to cover the expenses of his journey and pay his mercenary soldiers, he set forth for the Ebro.

The two Roman commanders, meantime, had already been informed of the Carthaginian decree brought by Himilco and were aware of Hasdrubal's intention. They now combined their two armies and crossed the Ebro to intercept him. They were convinced 'that if he and his troops from Spain once succeeded in joining Hannibal, who even by himself was an enemy that Italy could hardly bear, it would mean the end of Roman imperial power'. It should be remembered that the news of the disastrous losses inflicted on the Roman army at Cannae had probably reached the two men by this time and they were right to be concerned: but it was a concern which fired the spirit of the Roman soldiery, who had been made to realise by their generals that, although in a foreign field, they were fighting as much for their homeland and its peoples as if they were in Rome. The Carthaginian side, on the other hand, was filled with considerably less resolution. Most of the men were Spaniards, so Livy[5] relates, and 'naturally preferred defeat in their own country to being dragged off to victory in Italy'. Thus, when the two armies came together, the difference in their attitudes was quickly revealed. Hasdrubal's centre gave way, almost before the first javelin was thrown, causing his African cavalry on the flanks to turn and flee. His army was routed and he suffered heavy losses in men and equipment.

The scale of Hasdrubal's defeat meant that he was now abandoned by the waverers amongst his Spanish allies. The situation in which he found himself was, in fact, the complete reverse of that which prevailed in Italy, where the shift of feeling away from Rome, provoked by Hannibal's victory at Cannae, had spread as far as Sicily. Even Gelo, the son of Hiero II of Syracuse, was expressing his open contempt of his father's alliance with Rome. Indeed, Hannibal's successes had been so considerable that he had felt it possible to send his brother, Mago, to brief the senate in Carthage on the progress of his campaign and to plead with them for the reinforcements which they had so far appeared reluctant to provide. As we have heard, what he had to say was compelling and the senate made available to him a contingent of 12,000 foot, 1,500 horse, with 20 elephants. When this force had been assembled and he was on the point of setting sail for Italy, with an escort of sixty warships, news of the precarious situation which had arisen in Spain was received in Carthage. At the same time, further intelligence was received which suggested that a good opportunity had arisen to recover Sardinia. The Roman garrison on the island had been reduced, a change of governors had taken place and the people had grown tired of their Roman overlords.

In the light of this newly received intelligence, the senate now undertook a rearrangement of their plans. Mago, together with the warships and reinforcements the senate had allocated for Hannibal, was diverted to Spain, presumably because he was at hand and could immediately sail to stem a fast deteriorating situation. Hasdrubal the Bald, yet another commander bearing the same name, was despatched to Sardinia, with a force of similar size, to recover the island; and Bomilcar, a senior general, was placed in command of a convoy destined for Locri, on the 'instep' coast of Italy, with troops, elephants and supplies for Hannibal.[7] The need to send reinforcements to Spain was truly urgent but the digression to Sardinia at this stage (it proved an abortive operation, in any event) and the relegation of Hannibal's needs to a clearly low priority, with the arbitrary loss of his, by now, senior commander, Mago, suggests a surprising coolness towards his needs at a finely poised moment when Carthage might have been expected to provide him with hard support.

Rome, in the meantime, had been satisfied to allow the war in Spain to drift along with no sense of urgency, content that the land route from there to northern Italy should be blocked by the presence of her forces under Gnaeus and Publius Scipio. Nevertheless, she had provided them with such scant resources that, by the end of the summer of 215 BC, Publius and Gnaeus were constrained to write to Rome, listing details of their operational successes, and to protest that,

> there was no money left for the soldiers' pay and no clothing or other supplies either for the army or the ships' crews. As for the pay, the two commanders suggested that if the treasury were empty they might find means

of raising the money in Spain, though the other things would all have to be sent from Rome if there was to be any chance of keeping either the army or the province . . .The Senate unanimously admitted both the truth of the statement and the reasonableness of the demand; none the less they could not but remember the immense forces, both naval and military which they were already maintaining . . .

As a result of this pressure by the Scipios, the Senate agreed that there was no way by which the country could continue to exist simply on its assets: if it were to survive, it would have to borrow. As a result of this decision the financial state of the nation was laid before the assembly, to whom it was suggested, in blunt terms, that those who had made profits from the government contracts they had been operating should now undertake the task of providing what was needed for the army in Spain, on the understanding that, when there was once again money in the treasury, they would be the first to be paid. Upon this early hint of a windfall tax, three groupings of contractors came forward to suggest some slight amendments to the conditions being offered and, on that basis, to announce their acceptance of the work. Nevertheless, the resources allocated to the war in Spain continued to be thinly spread. Between the years 218 BC and 211 BC, the Roman strength there never exceeded two legions, except for the five years 210– 206 BC, following the disasters suffered in 211 BC by Publius and Gnaeus Scipio.

The Roman army in Spain had been strengthened during the winter of 212 BC by a contingent of 20,000 troops from the Celtiberes, a tribe which existed in the mountains between the Ebro valley and the headwaters of the Guadiana and Tagus rivers. As a result of this substantial reinforcement, the Scipio brothers appreciated that they were now in a position to destroy the enemy forces opposing them. The Carthaginians, however, had also been busy increasing their numbers. They had three armies in the field, with which to do battle against the Romans; one under Hasdrubal Barca, who was encamped nearer the Scipios, at a village named Amtorgis on the Baetis river; and two others, commanded respectively by Mago, his brother, and Hasdrubal Gisgo. These, according to Livy, were located some five days distant and had come together for operations. Additionally, the Carthaginians had provided themselves with a powerful asset, a strong force of experienced Numidian cavalry, commanded by the young Masinissa. He later was to become a worthy and trusted ally of Rome.

The Scipio plan was first to crush Hasdrubal Barca; they anticipated that, should he be summarily defeated, his other generals might take to the forests and remain a continuing operational hazard. In an effort to avoid this they divided their forces in two parts, of which Publius took two-thirds with the task of containing and destroying Hasdrubal and Mago. Gnaeus, with one-third of the original force, together with the Celtiberians, agreed to take on Hasdrubal Barca. Initially, the Scipios marched out their army as one column, headed by the Celtiberians. When they reached the river Baetis, and Gnaeus had drawn up his army in sight of Hasdrubal, Publius turned away and 'proceeded to his original assignment'. In the circumstances, it was an extraordinary decision, particularly in view of the time and space involved. The whole Roman army had been brought within sight of the notorious Hasdrubal Barca, with a prospect of outright victory against him and infinite possibilities for the future if he were killed or captured, and yet two-thirds of the Roman force was permitted instantly to abandon the field.

It was a disastrous decision and Publius was soon in trouble. Masinissa, perhaps informed of the approach of the enemy by galloper from Hasdrubal Barca, quickly moved to make contact with the Roman marching column. He then relentlessly harried it night and day, regularly descending upon its tail, cutting off men foraging for wood or fodder, attacking their camp at night time and generally allowing the soldiery no rest. Ultimately, Publius learnt that a party of some 7,500 Suessetani were marching to join the Numidians and he determined that this must not be allowed to happen. He left a small garrison, under a tribune, Tiberius Fonteius, to watch over his supplies and baggage, and broke out of camp at night to intercept them but, when he encountered them on the following day, the enemy tribesmen sensibly refused to form a conventional battle line and a confused running fight took place. Whilst this was progressing, the Numidian cavalry, whom he had hoped to evade, fell upon his flanks, and were soon followed by Mago and Hasdrubal Gisgo with their armies. Publius Scipio, as ever, was in the thick of the fighting, riding from one desperate situation to another, when he was killed, pierced through his right side by a lance. When the news spread to the soldiery, the line, such as they had been able to establish, broke, and only the arrival of darkness put an end to the slaughter which then ensued.

Gnaeus, whom we left on the river, appears to have been in no hurry to commit himself against Hasdrubal Barca and the latter, from his vantage point, was quick to observe how the numbers of the Celtiberian tribesmen opposing him heavily outweighed those of the Roman contingent. He contrived to make contact with them and induced them to withdraw, at some cost to the Carthaginian exchequer. Livy tells us, sardonically, that it was not, in Hasdrubal's view, an outrageous thing to have done, 'as there was no question of the Celtiberians turning their arms against the Romans . . . moreover, most of the rank and file were only too pleased with the prospect of returning home to see their families and belongings again'.[8] So the Celtiberian contingent of 20,000 men pulled up their standards, explained to their allies that a war at home demanded their presence and departed, leaving Gnaeus isolated from help and no match for the army which confronted him. He was also disturbed to note that Hasdrubal Barca had now been joined by Mago and Gisgo and correctly assumed that Publius had fared badly at their hands. That night, he wisely decided to withdraw, far and fast, but the enemy took up his pursuit at first light and crossed the river Baetis hot on his heels.

Again, the Numidian cavalry played a vital role, overtaking the Roman column, which suffered from a lack of horse with which to counter them, and pinned them down until the Carthaginian infantry could overtake them. Gnaeus was thus driven to take up a defensive position on high ground, placing his baggage in the centre, together with such horse as he possessed, and ringing it with his infantry. The hill he had been compelled to select was stony and treeless, 'so that no timber could be found for staves, no turves could be cut, no trench could be dug: for any work of fortification it was useless'. Gnaeus threw together a rampart of pack saddles, with their loads still attached, and such baggage as was unlikely to be required and settled down to await the arrival of the Carthaginian foot. When it came, his position was unsustainable and was quickly overrun. Gnaeus was said to have been killed in the first onslaught, twenty-nine days after the death of his brother and eight years after his arrival in Spain.

In due course, a substantial number of fugitives from these two unhappy episodes found their way back to the base camp established by Publius before his death. Fonteius, who commanded it, together with a knight, Lucius Marcius, who emerged at this crucial moment and, according to Cicero,[9] was a senior centurion, now collected together such remnants and garrisons of the Roman forces as they could find in southern Spain, probably no more than 8,000 foot and 1,000 horse, and retired north of the Ebro, where they prepared themselves for whatever the future might bring. Marcius, who had served under Gnaeus Scipio for many years and distinguished himself by his coolness in these trying circumstances, was unanimously elected as their commander by the soldiery.

The precise date and time of year of these events is uncertain but was probably late autumn 212 or early spring 211 BC. In Rome, itself, matters were looking brighter.

On 15 March 211 BC a meeting of the Senate was convened in Rome at which the state of the nation was discussed and the conduct of the war was reviewed. There had been substantial successes. Rome was arguably now sustaining twenty-five legions in the field, [10] the highest number throughout the duration of the war. In the operational year just closing, naval supremacy had been fully established in her coastal waters, Maximus Claudius Marcellus had retaken Syracuse, Capua had been placed under energetic siege, the citadel at Tarentum was still standing firm and the now accepted *Fabian Strategy* of indirect approach was containing Hannibal in southern Italy. His numbers and trouble-making ability, as a consequence, were being steadily reduced. Obversely, an army under Gnaeus Fulvius, guilty of ill-disciplined over-confidence on operations in Apulia, had been taught a sharp lesson by Hannibal, at a cost of some 16,000 men, and the army in Spain had received a rude set-back, with the serious loss of two valuable commanders. Nevertheless, despite the slim resources which had been fed to it, the Spanish campaign had continued to tie down Hasdrubal Barca and deny him the opportunity of marching reinforcements to the Carthaginian army under Hannibal in Italy.

Whilst these matters of policy and future operations were being discussed, a despatch was received from northern Spain, signed by Lucius Marcius, asking for clothing and supplies – and, doubtless, manpower. The senators gave immediate orders for his requests to be fulfilled but, whilst paying due recognition to his invaluable role in restoring stability to the two armies of the defeated Scipios, they took offence at his use of the title, pro-praetor, when signing his despatch.[11] They considered it 'a bad precedent that army commanders should be chosen by the troops or that the ceremony of an official appointment, with all due auspices, should be removed from the proper sanction of law and official control and abandoned to soldiers' whims in their camps abroad'. For this reason, in their response to Marcius, they refrained from addressing him by rank; and, upon the departure of the messenger, they issued orders to their staff officers to commence proceedings for the appointment of his replacement.

For the year ahead, the senators instructed that the whole effort of the war should be concentrated on Capua, for, apart from the contribution it made to the national economy, they believed that its recovery would recreate a general feeling 'of respect for the old alignment of power'.[12] They ruled that the conduct of this operation should rest with the two consuls of the previous year, Quintus Fulvius Flaccus and Appius Claudius, and they were instructed that they were to allow no respite until the city fell.

Hannibal, at this moment, was based in Bruttium. He was aware of the acute privations being suffered by the inhabitants of Capua and, we must presume, was concerned that the fall of the city could not long be prevented: he now determined to march to its relief. He was, according to Livy, torn for choice between the capture of the citadel at Tarentum and the attempt to save Capua: and Capua, rightly or wrongly, prevailed. Significantly, for he was eventually to march to Rome, he left most of his heavy baggage and all of his heavier armaments in Bruttium and set off on a forced march, with a select force of infantry and cavalry, supported by thirty-three elephants. He sent word to Capua, which caused considerable alarm when it became known to the Romans, that he proposed to synchronise his attack on the Roman lines with a sally in strength from every gate of the city.

The policy of the two proconsuls, throughout the siege they had been operating, was to starve the city into submission by constructing a ring of guard-posts and trenches around its walls, thus totally preventing its communication with the outside world and reducing opportunities for enemy sorties. They had made few serious attempts to storm it. The garrison within Capua, largely Campanian but supported by a relatively small Carthaginian contingent, outnumbered the Romans in infantry, albeit of poor quality. The Campanian cavalry, on the other hand, had proved itself notably superior to them in the few minor encounters which had taken place with the besieging force but its efficiency was now beginning to be affected by lack of fodder due to the 'scorched earth' policy practised by both sides. Polybius[13] expressed the situation very well:

> The position was that the Roman army did not dare to leave their camp and give battle because of their fear of the enemy's cavalry, but they remained

with complete confidence behind their entrenchments, secure in the knowledge that those same horsemen who had defeated them in pitched battles could not touch them there. The Carthaginians, on the other hand, could not stay encamped in that position with their cavalry, because all the forage in the surrounding countryside had been systematically destroyed by the Romans with that very end in view, and it was impossible to transport over such long distances sufficient hay and barley to feed so many horses and mules. For the same reasons the Carthaginians did not dare to attack an enemy protected by a trench and a palisade, being thus denied the support of their cavalry . . .

Hannibal's attempt to break through the Roman siege lines, supported by sorties from the city as he had planned, resulted in some savage fighting in which the consul, Appius Claudius, was wounded; but it soon became clear to him that he was making no headway at the cost of heavy losses. He now produced a plan which we must judge had been in his mind since the beginning, when he left 'most of his heavy baggage and all of his heavier armaments' in his Bruttian base. He determined to carry out a diversionary march on Rome, in the expectation that at least some of the besieging Roman army would follow him, enabling him to take on a reduced opposition on ground of his own choosing. He found a means of warning the garrison of Capua not to be concerned at his departure. He then secretly gathered together such boats as he could find on the Volturnus, prepared food for ten days and, employing the old ruse of leaving camp fires burning in a now empty camp, he crossed the Volturnus under cover of darkness and, having burnt his boats, marched for Rome.

The Senate had already received warning from deserters that some such action by the Carthaginian was a real possibility and a hurried meeting had been convened to determine their response to it. Some members had spoken out for the 'recall of every general and every man from the whole of Italy for the defence of the city', but Fabius Maximus, clearly perceiving Hannibal's purpose, argued that he had not dared to come near Rome after his victory at Cannae, so why should he hope to capture it after his rebuff at Capua? Ultimately, it was agreed to pass the problem to the two commanders at Capua to be resolved, for they alone would be aware what force Hannibal was bringing with him and how much could be spared by them without interfering with the blockade of Capua, which must be sustained under all circumstances. In the end, it was agreed, since his fellow commander, Claudius, had recently been disabled, that the discredited proconsul, Quintus Fulvius, should return to defend the city, with a force of 15,000 foot and 1,000 horse. With a commendable effort, Fulvius arrived in Rome, having crossed the Volturnus with difficulty, to enter the city by the Porta Capena, and before the appearance of Hannibal, to take up his position alongside the consular armies.[14]

Hannibal, meantime, was encamped 8 miles away, creating as much devastation and mayhem as possible. He then moved further forward, up the river Anio, to encamp 3 miles from Rome and from there, with some bravado,

The Temple of Vesta in Rome, where burnt a perpetual fire watched over by the Vestal Virgins. Its extinction carried bad portents for Rome. In 210 BC, Q. Fulvius Flaccus accused the Capuans of an attempt to extinguish the flames. (Livy, xxvi, 27) (By courtesy of the Italian State Tourist Board (E.N.I.T.), London)

rode up to the Porta Collina, accompanied by 2,000 horsemen, to survey the defences of the city. Fulvius, enraged by such arrogance, despatched his cavalry to drive him away and a skirmish took place within sight of the walls. Both Polybius and Livy suggest that, at this stage, Hannibal still aspired to capture Rome. We are, however, provided with no indication of his strength at this vital moment and, from what we have been told of his preparations for the relief of Capua, which in this instance was his prime intention, and the abandonment of his heavy armaments in Bruttium, it seems safe to judge that this thrust at the capital city was purely diversionary. It also enabled him to collect considerable plunder, particularly foodstuffs and meat on the hoof, for he was now operating in a region where his presence had previously never been anticipated. Before his invasion, the area north-west and north of the river Volturnus had been considered the heartland of the Roman Commonwealth. Hannibal had since devastated much of it and Fabius's scorched earth policy had increasingly added to its barren, empty state. Hannibal's march on Rome now provided the finishing touches.[15]

Traditionally, it is said that the two consuls in Rome, Galba and Centumalus, led their troops out of the capital on two successive days to offer battle to Hannibal but on both occasions each side was driven apart by freak storms which suddenly descended upon them, raining down giant hailstones upon friend and foe alike. Hannibal then decided to withdraw and content himself with 'ravaging the surrounding country and setting fire to the houses', whilst simultaneously accumulating a huge quantity of plunder and cattle. At the same time, he appears to have abandoned all intention of returning to Capua: perhaps he appreciated, for he was pursued and had to fight himself free, that he had put his hand into a hornets' nest. He now described a wide arc and, marching at speed through Samnium, Apulia and Lucania, returned to Bruttium, before emerging in front of the gates of Rhegium, on the Straits of Messina. Bostar and Hanno, the two officers he had deputed to organise the defence of Capua and who now found themselves abandoned, along with the men of the Carthaginian garrison, were understandably perturbed by this turn of events. We did not cross the Alps, so they wrote to him,[16]

> . . . to fight against Rhegium or Tarentum: the armies of Carthage should be where the Roman legions are. It was by meeting them face to face, by pitching our camps where they pitched theirs, and by risking the luck of the day that we were victorious at Cannae and at Trasimene.

After the realisation of their situation dawned upon the inhabitants of Capua, the senate entered into negotiations with the Romans for the surrender of the city. The majority of its members expressed their confidence in the clemency of Rome but twenty-seven senators that evening dined with Virrius, who had initially headed the movement to secede to Hannibal, and after supper in his house, committed mass suicide. Next day, the gate facing the Roman camp was opened and a legion marched in to take control of the administration. Under its orders, the remaining fifty-three senators were arrested, deprived of any gold and silver they might possess and in due course, were publicly scourged and beheaded. The settlement of Capuan affairs was thus in every respect admirable, wrote Livy:[17]

> . . . the most guilty were promptly and severely punished; the mass of free citizens was dispersed and had no hope of return; innocent buildings and city walls were spared the useless savagery of fire and demolition; and Rome, besides profiting by the city's preservation, was able to appear before her allies in the guise of a merciful conqueror. Capua had been a rich and famous city and all Campania would have wept over her ruins, and all the neighbouring peoples.

The capitulation of Capua expresses very clearly the dilemma which now engulfed Hannibal. He had, in the past, diluted the strength of his main body in order to provide garrisons to safeguard those many cities which had seceded to him. Rome, by this time, had fielded more armies against him than in any year since the commencement of the war; moreover, they were becoming increasingly experienced, were more willing to confront him, and were deployed over a much wider operational area than had previously proved possible. As a consequence, Hannibal could no longer guarantee his allies ready protection. Added to this, in view of the scale of the opposition now confronting him, it was essential that he should keep a strong force under his direct command. This meant abandoning some cities and withdrawing garrisons where he considered these to be under irreparable threat. In some cases, he had found himself compelled by circumstances to uproot friendly populations for operational reasons, a necessity not always welcomed by his allies. These sort of measures, writes Polybius[18], 'aroused indignation and exposed Hannibal to being accused of immorality and cruelty'. In truth, his war was failing and could only be revived by the arrival of Hasdrubal's army from Spain.

Immediately upon the fall of Capua, in late 211 BC, the Roman Senate authorised the despatch of a force of 6,000 foot and 300 horse to Spain, under the command of Gaius Nero, a general who had distinguished himself during the recent siege operation. It was decreed that he could select these numbers from the army he had commanded in Campania and that he should also be provided with an equal number of infantry by the allies of the Latin Confederacy, together with 800 cavalry. When these arrangements had been made he set sail without delay from Puteoli and made harbour at Tarraco, where he disembarked his army. He then beached his boats, armed their crews, embodied them into his infantry, and marched for the Ebro. There he joined with Tiberius Fonteius and Lucius Marcius and absorbed into his ranks the army of 8,000 foot and 1,000 horse they had salved from the earlier disasters in southern Spain. This brought the total strength of his force to 20,000 infantry and 2,100 horse. He then set about the task of re-establishing Roman influence north of the Ebro but it soon became clear, in the year that followed, that the Spanish tribes, who had almost unanimously abandoned Rome upon the deaths of her two generals, showed little enthusiasm for resuming their allegiance.

In March of the following year, a meeting of the senators in Rome, at their annual state of the nation appraisal, was encouraged by the military resources now available for allocation, largely arising from the capitulation of Capua. They decided, when discussing future strategy, that the moment had arrived for the longstanding war in Spain to be brought to a successful conclusion and announced their intention of despatching yet further reinforcements there, under a commander-in-chief of high quality. When they came to consider who this might be, there was a distinct lack of enthusiasm, amongst those eligible for consideration, to offer themselves for a task which, until now, had proved so conspicuously unsuccessful – principally, it should be repeated, because, as a matter of policy, it had been extensively under-resourced. Indeed, the reluctance of the assembled candidates was so marked that voices were to be heard suggesting that affairs in Spain had deteriorated to a degree where they were now irretrievable. In these circumstances, the Senate was driven to announce an election for a pro-consul 'to take over Spanish affairs, and the consuls announced the date'.

At this moment a young man, Publius Cornelius Scipio, son and nephew, respectively, of the two Scipios recently killed in battle in southern Spain, suddenly announced himself as a candidate for the command. As a young man of seventeen, he had led a cavalry charge to save his father's life at the battle on the Trebbia. Two years later, in the almost terminal confusion *post*-Cannae, he had, by his single-minded composure and determination, provided an example and a rallying point at Canusium for those who were determined that Rome should not fall into Carthaginian hands. Now, at the age of twenty-four, he was providing leadership to his countrymen again. His offer was greeted with a roar of approval from the assembly but was then followed by an expression of some doubts because of his youth. Scipio countered this by calling for an opportunity to speak,[19]

. . . and discoursed on his youth, of his appointment to the command, and of the coming war in such lofty and magnanimous terms that he kindled afresh the cooling ardour of the populace, and filled everybody with more confident hope than is usually inspired by trust in a mere promise or even by a reasoned deduction from facts.

A combination of many factors, wrote Livy, had set the young Scipio on a pinnacle, above the heads of mere men and for that reason 'the citizens of Rome entrusted the heavy burden of this important command to a man who had by no means reached full maturity'.

Scipio, accompanied by 10,000 foot and 1,000 horse, sailed for Spain from Ostia, at the mouth of the Tiber, with a fleet of thirty quinquiremes. He followed the coastline to Emporiae, where he landed with his army and marched to Tarraco, providing his men and animals with much-needed exercise after their long sea voyage, whilst simultaneously displaying the growing Roman military presence to doubting allies. At Tarraco, he was rejoined by his fleet which, as a mark of support, had been escorted from Massilia by four of their navy's triremes. He now returned these, beached his ships, for winter was coming, and called a meeting of delegations from tribes throughout the province, with the purpose of easing their anxieties about the recent unhappy fortunes of war. He then visited his troops, to heighten their morale, brief them as to his future policy, and express his confidence in their fighting ability.

One of the immediate actions of Scipio, upon his arrival in Spain, had been to obtain intelligence of the whereabouts of the Carthaginian armies. From this, he learnt that Mago was located in southern Portugal, east of the Pillars of Hercules;[20] Hasdrubal Gisgo was encamped on the Atlantic coast of Portugal; and Hasdrubal Barca was 'engaged in besieging a city in the territory of the Carpetani. Most important of all, each of these army commanders was situated at least 10 days' march from New Carthage.' Many of Scipio's senior officers encouraged him to attack one of the Carthaginian armies whilst they were so widely separated but their young general was a shrewd strategist in an age when the advantages of strategy, as opposed to battle tactics, were not always comprehended. He had already appreciated, along with the Senate in Rome, that possession of Spain provided the key for a Roman victory in Hannibal's War; but the sustenance of Carthaginian military operations in Spain inevitably depended upon the uninterrupted flow of essential stores, communications and an occasional interchange of reinforcements, between their homeland in North Africa and their Spanish base of New Carthage. If this latter link were removed, then Carthaginian resistance in the province would be neutered.

For these reasons, Scipio decided to seize New Carthage and passed much of his winter planning his assault upon it and gathering information about it:[21]

> He discovered first of all that it was virtually unique among the cities of Spain in possessing a harbour which could accommodate a fleet and naval forces, and that it was also conveniently situated for the Carthaginians to make the direct sea crossing from Africa. He also learnt that it was here that the Carthaginians kept the greater part of their money, all the baggage of their army and their mercenaries, the hostages they had taken from the whole of Spain and, most crucial of all, the fighting troops who garrisoned the citadel were only 1,000 strong.

The reason for this garrison being so extraordinarily weak was that the Carthaginian commanders considered their grip on the province to be so complete that it was beyond consideration that anyone should contemplate laying siege to the city, the defences of which were formidably designed and constructed, making full use of the land features upon which it stood.

Scipio told nobody of his intention, other than Gaius Laelius, the commander of his fleet. Rome had retained naval superiority in Spanish coastal waters and this was a factor he was determined to exploit, for if he were to fail it would provide him with a vital safety net. He now nominated Tarraco as his operational base and detached a garrison of 2,500 infantry and 300 cavalry, under Marcus Silunas, for its defence. He then concentrated the remainder of his force, 25,000 foot and 2,500 horse, at a forward assembly point at the mouth of the Ebro. He calculated, from the distances involved, that his task could be done before Hasdrubal, or any other of his army commanders, could arrive to interfere with him. He had, moreover, gleaned a vital piece of information from local fisherman, namely, that the lagoon upon which the citadel was situated was shallow and at low tide could be forded in many places. This knowledge formed the centre piece of his plan. Then, when all was ready, he issued secret orders to Laelius to meet him at New Carthage, and set forth, covering the ground at speed, by forced marches over a period of seven days. This suggests that he had moved to a forward assembly area before commencing this phase of his operation, for under no circumstance could he have marched from the Ebro in that time.

The harbour at Cartegena, New Carthage, as it looks today. (The Spanish Tourist Office)

New Carthage lay in a gulf, some 2½ miles long and a little more than a mile wide, the mouth of which was partially blocked by an island which allowed a narrow passage on either side. It was thus an ideal situation for a harbour. At the furthest end of the gulf a slender peninsula jutted out into the water, culminating in a rock in the style of Gibraltar, upon which the city was built. It lay in a hollow, overlooked on three sides by five hill features, the largest running the length of the southern stretch of the wall which surrounded the whole conurbation, including the high ground. The western reach of the defensive wall was constructed across open, level land. To its south and west the city was flanked by sea and to its north by the lagoon, about which Scipio had already learnt that the waters were at certain times so low as to be fordable, possibly at neap tides. He shrewdly told his soldiers that the sea god, Neptune, had personally briefed him upon this matter and thus gained their confidence for his plan.[22]

Scipio timed his arrival at New Carthage to coincide with that of his fleet. He then laid out his camp at the foot of the peninsula, where it emerged from the mainland, and threw up a rampart across its base, which reached from the southern coastline to the shore of the lagoon in the north. This defensive work was constructed so as to protect his force against outside attack whilst engaged in the business of the assault. On the other hand, he left open the flank of his encampment facing the city, possibly with the purpose of permitting untrammelled movement of reserves to and from his base. When this preliminary work had been completed, Scipio instructed his fleet to take up a blockading position and, in order to ensure that the highest attention was paid to detail, he visited each ship in turn to brief them upon their tasks. He then addressed his army, instructing them on what he required of them and charging them to remember[23] that, although they were about to assault 'the walls of one town, in that one town you will have taken the whole of Spain'. These words underlined his strategy of the indirect approach.

Scipio then commenced his attack by both land and sea, thrusting 2,000 selected men, carrying ladders, across the isthmus in the direction of the city whilst Laelius, with his fleet, and equipped with a variety of missiles, closed in to bring the walls under fire. As soon as Mago[24] heard Scipio's bugles sound the advance, he was ready with his response. He had already deployed his garrison, despatching half to the citadel and the remainder to a hill feature lying on the eastern side of the town. He had also marshalled 2,000 armed townspeople inside the east gate and, as the Romans advanced, they emerged from behind the walls to do battle. In a planned move, Scipio's men fell back upon their reserves and a furious fight developed until, overcome by sheer weight of numbers, the Carthaginians broke and fled. Many were killed on the battlefield; many more died as they fought to return through the town gates. The Roman assault force pursued so closely that they came near to bursting into the town and were enabled, due to the confused state of the Carthaginian defenders, to commence the task of scaling the walls. Their efforts, however, were eventually defeated, but more by the height of the walls and the casualties arising from overloaded ladders than by the garrison which, by this time, had rallied.

After this initial probing attack, Scipio withdrew whilst he waited for the tide to ebb, and his army took the opportunity of the respite to regroup, preparatory to a renewed assault, for which they were issued with an increased number of ladders. Then, at a carefully calculated moment, he recommenced his attack on the city walls, advancing in phased echelons, each one fresh and ready to take the place of the forward troops when ordered to do so.

The first phase of the assault was being withdrawn, having successfully fixed the attention of the defenders upon the main gate, when news was received that the tide was ebbing. Scipio had already stationed an assault force of 500 men behind a headland, on the edge of the lagoon but out of sight of events in the town. He now unleashed this party across the lagoon, where the water was so low that it had receded, 'uncovering shoal patches and leaving depths in some places up to a man's navel, in others scarcely up to his knees'. They found the battlements deserted and quickly made their way to the main gate, which they assailed and opened from the inside, allowing their comrades to pour into the town, with orders 'to exterminate every form of life they encountered, leaving none'.[25]

When Mago knew for certain that the city was lost, he surrendered to Scipio. The quantity of war material seized was vast. Indeed, Livy[26] remarks that, of all

*Publius Cornelius Scipio Æmilianus, Chartaginem funditus delevit.*

Scipio destroying Carthago Nova. (Drawing in the style of Giovanni Strandanus (1523–1605). The Royal Collection © 1997 Her Majesty Queen Elizabeth II)

the items the victors now found in their possession, the town was the least important. He quotes them in detail and they are worthy of note, for they indicate the catastrophic scale of the Carthaginian losses, both economic and military:

120 catapults of the largest sort, 281 smaller ones; 23 large and 52 smaller *ballistae*; countless 'scorpions' (catapults), large and small, and a great quantity of equipment and missiles, and, finally, 74 military standards. In

The continence of Scipio. Africanus restores a beautiful young prisoner to her Celtic lover, Allucius, after the fall of New Carthage. (From a painting by Pieter Codde. Bridgeman Art Library, CH 022878)

addition much gold and silver was brought to Scipio; it included 276 gold platters, each being a pound in weight; 18,300 pound of silver, either coined or in ingots; and a great many silver vessels. All this was handed over, weighed and measured, to the quaestor Flaminius. There were 400,000 measures of wheat and 270,000 measures of barley; 63 merchant vessels, some with their cargoes of grain and arms, besides bronze, iron, sail cloth, esparto for rope making and timber for ship building.

Equally remarkable was the attitude of Scipio himself, after such a profitable and decisive operation. He despatched Laelius to Rome by sea to provide the Senate with details of the victory. The latter took with him, in six ships escorted by a quinquireme, a selected number of prisoners, together with the unfortunate Mago and fifteen senators who had been captured at the same time. Scipio then gave his army a rest day and followed this by a regularly repeated five-day training and maintenance programme. No soldier or sailor was allowed to be idle and there was nothing 'on which the commander did not keep a careful eye, now with the fleet or at the docks, now attending the infantry manoeuvres, now watching all the work going on in the shops, in the armoury or in the dockyards'.[27]

When all in New Carthage was organised to his liking, Scipio left a garrison to hold the city and returned to 'winter' in Tarraco with his army and his fleet.

## CHAPTER X

# FINALE

> . . . as I have often said, while success in policy and victory in the field are great things, it requires much more skill and caution to make a good use of such success. So that you will find those who have won victories are far more numerous than those who have used them to advantage. This is exactly what happened to the Carthaginians . . .
>
> Polybius[1]

The situation of Scipio on his appointment to the Spanish command is comparable with that of Montgomery, who in 1942 arrived in the desert, 60 miles from Alexandria, to take over the 8th Army from General Sir Claude Auchinleck. Auchinleck, through a chain of unfortunate circumstances, although Commander-in-Chief, Middle East, had felt compelled to assume its direct command. He had been operating on necessarily slim resources and, after a successful forward thrust across the desert, found himself driven back from Tobruk to prepared defensive positions at Alamein, within a short march of the vitally strategic Suez Canal. The forced withdrawal led to his replacement. Montgomery, as the newly appointed Army commander, refused to be hustled into operations, as had been the experience of the unfortunate Auchinleck, until he felt fully prepared. It was essential, he later wrote, not only to have enough supplies to defeat Rommel at Alamein, but also to pursue him westwards until the ports of Tobruk and Benghazi could be relieved. He took two months building up the army and its morale,[2] whilst, from a beleaguered Britain, he received the reinforcements and equipment which circumstances had previously withheld from his predecessor.

Scipio Africanus, as the younger Scipio became known, like Montgomery, arrived at the right moment: and to say that is not to detract in any sense from the recognised military ability of either man. Until the despatch of Scipio, the younger, Rome had intentionally run her operation in Spain at minimum cost to herself, both in terms of outlay and manpower. The material cost of the expansion of her armed forces in the Italian peninsula, together with the devastation of her crops, by her own commander Fabius as well as Hannibal, had created for her treasury an embarrassing shortage of ready cash and resources. It was a situation which had made it necessary, on more than one occasion, for her commanders in the Spanish province, Gnaeus and Publius

Scipio Africanus on a coin,
c. 105 BC. (© British
Museum)

Scipio, to remind the Senate in Rome of their need, not only of clothing and equipment, but of money with which to pay their soldiery.[3]

Thus, the deaths of the two elder Scipios in battle, and the withdrawal of the remnants of their army to the line of the Ebro, had revealed a moment of crisis for Rome; but it had arrived at a moment when her fortunes were beginning to improve. In part, the immediate success of Scipio Africanus, and the changed atmosphere he brought to Spain, was due to the clear renewal of Roman interest in the province, now being visibly expressed, in particular by the increased scale of the resources he had been allocated for his task and which had been denied to his father. If Rome had already recognised the fact that pressure applied to Carthaginian forces in this, then, distant corner of the Mediterranean reduced the numbers of enemy troops available for operations elsewhere, particularly in Italy, Spain had not ranked high on her list of affordable priorities. Her circumstances had now changed and Scipio Africanus arrived with sufficient reinforcements to cast a different light on the future.

Nevertheless, nothing should be allowed to detract from the performance, judgement and strategic vision displayed by the young general. His choice of New Carthage as his first objective is an early example of this; it was not only employed by his enemy as a main base for land operations but also as a seaport, which provided a vital link with North Africa and Carthage itself; its loss was to prove a devastating blow. Now, with this great prize in his possession, his next task was to seek out and destroy the three Carthaginian armies, summarily cut off from their main logistical base, before they could unite.

The nearest of these was that of Hasdrubal Barca, encamped near Baecula, on the upper reaches of the Guadalquivir; and it was to attack him that Scipio marched from Tarraco in the spring of 209 BC. The morale of the Roman legions was high, so much so that when the cavalry outposts which protected the Carthaginian lines were first encountered, his column, wasting no time upon the customary establishment of a camp, drove them in with such zest that 'the Roman standards were all but carried through the gates'. That night, Hasdrubal pulled back to a nearby hill, the flanks and front of which were surmounted by a wall-like rim and the rear of which was covered by a river.

It was clearly a difficult feature to attack and Scipio was concerned that the other two Carthaginian generals might arrive whilst he was engaged in a prolonged assault: speed was therefore of the essence. For this reason, he retained his main body securely inside the encampment he had constructed on the previous evening, whilst he thrust his light troops forward to gain a foothold on the lower 'step' of the feature. When that had been successfully achieved, he released his heavy infantry in an encircling movement which was conducted so rapidly that Hasdrubal was caught unprepared. The Carthaginian front line recoiled and fractured upon being attacked from the rear, and the Roman assault force broke through its ranks to take hold of the enemy fortification on the summit. The Carthaginians suffered 8,000 killed during the fighting, whilst a further 10,000 foot and 2,000 horse were taken captive. Hasdrubal's army was thus severely weakened. He now made a seemingly pre-planned withdrawal along the line of the Tagus, in the direction of the western Pyrenees and a pass into Gaul which, some 2,000 years later, was to be used by Wellington after the battle of Vitoria. Both Livy and Polybius make the point that Hasdrubal took his money and his elephants with him, but Livy[4] suggests (and, if true, it was a significant display of low morale) that he had already despatched these to a rear assembly area prior to the battle.

Despite pressure from his senior officers, Scipio determined not to pursue Hasdrubal into the mountains but returned to Tarraco. It was a wise decision, for two other Carthaginian armies, under Mago and Hasdrubal Gisgo, were on the move in his vicinity. They possessed a strength superior to his own and he could well have found himself trapped by them in the forest of Castulo, and cut off from his established base, had he delayed his departure.

Within a short time, probably in the autumn of 208 BC, the three Carthaginian generals came together to hold a council of war. They had been widely separated, Gisgo and Mago having been deployed in Further Spain, whilst Hasdrubal Barca had been encamped in the Baecula region. Gisgo felt that the extreme western Spanish tribes were as yet not fully aware of the scale of the disaster inflicted upon their enemies by Scipio, and still possessed some loyalty to Carthage. Mago and Hasdrubal Barca totally disagreed with him: they expressed the view that the whole Spanish population, both tribally and individually, were flocking to the Roman cause and that this would remain the situation until their Carthaginian troops 'were either moved to the remotest parts of the country or carried into Gaul'. Spanish troops in the pay of Carthage were being affected by these feelings. For this reason, whether approved or not by the senate in Carthage, Hasdrubal Barca should go to Italy, 'for Italy was the main theatre of the war and his going there would take all the Spanish troops out of Spain and at the same time far away from the sound of Scipio's name'. They proposed, therefore, that Hasdrubal Barca's army,[5]

> . . . weakened by desertions and by the losses incurred in the recent defeat, should be made up with Spanish troops and that Mago should hand over his forces to Hasdrubal, son of Gisgo, and cross to the Balearics with a supply of money to hire auxiliary troops. Further, that Hasdrubal, son of Gisgo, should take his army deep into Lusitania and avoid action against the Romans; that Masinissa should have 3,000 of the best available cavalry for a roving commission through Hither Spain, helping allies and raiding enemy towns and farms.

In this manner, Hasdrubal Barca set out to bring relief to his brother, Hannibal, but, due to the delays and circumstances inflicted upon him by the Scipio family, he now came from Spain brandishing a broken sword rather than the weapon of burnished steel of yesteryear. His progress eastwards, through the northern foothills of the Pyrenees, appears to have been unreported but nevertheless the very rumour of his coming created increasing tension and anxiety in Rome. The first firm indication that he was on his way came from Massilia, whose senate despatched envoys to their ally with the news that

*Above and opposite:*
Typical views of the
western Pyrenees, through
which Hasdrubal would
have marched in 208 BC to
descend, like his brother
Hannibal, into the Po valley.
(Mary Spiller)

Hasdrubal had crossed into Gaul, bearing a large quantity of gold for hiring mercenaries, and that the tribes were in a high state of excitement. The Romans returned the messengers home at once, together with a Roman intelligence team, with instructions to recruit urgently a network of friendly Gallic chieftains in the task of information gathering. Soon, their worst fears were confirmed by reports that Hasdrubal assuredly was on his way, together with an immense army, and that he intended to cross the Alps in the coming spring of 207 BC. The only thing which prevented him from doing so immediately was the depth of the winter snows still lying on the summit of the mountains.

It was not long before the excitement in the capital was further increased by yet another report, on this occasion from praetor Porcius, from his advanced position on the frontiers of Cisalpine Gaul. News had been received by him that Hasdrubal had broken winter camp, was already on his way across the Alps, and that 8,000 Ligurians had been conscripted and armed and stood ready to join him in Italy. He proposed to advance and keep watch on the situation but he warned that his numbers were too inadequate for him to be able to do much. At this juncture, the Senate, in a hastily arranged meeting, urged their consuls to take the field without delay with three clear purposes in mind: Hannibal was to be pinned down in Bruttium and prevented from joining his brother in the north; Hasdrubal was to be met as he descended from the Alps into the Po valley; and

the tribes of Cisalpine Gaul and Etruria, for the latter were also displaying disturbing signs of restlessness, were to be restrained from joining him.

Meantime, at the far, southern end of the peninsula, Hannibal's situation was weakening further. Following upon the fall of Capua and his brief appearance before the gates of Rome, he had withdrawn to Bruttium. Because of his depleting numbers, he had, as we have already seen, little protection to offer his allies. Indeed, many of them, persuaded by his obvious military limitations, were turning back to their old allegiance with Rome. In general terms, it was his policy to avoid battlefield confrontation wherever possible and to continue to deny to Rome the use of any of the cities which had fallen into his hands, or might still be converted to his cause. If, through force of circumstances, he found it necessary to abandon any of them, and Rome was equally savage with those who had transgressed, he did not permit the unfortunate inhabitants the option of making unlikely peace with their old allies. However steadfastly they may have served him, he levelled their cities to the ground and transported their peoples behind his steadily reducing frontiers. This policy worked for him in two ways: it maintained his recruitment pool, and added to the agricultural desert along his northern frontiers, making it logistically difficult for Roman operations.

The year 209 BC, which witnessed the seizure of New Carthage by the young Scipio, saw a continued improvement in Roman affairs. The able Quintus Fabius

Maximus, author of the controversial but successful *Fabian Strategy*, was appointed consul for the fifth time in his career, as well as leader of the House of Senators. Quintus Fulvius Flaccus, who had served under Fabius, *post-Trasimene*, was appointed consul for the fourth time. The Senate, when confirming the nominations, announced that both men were to serve in Italy, Fabius to command in the region of Tarentum, where the citadel was still tenuously held in Roman hands, and Fulvius, in Lucania and Bruttium. The Senate also agreed that Marcellus, as proconsul for yet another year, should continue to command the legions in Lucania with which he had distinguished himself so well against Hannibal. When the appointments had been promulgated, Fabius left at once to assume his duties at Tarentum but, before his departure, by letter and by word of mouth, he urged his military colleagues, operating on his flanks, to contain Hannibal's activities, 'with all possible vigour', whilst he addressed himself to the recapture of Tarentum. If only this last remaining bastion of enemy activity of any importance could be taken, he emphasised, then Hannibal would have no cause to stay in Italy.

Marcellus displayed his customary dash. As soon as sufficient spring forage was available in the countryside, he wasted little time in taking the field to seek out Hannibal. He fell in with him at Canusium, where the latter, in line with his policy, was endeavouring, with little luck, to persuade the people of the town to renounce their allegiance to Rome. Hannibal had received warning that Marcellus was approaching and, in an effort to avoid an encounter with him, he withdrew. Marcellus hotly pursued him and, that evening, caught up with the enemy whilst he was fortifying his encampment. He dug in nearby and, next morning, again marched out to take up traditional battle positions, displaying his desire for combat. Hannibal's men, who, according to Livy,[6] were weary of the almost contemptuous harassment of them by Marcellus, accepted the challenge and, charging the Roman line with pent-up ferocity, drove it uncompromisingly from the field. Next day, battle was again joined, during the course of which, in the two-day encounter, Marcellus's army suffered a loss of four standards, together with more than 5,700 killed and many wounded. If Livy's figures be accepted, Hannibal suffered 8,000 dead, with the loss of five elephants. Both sides then drew apart to lick their wounds, Hannibal returning to Bruttium.

Fabius, meantime, had stormed Manduria, a town in Salentine territory, and had captured within it about 4,000 men and a considerable quantity of material. He then turned toward Tarentum but first sent a message to Rhegium that the 8,000 brigand corps garrisoned there was to be released against nearby Caulonia, sympathetic to Hannibal.[7] Upon arrival at Tarentum, with typical patience and attention to detail, he commenced preparations for a seaborne assault on the city. He armed many of the larger ships lying in the harbour with 'catapults, stones and every variety of missile weapon', so that they might give effective long-range covering fire to an assault party. The merchant vessels, including many of the lighter ones dependent only upon oars, he equipped with ladders and light artillery.

Whilst he was engaged in these preparations an incident occurred which, in Livy's words, was 'almost too trivial to mention'. It was nevertheless to bring about the collapse of the city's defences. The garrison provided by Hannibal for Tarentum contained a Bruttium contingent, the commander of which 'was desperately in love with some woman or other who had a brother serving in Fabius's army'. The woman informed her brother of the connection with this wealthy, influential stranger (we are not told whether she had any affection for him) and he at once recognised the opportunity which now presented itself. He told Fabius of his sister's attachment and, with his commanding general's approval, inveigled his way into the city, posing as a deserter. There, 'having satisfied himself as to the fellow's lack of character', the brother and sister persuaded the 'love-sick captain' to betray his trust. In short, it was planned that whilst trumpets in the citadel and upon the ships in the harbour were sounding the assault, thus attracting the defenders of the city to what appeared to be the threatened quarter, Fabius's men would scale the wall where the Bruttian contingent would be on guard, warned not to oppose them. This is the way it worked out. The Romans, having reached the battlements unchallenged and unopposed, descended into the town and broke open the gates, to admit the main body of troops. The almost habitual indiscriminate slaughter then commenced, the Roman soldiery 'butchering Carthaginian or Tarentine alike': and, despite Bruttian participation in the act of treachery, many of their kinsmen were killed, 'either by mistake or because of the inveterate hatred the Romans felt for them'.

The fall of Tarentum delivered yet another wounding blow to Carthage. It is not easy, on the face of it, to understand how Hannibal permitted it to happen without intervening, unless he judged that he did not possess the military strength. He was normally armed with an extraordinarily efficient intelligence-gathering service; but when Fabius commenced his assault on the seaport, we find him at Caulonia, which had but recently been subjected to a diversionary attack by a rag-tag force of 8,000 Sicilian outlaws and Bruttian deserters based on Rhegium. Here, as might be expected against such opposition, he had little difficulty in raising the siege. Livy relates that when news was brought to him that Tarentum was under attack, he set out to its assistance immediately, marching day and night. When he arrived, and learnt that it had fallen, he took up a position some 5 miles from the town, where he remained for a few days before withdrawing westwards, along the coast, to Metapontum. Again, we are left with a sense that we are watching a public relations ploy, with Hannibal doing what he could with limited resources but avoiding full-scale confrontation, with its risk of considerable loss of manpower and possible defeat.

Nevertheless, Hannibal was always eager to seize an opportunity when one presented itself, as it was to do in the following year, 208 BC. Marcellus, for the fourth occasion, and Titus Quinctius Crispinus had both been elected to the consulship. Crispinus, ambitious to make an instant success of his tenure of office and conscious that Fabius had enhanced his already considerable reputation yet further by retaking Tarentum, now determined to make a similar attempt on the port of Locri in Bruttium. He was dissuaded by the sudden arrival of Hannibal and marched to join Marcellus at Venusia, where they established camps within 3 miles of each other. They were followed there by Hannibal, who also set up camp nearby.

Situated between the opposing forces there was a hill covered with trees. Both protagonists recognised its importance but each had refrained from using it until they knew more about the slope, out of their vision, which confronted the enemy position. Hannibal, a master of the art of irregular warfare, saw a possible ambush position in the wooded high ground and, under cover of darkness, despatched a squadron or so of Numidian cavalry to conceal themselves in the trees. Meantime, many senior ranks in the Roman camp had expressed their unease that such a feature, so close to their lines, should be left unoccupied. The two generals then made the astonishing decision to carry out a joint and personal reconnaissance of the feature, together with a group of staff officers and senior commanders.[8] 'Once we have seen the hill', said Marcellus, 'we shall be in a better position to make a decision.' The Numidians, from their high position, watched as the two men left their camp, escorted by two squadrons of cavalry, largely Etruscan, with some Fregellae, and sprang the ambush with perfect timing. The consuls were trapped: they could not make the summit, which was held in enemy hands, and they were being assailed by cavalry from the rear. Marcellus was killed in the first onslaught and Crispinus was wounded, together with Marcellus's son. The Etruscans deserted almost as soon as they came under attack. Livy[9] writes that,

> . . . when (the Fregellae) saw that both consuls had been hit, Marcellus, indeed, run through with a lance and falling at his last gasp from his horse, then they too, the few who survived, took to their heels with the consul Crispinus, who himself had two javelin wounds, and the young Marcellus, who was also wounded. Manlius, the military tribune, was killed, and Arrenius was taken prisoner. Of the consuls' lictors, five were captured or got away with Crispinus. Of the mounted troops, 43 were killed, either in the fight or whilst trying to escape, and 18 were taken alive.

Crispinus, who was to prove to have been mortally wounded, appointed the young Marcellus to take over his father's army at Venusia and then set out for Capua, borne in a litter. Hannibal had returned once more to Bruttium after making this important coup, and Crispinus, by deploying his forces in this manner, covered the main trunk roads northwards, the *Via Appia* from Bruttium and the *Via Latina* from Tarentum. At the same time he despatched a report to the Senate, bringing them up to date with the consequence of these disastrous events and voicing his concern that Hannibal's attention might once again turn towards Tarentum.

As the year 208 BC came to an end, an atmosphere of crisis was beginning to develop in Italy, created by the knowledge that the arrival of Hasdrubal in Cisalpine Gaul was imminent and enhanced by the deaths of the two consuls. The Senate, after carefully considering the replacements of these two men, appointed Gaius Claudius Nero as their first choice. Senate members considered him to be head and shoulders above all the other candidates. The second consul to be appointed was Marcus Livius: he was an odd selection, for his previous performance in office had ended in disgrace. He had been condemned for dishonesty in 219 BC, when conducting the war again Demetrius of Pharos. He always considered himself to have been grievously wronged and, as a consequence, had withdrawn from public life: but, says Livy,[10] 'he still kept his old clothes and his long hair and beard and clearly showed, both by his dress and his countenance that he had never forgotten his disgrace'. Selected as a cautious and prudent colleague for the temperamentally fiery Nero, he was now recalled from this strange retirement and compelled once again to accept public office. These two oddly incompatible men were destined to frustrate the second great Carthaginian assault on Italy during Hannibal's War.

Unusually, for the geographical deployment of the consular armies was customarily left to the officers concerned, the Senate in this case specified the new consular areas of operation: one was to have the task of containing Hannibal in Bruttium; the other, of standing guard against the arrival of Hasdrubal in northern Italy. The Senate pressed the two men to take the field as urgently as possible.

Nero was the first to leave: he opted for southern Italy where, upon arrival, he put together an army of 40,000 foot and 2,500 horse, leaving his praetor, Quintus Claudius, with a task force made up of the balance and with the role of safeguarding friendly towns from harassment by Hannibal. He then went in search of his enemy, whom he found at Grumentum, in Lucania. Here, Hannibal had assembled all the troops he had deployed on garrison duty in Bruttium, together with the main body with which he had recently 'wintered'. He was about to commence an unambitious round of marches to reassert his influence on local towns, dissuading them from seceding to Rome. Nero engaged him immediately, with some considerable success, inflicting upon him losses of 8,000 killed, 700 prisoners, 9 standards and 4 elephants.[11] He then pursued him remorselessly as Hannibal withdrew from Grumentum to Venusia, and from Venusia towards Metapontum, from where he retraced his tracks once again to Venusia. From Venusia, again, he marched onwards to Canusium, where the two sides encamped within some 500 yards of each other, with Nero tenaciously hanging on to Hannibal's coat tails.

An incident now occurred which was to change the course of the war. Whilst in Cisalpine Gaul, Hasdrubal had sent to Hannibal a message giving details of his movements and of a proposed meeting place for their two armies. He had entrusted the document to an escort party of four Gallic and two Numidian horsemen. With extraordinary courage and ingenuity, this group rode the length of the peninsula unobserved and had been trailing Hannibal from Metapontum when they mistook their route and found themselves at Tarentum. There, unhappily for them and, as it was to prove, for Hasdrubal, they were discovered by a Roman foraging party and brought before Quintus Claudius, where, under threat of torture, they confessed their role. They were then despatched to Nero, escorted by two troops of Samnite cavalry. It was Hannibal's misfortune that, for the second time in his campaign, a message of such crucial operational importance should have fallen into enemy hands.

Nero, upon receipt of this captured document, which announced Hasdrubal's intention of meeting with Hannibal in Umbria, was aware of the powerful threat which would be posed, particularly to the city of Rome, if the two Carthaginian armies were allowed to join together. He also recognised the folly of a situation 'whereby each consul should fight only within his prescribed area, using only his own troops against an enemy assigned to him by order of the senate'. He now determined to march with a select force to join Livius, whilst leaving his main body encamped, confronting Hannibal, under his second-in-command, Quintus Catius. For this purpose he selected 6,000 horse and 1,000 foot, and despatched gallopers ahead to make the necessary logistical arrangements along his route, including the dumping of rations and the provision of extra horses and mules to transport those of his men who fell out through fatigue. As a cover plan, he announced that the purpose of the operation was the seizure of a nearby Lucanian town, with its Carthaginian garrison.

Simultaneously, he despatched a letter to Rome telling the Senate of his plan, whilst at the same time warning them of the threat to the capital. He advised them to transfer a legion from Capua for the defence of the city, to raise fresh troops within Rome itself, and to take the precaution of sending the city army northwards, along the *Via Flaminia*, to hold Narnia. There, should Hasdrubal break through, they would have the dual role of contesting the trunk road and of providing a fall back position for Livius.

Whilst all this was going forward, Livius, also, had been preparing for operations. Aggrieved that he had been compelled to return to office, he had delayed taking up his duties in the field until he was satisfied he had the resources with which to undertake the task he had been given. Livy[12] emphasises that his requirements were discussed with great harmony and that reinforcements were despatched to him from many areas:

> The slave-volunteers were attached to the XIX and XX Legions; according to some chroniclers powerful auxiliaries were sent by Scipio from Spain to join (him) – 8,000 Spanish and Gallic troops, 2,000 Roman legionaries, 1,800 mounted troops, part Numidian, part Spanish. These were brought over by sea by Marcus Lucretius. Some 3,000 archers and slingers were also sent by Gaius Mamilius from Sicily.

He then marched northwards. The details of his initial encounter with Hasdrubal are obscure but he appears to have made contact with him as he progressed along the northern extremity of the *Via Flaminia*, in the neighbourhood of Sena, south of modern-day Rimini. The two armies then came to a halt, erected fortified encampments within a few hundred yards of each other, and prepared for battle. Occasionally, they emerged to draw themselves up in line and assess the numbers and state of readiness of the enemy. Joined with Livius was praetor Porcius Licinus, who, until now, had been deployed on the northern frontier, watching for Hasdrubal. He had then shadowed him southward, employing every delaying tactic against him and harassing his column by pin-prick attacks on his flanks and rear.

Nero's march from Canusium was a triumphal occasion. Men and women flocked from the farmhouses and villages to line the route as the soldiers passed, hailing them as 'their country's defenders, champions of the City and imperial power of Rome'. The soldiery bore nothing but their weapons but they had no need to do otherwise. Everything they required for themselves or for their animals was thrust upon them as they marched. Impelled by this surge of patriotism, Nero's fighting strength swelled in numbers as he advanced: old soldiers joined his column and young men competed with each other to enlist in his ranks. As he drew near to Livius, he sent staff officers ahead to enquire whether he should arrive openly, in daylight and occupy a separate camp, or whether he should move in after dark and in secret. Livius chose the latter option and directed that Nero's party should be found accommodation within his existing lines; for if he were to enlarge the camp, Hasdrubal might guess that he had been reinforced.

That night a council of war was convened at which the future was discussed. Many voices were raised in opposition to immediate action, arguing that the new arrivals from the south should be allowed a period of rest before being committed to action. Nero did not accept this: his forced march to join Livius was worthy of success because of the speed and unexpectedness of his arrival. To delay action further, he proclaimed,

> . . . was to betray the camp at Canusium . . . No: the signal for battle must be given immediately; they must take advantage of the fact that both their opponents were unaware of the real situation, that Hannibal did not know that the army opposed to him had been diminished, or Hasdrubal that he was faced with stronger and more numerous forces than before.[13]

Upon hearing what Nero had to say, there was no further argument. Operational orders were issued, the council of war was dismissed and next morning the army moved out of camp and formed into line, to find Hasdrubal's troops already drawn up in front of their entrenchments.

Hasdrubal had already, with great awareness, begun to suspect the worst. He had ventured forth on a reconnaissance, escorted by a small cavalry patrol, and he had noted, in the enemy's ranks, some battleworn shields he had not previously observed, together with a number of 'unusually stringy' horses. It seemed to him, also, that the opposing army was larger than usual. He at once ordered the retreat to be sounded and then despatched a number of patrols to see what evidence could be found that Nero was present. They brought back little information, except that, when duty trumpet calls were being made, 'the trumpet sounded once only in the praetor's camp and twice in the consul's', thus indicating the presence of two consuls. If this were indeed so, it suggested that Hannibal had been defeated. He decided to move: he immediately ordered all camp fires to be extinguished and, after dark, his army packed its gear in silence and moved out of camp, northwards, towards the Metaurus river. His guides, however, were untrustworthy, with the result that he lost his way in the dark and failed to find his crossing place. Next day, whilst he was still searching for it, he was overtaken by the Roman army, with, almost inevitably it might be thought, the irrepressible Nero riding in the van with the cavalry contingent.

The battle which now followed raged throughout the morning, and the Carthaginians, worn out with marching in full equipment and with lack of sleep,

Hannibal with the head of
his brother Hasdrubal,
whose death caused
Hannibal much distress.
(From a painting by
Giovanni-Battista Tiepolo.
Bridgeman Art Library,
MAM 065657)

suffered heavy casualties. The poor fellows, wrote Livy, gasping with thirst and heat, were killed or captured by the hundred. Livy puts the number of their dead at 57,000, with 5,400 prisoners. Polybius,[14] probably more reliably, puts their losses at 10,000 killed and 2,000 prisoners. Many others of the enemy, notably tribal contingents from Cisalpine Gaul, streamed away from the battlefield, making their escape northwards. Some wanted to pursue them but Livius, surveying the carnage surrounding him, said there had been enough killing and let them go. The Carthaginian general, Hasdrubal, brother of Hannibal, was amongst those who died. Hasdrubal's fame, wrote Livy,[15]

> . . . rests upon many exploits but more than all upon his conduct in this last battle. It was he who kept his men going with words of encouragement, sharing their perils; he who rekindled the courage of the weary and the faint hearted, cursing their slackness or entreating them to rally; he who called back the fugitives to the colours and again and again forced them to fight on. When at last no doubt remained that the day was lost, he refused to survive the great army which had followed his fame, and setting spurs to his horse galloped straight into the midst of a Roman cohort. There, still fighting, he found a death worthy of his father Hamilcar and his brother Hannibal.

The Roman victory on the Metaurus, although Livius is given credit for the outcome, owed much to the clarity of mind, the determination and physical urgency of consul Gaius Claudius Nero. His march, both to and from the battlefield, and his conduct upon it, where he led a vitally important encircling attack upon the Carthaginian flank and rear, was truly remarkable. If we are to believe Livy, his return to Canusium was even more so, for he relates that Nero started back for Apulia the night after the battle and 'returned even more quickly than he had come, and in less than six days had reached his camp close to Hannibal's lines'.[16]

Nero carried with him Hasdrubal's head, which 'he had carefully preserved throughout his march' and, upon his return, caused it to be flung into Hannibal's lines. There it was retrieved by one of the enemy pickets and carried to the Carthaginian commander-in-chief. At the same time, Nero released two of his African prisoners and sent them across to the enemy camp, so that they might provide a full account of the battle. The news of the double calamity, the loss of the battle and the death of his brother, caused Hannibal great personal distress. It is said that when he learnt of it, and was shown the ghastly evidence, he exclaimed: 'Now, at last, I see the destiny of Carthage plain!' Immediately, he appreciated the dangers which now confronted him and gave orders for the instant withdrawal of his army to Bruttium. He also called in his outlying garrisons, and arranged for the transfer to Bruttian territory of all those Lucanians who still gave him their allegiance, together with the entire population of Metapontum. From this moment forward, Hannibal undertook no further major operations. Indeed, Livy[17] records that he spent the following summer in the vicinity of the temple of Juno Lacinia, where he dedicated an altar with a long inscription of his achievements, written in Punic and in Greek

It might have been expected that Rome, following upon her success on the Metaurus, would now have concentrated her force and pursued the disheartened Hannibal to his destruction. On the contrary, she was content to ignore him. Livy relates that throughout the whole of the year, subsequent to the defeat of Hasdrubal (206 BC), no direct action was taken against Hannibal, even though it was evident that 'everything around him was tumbling into ruin'.

Equally extraordinarily, the authorities in Carthage continued to put the major part of their military effort into retaining their hold on Spain, which, by now, under pressure from Scipio, was on the point of finally slipping from their grasp. They seemed to fancy, Livy[18] comments, 'that in Italy all was well'. By their actions, and the orders which they issued to their unfortunate commanders, this appears to have been their belief but it is not easy to understand, in face of the facts, how they could have reached such a conclusion.

Scipio, after convincingly defeating Hasdrubal Gisgo in battle and forcing him to flee the province, had driven Mago to seek refuge at Gades, today Cádiz, in Further Spain, then utilised by the Carthaginians as a port after the loss of New Carthage. Scipio finally achieved the subjugation of Spain at the end of 206 BC. He then returned to Rome for the consular elections, having handed over command to his pro-praetors, leaving with them the responsibility of stamping out the last vestiges of Carthaginian power.

At about this same moment, Mago, who was preparing to depart for North Africa, received orders from Carthage to sail for Italy with the fleet under his command. He was instructed to hire as many Gallic and Ligurian mercenaries as he could find and, after landing in Italy, to join forces with Hannibal 'in order to prevent the Carthaginian war-effort, begun with great vigour and even greater success, from petering out'.[19] It was, in the circumstances, a completely impractical order, which totally ignored the military pressures now being applied to Carthage in general and Hannibal in particular. At the same time, Mago was handed a large sum of money to finance this new enterprise and, before leaving, he adroitly took the opportunity to raise an even larger total from the unfortunate people of the town, emptying their treasury, robbing their temples and prising from individual citizens whatever gold and silver they might possess.

Mago spent the coming winter months on the most westerly of the Balearic Islands, inhabited by Carthaginians. Here he recruited many of the reinforcements he needed and, in the spring, with a fleet of thirty warships and a large number of transports, he set sail for Genoa where he landed with a force of 12,000 infantry and 2,000 cavalry. Here, he made an alliance with the Ingauni, established a base in their territory at the port of Savo, and engaged their sympathy by providing them with military assistance in their war with the Epanterii, a highland people of the Maritime Alps.

During this same period, Scipio, appointed consul for the year 205 BC, had also been occupied with planning for the coming campaigning season. Whilst commanding in Spain, he had made important friends with many powerful African leaders, including Syphax, king of the Maesulii, to whom he had at one time despatched a military infantry team to help train his soldiers, and Masinissa,

King Syphax on a Numidian coin. (© British Museum)

now king of Numidia. The latter's young nephew, Massiva, had fallen into Scipio's hands at the battle of Baecula and he had calculatedly returned him to his uncle with gifts and suitable honours. The two men had already met clandestinely in Spain, when Masinissa was still serving Mago as cavalry commander of the Numidians. The Numidian had then hinted at an alliance against Carthage were the war to be carried to Africa and Scipio be appointed to command.

King Masinissa on a Numidian coin. (© British Museum)

Scipio had long recognised the military advantages of launching a direct assault against Carthage on African soil. Indeed, it had already been Roman policy for many years of the war to carry out diversionary seaborne raids along the Carthaginian coast of North Africa. Thus, when appointed consul, he strongly advocated this tactic in his address to the Senate in its annual assessment of the war. His thinking was opposed by Fabius and coolly received by other members, on the tenuous but not insuperable grounds that, with the waters of the Mediterranean lying between them, the consular armies would be unable to give each other mutual support. Ultimately, after lengthy and sometimes heated discussion, the Senate decided that one consul throughout the coming year was to have responsibility for Sicily. He was also granted permission to cross to Africa if he judged it to be in the public interest, but they restricted his naval support to a meagre thirty warships, thus rendering such an operation difficult to carry out on any significant scale. The other consul was given charge of operations against Hannibal in Bruttium.

When lots were drawn, command of the army in Sicily fell to Scipio, a role which opened the way for him to carry the war to Carthaginian Africa. Thus, one of his earliest actions upon arrival on the island was to despatch Gaius Laelius, his second-in-command, to raid the African coast, where he devastated the countryside around Hippo Diarrhyus, modern-day Bizerta. In part, the said visitation may have been motivated by the hope of making renewed contact with the Numidian leader, Masinissa. If so, he was fortunate, for Masinissa came to meet Laelius on the coast, urging Scipio not to delay his invasion, since morale in Carthage was low and their ally, Syphax, had his hands full with local wars. Although he was still forbidden to return to his country, where he was a contender for the throne, Masinissa undertook to raise for Scipio 'a by no means contemptible force of infantry and cavalry'.

The appointment of Scipio to the Sicilian command, followed so swiftly by this raid, created alarm in Carthage. At a hurriedly convened meeting, it was agreed that a variety of counter-measures should be set in hand, the most important of which were aimed at distracting Roman attention from landings in Carthaginian Africa. A delegation was sent to King Philip V of Macedonia, promising him 200 talents of silver if he were to invade either Sicily or Italy. Further delegations were also sent to Hannibal and to Mago, urging them to use every means of discouraging a Roman assault on their homeland, particularly by Scipio. At the same time, reinforcements of 25 warships, 6,000 foot soldiers, 800 horse, together with 7 elephants and a further large sum of money were sent to Mago, with instructions that, on the strength of these additional resources, he was to move nearer to Rome and join forces with Hannibal.[20] Again, with both

Table 5: Allied State Contributions to Scipio's Fleet.

| Serial No. | State | Material etc. |
| --- | --- | --- |
| 1. | Caere | Grain for the crews and sundry supplies |
| 2. | Populonium | Iron |
| 3. | Tarquini | Sail-cloth |
| 4. | Volaterrae | Timber for keels and garboards: grain |
| 5. | Arretium | a. 3,000 shields; 3,000 helmets; with a total of 50,000 pikes, javelins and spears<br>b. Axes, shovels, sickles, basins and hand-mills to equip 40 warships<br>c. 120,000 measures of wheat, plus funds for travel allowance for crews |
| 6. | Perusia, Clusium Russellae | Grain and fir for shipbuilding |
| 7. | Camerinum | A fully equipped cohort, 600 strong |

Many others provided volunteers for service with the fleet.

men located at opposing ends of the peninsula, this was yet another order from Carthage completely divorced from military reality.

When these latest reinforcements reached Mago, he called a meeting of representatives of the peoples of Cisalpine Gaul and of Liguria. Pointing to the new arrivals, he told them that he had been sent to restore them to liberty but added, realistically, that there was little he could achieve unless he received their substantial support. The Cisalpine tribes were reluctant to commit themselves because of the proximity of the two Roman armies already closely watching their behaviour. The Ligurians were willing to help but required two months in which to raise the necessary troops. Mago, meantime, commenced recruiting volunteers but kept his distance from Roman forces, by remaining in the area of the Maritime Alps, until he could raise the manpower necessary for the task he was being asked to undertake. Rome responded to his recruiting drive by moving two legions from Etruria to Ariminum and replacing them by a pair of city legions. Clearly, the route to Rome for Mago, when the moment came to take it, would be heavily contested.

The Carthaginian landing in the north of Italy left Scipio, and indeed the Roman planners generally, unperturbed. The Roman general continued to direct his attention and considerable intellect to the invasion of Carthaginian Africa. He had been granted no authority to raise fresh troops for the purpose but did possess the Senate's consent to take volunteers. Likewise, he was permitted to accept contributions, in cash or in kind, for the construction of new vessels. These were made to him in generous quantities (see Table 5, opposite) by allied communities before he left Rome. In all, the keels of 30 ships were laid, 20 quinquiremes and 10 quadriremes, and, under the keen eye of Scipio himself, who permitted the workmen and shipwrights no respite, they were launched, fully equipped and rigged, forty-five days after the timber for them had been felled.

Under this rigorous leadership, a high state of readiness was soon achieved and Scipio was able to announce, probably in the early summer of 204 BC, that, with God's blessing, he would sail for Africa on the next fair wind. The invasion port he had selected, from which to launch his attack, was Lilybaeum. Every soldier in Sicily, both mounted and unmounted, together with every warship and transport vessel in the fleet, had been concentrated there, 'making the town too small to contain the men and the harbour too small to contain the ships'. The administrative arrangments for the embarkation are outlined in Livy's annals and provide an interesting record of the detailed planning of the expedition undertaken by Scipio and his staff. The purpose of the operation, he announced for the benefit of the public, was to draw Hannibal from Italy and transfer the war to Africa. The fleet then set sail, the dense crowd at the water's edge making 'as thrilling a spectacle for the troops on board as the fleet itself made for the watchers on shore'. At dawn, next morning, after silence had been called for by a herald, he uttered the following uncompromising prayer:

> O Gods and Goddesses of the seas and lands, I pray and beseech you that whatsoever things have been done under my authority, are being done, and will be done, may prosper for me and for the people and commons of Rome, for our allies and for the Latins who follow my lead, authority and auspices, and those of the Roman people by land, river and sea; and that you will graciously assist all these our enterprises and bless them with a rich increase. And I pray that you bring the victors home again, safe and sound, enriched with spoils and laden with plunder to share my triumph when the enemy has been defeated; that you grant us the power of vengeance upon those whom we hate and our country's enemies, and give to me and the Roman people means to inflict upon the Carthaginian state the sufferings which the Carthaginians have laboured to inflict upon us.[21]

Scipio headed, firstly, for Cape Bon but, on making landfall, decided to sail further down the coast and ultimately came ashore at modern-day Cap Farina, about 12 miles north of Utica. His arrival, with the large-scale disembarkation of men, animals and supplies, created panic amongst the local towns and farms. The countryside was filled with refugees, the whole confused scene being magnified by large herds of cattle, amongst the throng of people, being driven inland by their owners. An early and welcome visitor to Scipio was Masinissa, accompanied by a personal escort of some 200 cavalrymen.

Scipio's first task was to provide himself with a firm base from which to operate, preferably a seaport, and for this purpose he laid siege to Utica but the defences of the city proved too strong for him. With winter approaching, he was compelled after forty days to relinquish his efforts to reduce the city and found for himself a hill site some 2 miles to its east. Although it was not ideal, he was well provisioned, with foodstuffs from the surrounding countryside and supplies brought by sea from Sicily, Italy and Sardinia. Here, whilst waiting and preparing for the coming campaigning season, he entered into negotiations with Syphax, first, in an unsuccessful effort to persuade him to abandon his alliance with Carthage and then, latterly, to persuade him, with his commander, Hasdrubal Gisgo, lately from Spain, that he, Scipio, was eager for peace. He also used this time to collect intelligence and make operational plans for the future. It is clear from his actions that he had no intention of tackling the capital city of Carthage until he had crippled the enemy in the field.

One of the pieces of information brought to Scipio during these months was that the nearby camps of Syphax and Hasdrubal were constructed in some cases of timber and others of dried reeds and were highly inflammable. With this simple but important knowledge in mind he planned an assault on their position, with half the Roman troops, together with all the Numidians, under command of Laelius and Masinissa, to attack Syphax's camp, whilst he himself advanced towards Hasdrubal's lines, delaying his advance so that his troops were the last to arrive. Laelius, judging the right moment, then sent forward his light troops to set fire to the huts and the flames spread with enormous speed. Masinissa, meantime, circled the position to cover the rear exits. The outcome was total disaster for the Carthaginian army. The casualty figures quoted by the annalists Livy and Appian are so large as to be wholly unsustainable, but are useful in that they indicate very considerable Carthaginian losses.[22] Scipio followed this success a few weeks later with another victory of equal importance, when he marched inland to defeat the reorganised armies of Hasdrubal and Syphax, in the area of the Great Plains, and inflicted upon them further heavy losses.

Following upon this, Scipio now felt confident, for the first time, to turn towards Carthage. Largely unopposed, he briefly occupied Tunis, from whence he had a clear view of the capital, barely 15 miles distant. This new threat, together with the capture of their ally, Syphax, by Laelius, delivered a severe blow to Carthaginian morale. It was decided to send thirty senior members of their government to Scipio to make overtures for peace. Livy[23] contemptuously writes,

> . . . when they entered Scipio's headquarters in camp, they prostrated themselves like the courtiers of an eastern monarch (having, I suppose derived that practice from the country of their origin) and their words were fully in keeping with such fawning, as they proceeded, not to excuse their own error, but to transfer the original blame to Hannibal and the party which supported his power. They asked pardon for their country, now twice brought low by the reckless policy of its people and able to be saved a second time only by the goodwill of its enemies . . .

Scipio responded by stating his terms for a truce, namely that Carthage should hand over forthwith all prisoners of war and deserters; withdraw her armies from Cisalpine Gaul and Italy; surrender all her warships, leaving herself with a balance of twenty; and, additionally, that Carthage should provide to the Romans 500,000 measures of wheat and 300,000 of barley, together with 5,000 pounds of silver.[24] He gave the envoys three days in which to go away and consider these arrangements, after when, if accepted, they would be required to make an armistice with him and send envoys to Rome to agree a formal treaty. They quickly returned to Scipio with acceptance of his terms and despatched a delegation to Rome, where they were not admitted into the city. They were, alternatively, lodged in the Villa Publica outside the walls, and granted a hearing by the Senate, sitting in the temple of Bellona.

A prime clause of the terms proposed by Scipio was his demand that Hannibal and Mago should immediately be withdrawn from their theatres of operation in Italy and in Gaul. The annalists differ in their records of how this was achieved.[25] Livy relates that the Senate, in discussion on this point, decided that the peace terms should be rejected until the withdrawal and final destination of both men had been determined and agreed. Appian records a ruling that the final decision and completion of the terms should be left to Scipio. Polybius and Cassius Dio are both in agreement that the document containing the terms was signed in Rome by the Senate. Dio, more probably, adds that the Carthaginian delegation was not granted an audience until it was known that both enemy generals, with their armies, had departed from Italian soil. In the circumstances in which they found themselves, the orders to return to Carthage cannot have been unwelcome.

Since his arrival in northern Italy, Mago had been unsuccessful in obtaining the open support of the tribes of Cisalpine Gaul, without which his mission to Italy stood little or no chance of success. In order to arouse their interest in his cause, he marched, in the summer of 203 BC, to the tribal territory of the Insubres. There, by chance, he encountered a Roman army under the praetor Quinctilius Varus and the proconsul Marcus Cornelius, and, in a sharp battle involving the deployment of Carthaginian elephants, he received a serious wound in the thigh. When he was seen to fall, his line was shocked to a standstill, then crumbled and a rout soon developed. Mago, already heavily doubtful about the future, pulled back to the coast and there met envoys from Carthage who had landed a few days previously in the Gulf of Genoa. They brought him orders to return to Carthage at the earliest possible moment. Mago, a sick man, embarked his troops at once and set sail for home but his fleet had barely passed Sardinia when he died of his wounds.

Hannibal was already prepared for his recall. He had weeded out those of his men he considered to be unfit for further service and had despatched them for garrison duty to those Bruttium towns still displaying loyalty to him. They must have been guaranteed a doubtful future. The remainder he embarked and, with them, returned to Africa. Hannibal's war on Italian soil was over. It is said that, when the emissaries from Carthage delivered their message to him, he exclaimed, in frustration and with some justification:[26]

> For years past they have been trying to force me back by refusing me reinforcements and money; but now they recall me no longer by indirect means, but in plain words. Hannibal has been conquered not by the Roman people whom he defeated in battle so many times and put to flight, but by the envy and disparagement of the Carthaginian.

CHAPTER XI

# HANNIBAL'S GENERALSHIP

Where, are now the great Empires of the World and their great Imperial Cities? Their Pillars, Trophies and Monuments of Glory? Show me where they stood, read the Inscription, tell me the Victor's Name.

Thomas Burnet (1635–1715)[1]

On, on, you madman, drive
Over your savage Alps, to thrill young schoolboys
And supply a theme for speech day recitations!

Juvenal, *Satire X*[2]

Military command is defined as the authority vested in an individual for the direction, coordination and control of military forces.[3] Thus, when we are discussing the quality of a general such as Hannibal, it is necessary, if we are to be fair in our assessment, to be certain of the tempo of war at which he is to be judged. That is to say, whether at the level of grand, military or simply operational strategy.

In ancient times the application of grand and military strategies was frequently exercised as a whole: grand strategy being the application of national resources to achieve policy objectives set by the government of the nation at war, and military strategy representing the application of military resources, to theatre commanders, to achieve those objectives.[4] These definitions at once place us in a quandary, for we are unable to say with certainty that it was Carthage herself who set the objectives for Hannibal's War: nor, if she did so, are we able to detail them with any accuracy. If we are to accept Polybius,[5] it was the firmly held belief of the Roman historian Fabius that Hannibal, in total defiance of the wishes of the Carthaginian senate, had launched himself into war with Rome entirely on his own initiative. Indeed, when the terms of the subsequent peace treaty were being negotiated by the defeated Carthaginians, their envoys spared no effort to shift total responsibility for the war on to Hannibal. He had, they declared, 'without order from the senate, crossed both the Alps and the Ebro and, on his own private initiative, had made war not on the Romans only but, before that, on Saguntum'.[6] Polybius, generally considered a reliable historian, appears to reiterate Hannibal's responsibility. He relates that, as soon as the young general was appointed to command, 'it became clear from the measures which he then set in hand that his purpose was to declare war on Rome'.[7]

We are not, of course, in a position to say whether or not Hannibal was, by this behaviour, acting under orders. Livy,[8] a romantic historian who writes of Hannibal's War in vivid, heroic phrases, suggests that this might have been the case. 'From the very first day of his command,' he tells us, 'Hannibal acted as if he had definite instructions to take Italy as his sphere of operations and to make war on Rome': but we should not forget that the Carthaginian senators had a direct opportunity to deny Hannibal and avoid conflict when confronted by the Roman envoys, led by Quintus Fabius Maximus[9] before the outbreak of hostilities. 'We bring you peace and war – take what you will!' he told the senate. They accepted war and vowed to fight it to the end, albeit perhaps dragged unwillingly into the situation, compelled by personal pride and Hannibal's impetuosity.

Nevertheless, if we read Livy's above statement in the context of the definition of grand strategy, then Carthage should have been militarily committed not only to provide the resources he needed for his Italian campaign but, at the same time, to state a clear objective for him to pursue. Livy's words make little sense unless the task allocated to Hannibal, *to take Italy as his sphere of operations and make war on Rome*, formed part of a greater, more coherent whole. Truly, Carthage, throughout the period of Hannibal's War, retained tight control over the allocation of military resources, supplies and reinforcements to her armed forces within her various theatres of war, but she understandably and visibly granted the highest priorities to the defence of both her African base and her increasingly prosperous trading empire in Spain. It is notable that, in 216 BC, the crucial year of the Roman army's calamitous defeat at Cannae, it was Carthage who ordered Hasdrubal, then commanding in Spain, to 'march for Italy at the earliest possible moment'[10] and join forces there with his brother, Hannibal. If Hasdrubal had been successful in doing so, and had arrived in the peninsula amidst the disarray following Cannae, it is more than probable that Rome's Italian alliances would have collapsed and the war would have been won. Carthage, however, was extraordinarily out of touch with events in the field and Hasdrubal, upon receiving these instructions, was constrained to remind them that

> . . . if he did have to leave Spain the whole country would be in Roman hands before he could cross the Ebro. He went on to say that he had no troops and no adequate commander to leave in his place, not to mention the fact that the Roman commanders in Spain were men whom it would be hard to resist even on equal terms. Consequently, if the Carthaginian government were interested in Spain at all, they must send someone with a powerful army to take over from them . . .

As a result of this strongly worded assessment of the situation by Hasdrubal, Himilco was despatched from Carthage with a fully equipped force and an enhanced fleet 'to hold and protect Spain'; but the orders for Hasdrubal to march for Italy were not withdrawn. In other words, it was the clear intention of the Carthaginian senate that Himilco should take over from Hasdrubal.

The Roman military opposition in Spain, astutely led by Gnaeus and Publius Scipio and invariably well informed, were in no doubt as to what was happening. They were quick to recognise the danger. They explained to their troops that, although campaigning in a foreign land, their performance on the battlefield was as important as if the enemy were in Italy, at the very gates of Rome itelf: they called for a supreme effort. They then combined their forces and succeeded in bringing Hasdrubal to battle, near Ibera, on the river Ebro, where, in savage fighting, they inflicted heavy casualties upon him. This outcome, with the consequent disaffection of many Spanish tribes in favour of Rome, rendered it impossible for Hasdrubal to march at once to Italy as he had been instructed. In the event, the uncertain situation in Spain which now developed held him there for a further nine years.

Hasdrubal's battle on the Ebro, and the delay which resulted from it, was one of the decisive moments of Hannibal's War: but the importance of the incident is rather to be found in the apparent determination of the senate to get reinforcements through to Hannibal at this vital moment, despite the risks and obvious difficulties involved. The threat to their homeland so quickly recognised by the Roman commanders in Spain, was, for their part, seen by the Carthaginians as a culminating thrust to bring down an enemy, whose army had already been decimated by Hannibal at Cannae. It is not easy to believe that the planning arrangements which had brought the war to this successful stage, each phase of which, for logistical reasons alone, would have required the authority of the Carthaginian senate, had not already been agreed with them before it had been embarked upon. It was, after all, the senate who ordered Hasdrubal to Italy; the senate who continued to insist upon his departure after relieving him by Himilco; the senate who ultimately must have sanctioned his prolonged stay in Spain; the senate who, in the same year, quizzed Mago, with some dissent, when he arrived from Italy to seek from them, on behalf of his master, additional resources and money;[11] and the senate who, ultimately, after seventeen years of war, recalled Hannibal to North Africa to defend Carthage against Scipio Africanus.

In the face of these facts, there can be little doubt that the Carthaginian senate exercised supreme command of the war, that their purpose was the conquest of Rome and that Hannibal's role, as correctly defined by Livy, was *to take Italy as his sphere of operations and make war on Rome*. Polybius[12] believed otherwise: everything that befell both peoples, he opined,

. . . the Roman and the Carthaginian, originated from one effective cause – one man and one mind – by which I mean Hannibal. It was he who beyond any doubt was responsible for the Italian campaign in Italy and who directed that in Spain, first through the elder of his brothers, Hasdrubal, and later through Mago: these were the generals who killed the two Roman commanders in that country, Publius and Gnaeus Scipio. Besides this he also managed affairs in Sicily, first through Hippocrates and later through Mytonnes, the African. He was also active both in Greece and Illyria, where he succeeded in stirring up trouble and causing alarm to the Romans . . .

It is, however, easier to believe, and the evidence suggests this to have been the case, that Hasdrubal and Hannibal each commanded their own theatres of war under the supreme direction of Carthage; that Hasdrubal assumed responsibility for the conduct of the war in Spain upon the departure of Hannibal for Italy; and that Hannibal commanded the Italian theatre, an area which seemingly included Sicily, at his own behest, and gave him the authority to seek allies in Illyria and Greece. It is thus as a field commander, in a defined theatre of operations, that we need to consider Hannibal's generalship.

Hannibal was brought up, from an early age, in a war environment. His father, Hamilcar Barca, had led the Carthaginian army in the First Punic War and, in the estimation of Polybius, who wrote from the unbiased viewpoint of a Greek national, he had displayed himself as the greatest general on either side of the conflict, both in daring and in genius. After the conclusion of the war, Hamilcar played a prominent role in the reconstruction of Carthaginian fortunes by leading an expeditionary force to Spain, 'where he proceeded to establish the power of Carthage over the peoples of Iberia'. It is said, traditionally, that, whilst Hamilcar was preparing a sacrifice for a successful outcome of the enterprise upon which he was embarking, he was approached by young Hannibal, at that

Hamilcar punishing the insurgent mercenaries. (The Mansell Collection)

time only nine years of age, who asked to be allowed to accompany him. Hamilcar then led the boy to the altar and made him solemnly swear, 'with his hand on the victim', that as soon as he was old enough, 'he would be the enemy of Rome'. This incident, if it ever happened, is sometimes said to have been one of the origins of the Second Punic War.

Hamilcar Barca on a coin from New Carthage. (© British Museum)

Hamilcar worked unsparingly and successfully at expanding Carthaginian influence and prosperity in their new-found territory until, in 229 BC, he lost his life in a war against one of the more powerful and recalcitrant Spanish tribes. He was succeeded by his son-in-law, Hasdrubal, who for a period of some eight years distinguished himself by his diplomatic and administrative skills, both of which he employed to forward the interests of the province, in preference to the exercise of military force. His governance was abruptly terminated in 221 BC, when he was assassinated in a revenge killing. He had, however, some years earlier, written to the senate requesting the presence of Hannibal with the troops in Spain, although the latter was still 'little more than a boy'. The request was grudgingly conceded by the senate, many of whose senior members saw it, probably very accurately, as a move to ensure the succession of yet another member of the Barca faction to a position of power. Thus it happened that Hannibal had already served three years under Hasdrubal's leadership before himself being appointed, at the age of twenty-five, to Carthage's Spanish Command.

Hannibal's early years of service in Spain were to prove invaluable in preparing him for the great campaign which lay ahead. They provided his first taste of command and gave him the opportunity of serving alongside the many mercenary soldiers, of diverse origins, from amongst whom Carthage enlisted her field army: infantry from Liguria, North Africa and Spain; shot-slingers from the Balearics; and light cavalrymen from Numidia and Libya, being some amongst others. He learnt to communicate with them, to understand their motivation and to appreciate their particular skills and military qualities. It was at this time also, in the colonial wars which accompanied the territorial expansion of Carthage in south-west Spain, that Hannibal developed the tactical originality he was later to display so incisively in battle on the shores of Lake Trasimene; during his break-out from the trap set for him by Fabius at Mount Callicula; and at Tarentum, when, under the nose of the Romans, he extracted the Tarentine fleet from the Inner Harbour by transporting it overland to the high seas, where it was used to blockade the already besieged Roman citadel.

Vegetius, the author of the ancient military training text book *Epitoma rei militaris*,[12] when considering Hannibal's military education, suggests that, just as Carthage employed a Spartan general, Xanthippus, to reform and successfully lead their army against the Romans in 256 BC, so did Hannibal obtain the services of a Spartan tactician when he was about to invade Italy, using him, perhaps, in the nature of a chief of staff. Be that as it may, his early years campaigning in Spain were well spent. Colonial wars, as the British discovered in their days of empire, many centuries later, have always proved good training grounds for young generals. By their very nature, they present wide-based

An example of the terrain of the eastern Pyrenees, near Prats de Mollo, crossed by Hannibal as he marched from Spain into Gaul. (Roger Day)

intricate logistical problems and the tactical situations they provide in the field almost invariably demand unorthodox solutions.

It was thus with a background of colonial experience that Hannibal entered upon his Italian adventure, to engage an enemy rigidly educated in conventional warfare and generally unprepared for the military disaster now about to engulf his homeland. Equally, it might be said that Spain was not as prepared for Hannibal's departure as some ancient historians suggest, despite the Carthaginian's carefully planned cross-posting of tribal contingents to and from North Africa, before he set forth, to ensure the loyalty of the armies he left behind.[13] Many tribes in south-east Spain had been angered by Hannibal's progress through their territories to the Pyrenees, ripples of tribal unrest following the sack of Saguntum continued to be experienced west of the Ebro and there was the worrying expectation of the imminent arrival of a Roman army in aid of the Saguntines. Hannibal's plan clearly anticipated more stability than this: he had, after all, before entering into Gaul, returned some 10,000 troops to Spain with the hope that, as a consequence, they would be 'well disposed' towards him and that 'if he were ever in need of reinforcements they would all enthusiastically respond'. Events were to show that he would have done better to take them with him, despite the help he was soon to receive from his Celtic allies in Cisalpine Gaul and, later, from the peoples of southern Italy.

*Opposite*: Hannibal swearing eternal enmity to Rome. (From a painting by Jacopo Amigoni. Bridgeman Art Library, AGN 035452)

The continuing lack of strength of Hannibal's army, the diminution of its quality by the recruitment of uncertain tribal replacements and the manpower drain imposed upon it by the necessity to garrison importantly sited cities which had ceded to him, produced a series of other problems. In the five years onwards from 218 BC, Hannibal is recorded by Livy as having besieged thirteen towns and cities in Italy, of which he carried not one by direct assault: four, he reduced by siege; at six, he was rebuffed; and in three cases, one being Tarentum, where he gained entry by subterfuge, they surrendered to him. In some other instances, he veered away without committing himself to attack.

Occasionally we hear that this apparently weak operational performance originated from Hannibal's lack of siege equipment, which he appears to have left behind with his brother, Hasdrubal, along with his heavy baggage, when the two parted company at the Pyrenees. This is an unjustified assumption, for Hannibal could easily have manufactured siege engines, catapults and similar machines during the long hours spent in winter camps. It is more probable that Hannibal did not wish to possess equipment of this nature, since it would have reduced his speed and mobility on the march, an asset which he valued greatly. His lack of success in laying siege to cities, in particular the seaports which would have been of such benefit to him had he been able to gain the use of one of their harbours, was due to his lack of numbers. An army besieging a city necessarily remains in one place for a long time: it therefore becomes vulnerable to attack for its own part and, unless it possesses sufficient numbers, can become trapped. Hannibal did not intend to allow this to happen, as he illustrated, with no great result, in the year 214 BC, when he descended, darting like a bluebottle, first upon Cumae, then briefly upon Puteoli, before returning to demonstrate, rather ineffectively, before the gates of Naples. He then passed onwards to Nola, before turning southwards for no more than a glance at Tarentum.

In no place, during these sorties, did he achieve any marked operational success: rather does he convey the impression of a commander with a touch of desperation in his actions. The heroic march with which he had signalled his arrival in Italy, with victories at Ticinus, Trebbia, Trasimene and Cannae, had now been reduced, by Rome's tight control of her coastline, to a guerrilla campaign, south of the Volturnus.

It was at this moment that Hannibal wrote to the senate in Carthage, despite his many problems, telling them that the time had come 'to win back Sicily as the national honour demanded'. We have already noted the strategic importance of this island, centrally situated in the Mediterranean, at a crossroads of wind and tide and but a stone's throw from the Italian mainland. More than 2,000 years later, it was to be the objective of yet another army, also based near Carthage and contemplating the invasion of Italy and the capture of Rome. Its war planners, as had those of ancient Carthage, regarded 'the taking of Sicily as an indispensable preliminary' to these events.[14] Hannibal, with his room for manoeuvre on the Italian mainland increasingly restricted by his enemy, and with the hope of reinforcements from Spain no longer immediately realistic, now pinned his hopes on Sicily and the opening of a new maritime route to a southern seaport, the opening of which might resolve his problems. His twin immediate objectives thus became the conquest of Sicily and the capture of Tarentum, a seaport equally acceptable to shipping from Greece should Philip of Macedonia be willing to ally himself with Carthage. To this end, he now turned towards Tarentum and appointed two 'agents', Hippocrates and Epycides, as his military representatives in Sicily.

At almost every step of his contest with Rome for Tarentum, the Roman generals displayed better anticipation and planning than the Carthaginian, probably as a result of superior military intelligence. Upon Hannibal's first approach, Valerius, the district commander with responsibility for the fleet at nearby Brundisium, had swiftly despatched Marcus Livius to organise the defence of the town. Later, Hannibal, having penetrated Tarentum's defences by subterfuge, failed to capture the citadel at his first strike. Livius had been momentarily in his hands but slipped away by rowing boat to command the citadel which covered the inner harbour. Then, having captured the town and laid siege to the citadel, which was thinly garrisoned and had sparse resources, he allowed it to be reinforced by a Roman contingent from nearby Metapontum. Finally, when the siege had reduced the citadel to near starvation, a convoy of twenty ships, carrying grain from Etruria in northern Italy, was allowed to slip into Tarentum harbour, despite the presence of the Tarentine fleet.

In view of the importance of Tarentum to the Carthaginian cause, these failures in command were crucial. They were caused partly by bad luck but mainly by Hannibal's determination not to appear to abandon his allies, nor his garrisons in their cities, in the Volturnus area of northern Campania and Apulia. He almost invariably wintered amongst them but he was, nevertheless, constantly under pressure to do more for them. For this reason, his attention was being deflected from the main tasks which confronted him. This became particularly clear in the incident involving Muttines of Hippacra, whom he had sent to Sicily as his representative to replace Hippocrates, the latter having perished, with Himilco, in the Syracusan plague.

Muttines, as we have already witnessed, quickly distinguished himself in the field as a courageous, successful and popular commander, unlike Hanno, whom he found in command, based at Agrigentum, who was generally disliked. Livy,[15] in his usual lively style, has described the outcome of the quarrel which ensued. It was upon Muttines and his Numidians that all hopes for victory in Sicily were centred:

> Muttines was out on raids all over Sicily; he was plundering Rome's allies at will; neither force nor stratagem could cut him off from Agrigentum and nothing could stop him from coming out on foray whenever he wished to do so. His continued success had for some time been casting a shadow on Hanno's reputation as a commander-in-chief, and it ended in producing jealousy and dislike, so that Hanno no longer took pleasure even in a victory because it was Muttines who won it. In the end he deprived Muttines of his cavalry command and transferred it to his son, in the belief that the loss of the command would involve the loss of his influence with the Numidians. The result was far otherwise . . .

The fate of the army, indeed the fate of the Carthaginian nation, was to depend upon the outcome of these personal animosities. Hannibal, at this time, was engaged in a battle of no particular significance at Salapia, in mid-Apulia. He would have been better employed in resolving this calamitous dispute which left Muttines feeling not only rankled by such blatantly unfair treatment, but deeply insulted. As a consequence, the African had sent a secret message to the nearby Roman commander Laevinus proposing a plan which would put Agrigentum into his hands. The offer was accepted and the plan agreed: and, when Muttines' Numidians opened the gates after having killed the sentries or caused them to flee, a Roman contingent entered the town and advanced upon the forum. Hanno heard the noise and confusion created by these events and imagined it to be 'nothing more serious than yet another mutiny of the Numidians'. He went down to the centre of the town to see what was happening and found it in the hands of enemy soldiery. He turned at once and, Livy narrates, taking Epicydes with him, 'they were lucky enough to find a small vessel in which they crossed to Africa, *abandoning Sicily . . .*'.

The last two words of Livy's quotation in the above paragraph are placed in italics because of their importance and the tone of finality with which they are written: from this year forward (210 BC), despite the anticipation of Hasdrubal's arrival from Spain, there was little to provide Hannibal with any hope of victory.

How, then, should we assess the performance of this obviously charismatic commander? Hannibal was a remarkable leader of men; he maintained the war with Rome in Italy, in Polybius' words, for more than sixteen continuous years, 'without once releasing his army from service in the field but keeping the vast numbers under control without any sign of disaffection towards himself or towards each other'. He is also widely and rightly recognised as a great tactician. Ancient armies were organised and trained to test each other in the open field. A battle, as a generality, did not become possible until the enemy had left his camp, and placed himself in country practicable for a set-piece confrontation. Hannibal avoided this custom whenever possible, favouring unorthodox tactics such as the ambush he set for Flaminius on the shores of Lake Trasimene. The manner in which his centre deliberately collapsed at Cannae, falling back and luring the Roman heavy infantry into a trap sprung by his flanking infantry, is another example of his careful tactical planning. In part, it was this unpredictable aspect of his field tactics, a legacy of his colonial training, which persuaded Fabius to adopt a strategy of indirect approach.

It was in strategy, however, that Hannibal was at his weakest: during the long years of his war he made three fundamental errors, leaving aside the question of whether he was correct to evade contact with the elder Scipio on the Rhône. Any single one could be said to have lost Carthage the Second Punic War:

- His first error was to cross the Ebro before his Spanish base had been properly secured. When in Italy, he was hoping to receive early reinforcements from Spain but these were denied him due to the vigorous fighting which erupted there after his departure from it.

- In Italy, he achieved a series of victories, the last of which, at Cannae, was startling in its scale. It could, nevertheless, be argued that despite, its remarkable outcome, it contained his second vital error, namely, that he failed to maintain his offensive momentum after the battle. He should have pursued the remnants of the Roman army to the shelter they sought in Venusia and Canusium and not allowed them time for reorganisation. Had he done this, he might still have brought about the collapse of Rome visualised by Maharbal. He chose, rather, to delay and allow his men the free run of the battlefield so that they might collect the 'enormous quantity' of booty scattered upon it.[16]

- He should have changed his command structure when the fighting spread to Sicily, for the complexion of the war had then altered and possession of the island held far greater strategic importance for Carthage than the retention of a steadily decreasing, tenuous and hotly contested foothold in southern Italy. His failure to take direct command in Sicily permitted the disastrous quarrel with Muttines which caused Hanno to abandon the island.

But the question remains, and the answer can only be surmised, as to how much Carthage itself was responsible for its own military misfortunes. By the year 203 BC, Hannibal had been driven into the toe of Italy, dependent still upon his Bruttian allies, many of whom had long since begun to question their wisdom in continuing to support him. At the same time, Sicily was becoming an armed base, preparatory for the war in North Africa, where Roman troops were assembling for a final assault on Carthage. As the situation deteriorated, the senate determined to recall Hannibal. Hannibal, a soldier by now of considerable experience, can have entertained few doubts about the fragility of his situation. Indeed, Livy records that he had already foreseen his own recall: his ships were in readiness and his plans for departure were prepared. His army had been pruned of unfit soldiers, he earmarked these for local garrison duty, and those whose loyalty was in doubt had been set aside. Appian[17] relates that, additionally and before setting sail, he slaughtered some 4,000 horses and a large number of pack animals, probably because of limited shipping space.

This very apparent last-minute recall for Hannibal, and the seeming facility with which he found the ships for his return, for the area had very obviously become a hotbed of military and naval activity, poses a number of questions we can do little more than ponder. Livy suggests a political answer for the delayed summons to return and tells a story[18] of how, when the emissaries arrived to call him home, 'Hannibal groaned and gnashed his teeth and could hardly refrain from tears'; and, when they had delivered their message, he is said to have exclaimed, in frustrated anger, that for years his country had denied him resources in order to drive him ignominiously home and he blamed the Carthaginians for his defeat. It could equally have been that these resources were denied to him by his own lack of vision.

There can be no doubt that Hannibal's qualities have been highly rated. Napoleon Bonaparte compared his talents with the skilled generalship of Frederick the Great and of Alexander. Dodge, the American military historian, considered that 'as a soldier he stood alone and unequalled'. Montgomery of Alamein saw him as a poor strategist but a born leader and a man of courage whose 'tactical genius at Cannae can compare with the conduct of any battle in the history of warfare'. Polybius wrote with admiration of his 'generalship, courage and power in the field' and commented particularly upon his ability to persuade men, of various races and with little in common, 'to give ear to a single word of command and yield obedience to a single will'. Others, of which the eminent historian Mommsen is one, have eulogised that he was 'a brilliant individualist', 'a military genius of heroic status' and have seen him as 'the greatest of soldiers'.

Are these adjectives truly justified? Arnold Toynbee perhaps reached a more balanced judgement when he wrote that, although the Romans produced no hero of Hannibal's status, their corporate heroism and his individual heroism were worthily matched. He might have added that, once the surprise of Hannibal's initial invasion had been absorbed, and they had learnt the tactical lessons in which the Carthaginian army were so well rehearsed, the Roman performance improved until, in almost every aspect, it more than equalled anything he could produce. It is easy to accept Hannibal as a man of courage and a great commander of men but it should be tempered with the knowledge that his three decisive victories, on the Trebbia, at Lake Trasimene and at Cannae, were all gained over generals schooled in the thought of inflexible, massed infantry warfare. Once Rome found his measure, things were never the same again.

There is one final comment to be made. As I have said in my introductory chapter, it is a principle of war that, in every military operation, it is essential to select carefully and define the grand objective. Moreover, whatever the ultimate aim, each phase of the campaign and each individual operation must be directed towards the achievement of the final result, albeit with a more limited purpose of its own. But, in the case of Hannibal's War, the decisive intermediate steps, *post-Cannae*, so necessary for a coherent plan, are sadly missing. Hannibal's failure to concentrate his effort and resources on the seizure of Sicily, when his operation in southern Italy began to unravel, is incomprehensible.

It was not simply Hannibal's genius as a leader of men and as an original tactician which kept the war in Italy alive for so long. Fabian's strategy of isolation and containment, whilst the war was being fought on battlefields more advantageous to Rome, also had much to do with it. If Hannibal, wrote Polybius,[19] had begun his bid for power

. . . with the other parts of the world and finished with the Romans none of his plans would have failed to succeed. But, as it was, commencing with those he should have left to the last, his career began and finished in this field.

# EPILOGUE

The treaty signed in Rome was broken before the ink was barely dry. Indeed, when the Carthaginian envoys, accompanied by a Roman delegation, returned to North Africa to witness the countersigning of the document by Scipio and the senate in Carthage, they found their two peoples again at war.

In their absence, a disaster had occurred to a Roman supply convoy sailing from Sicily with 200 transports and escorted by 30 warships. It had encountered a storm and been blown off course, some vessels to the island of Aegimurus, which dominated the entrance to the Bay of Carthage, whilst others had found shelter at Aquae Calidae, lying eastward across the bay and directly opposite the city itself. The convoy, without doubt, had penetrated Carthaginian territorial waters and Livy, himself a Roman, relates that all the transports had been abandoned by their crews. The affair was discussed at an angry meeting of the Carthaginian senate, at which it was decided, and it must be remembered that they were not yet aware of the signing of the treaty in Rome, that Hasdrubal Gisgo should take fifty ships and sail first to Aegimurus and then along the coastline of the bay to collect such shipping as he might find. The salvaged vessels, with a great quantity of stores, were then towed stern-first to Carthage, where they were retained as captured material.

Scipio was irate at this turn of events. Fate had not only robbed him of much-needed supplies and necessities destined for his own army but had presented them to his enemy, thus making good many of the shortages his operations had inflicted upon them. He accused the Carthaginians of breaking the truce he had already agreed with them. He sent three envoys to remonstrate with them. They addressed both the senate and a popular meeting, at which, in uncompromising terms, they reminded the people how their representatives, but recently, had abased themselves at the feet of Scipio and his council to plead for peace. Now, they remarked, doubtless encouraged by the approaching return of Hannibal, they had rediscovered their courage.

These were hardly the words to restore passive relations. A more diplomatic approach might have resulted in a different outcome. The Carthaginian senators were enraged at the manner in which they had been addressed. The majority saw no reason why they should surrender the windfall of ships and supplies which the gods had bestowed upon them. Moreover, treaty obligations nothwithstanding, it was generally held that this event, with Hannibal's imminent return from Sicily, now opened the way for the restoration of their fortunes. An influential group was prepared to go further than mere aspiration. They plotted to bring about an instant return to war by arranging the destruction of the envoys on their way home, together with the Roman quinquireme in which they were travelling. In the event, the ship was severely damaged and the envoys escaped but the effect was as they had planned it. The Romans, probably justifiably, considered they had been treacherously attacked and the war was resumed. Scipio, to demonstrate his displeasure, 'no longer accepted the submission of those cities which offered to surrender, but took each place by storm and sold the inhabitants into slavery'.

At this juncture Hannibal returned home. He disembarked with his army at Hadrumetum, some 100 miles south of Carthage, but his strike power was now considerably reduced by the defection of Masinissa to the Roman cause, with the powerful wing of Numidian cavalry which had performed so effectively in the past for the Carthaginians. Recognising the vital contribution which this contingent of horse would provide to his enemy, Hannibal timed his move in an unsuccessful attempt to intercept Scipio as he marched up the Mejerda valley, before he linked with his cavalry support. Today, at the heart of the Mejerda valley, lies Medjez el Bab, attacked in 1942 by a British infantry brigade during the war in the Western Desert and recognised by both contestants as strategically vital. It was here that Field Marshal Kesselring interestingly reminded the commander of the occupying German forces that 'he who holds Mejerda, holds Carthage'.

As the forces of the two empires came together at Zama, Hannibal at once recognised the serious significance of his failure to bring Scipio to battle before the arrival of Masinissa. He sought a parley and both men agreed to meet. Two days later, the two commanders rode out from the ranks of their armies, each accompanied by an interpreter and escorted by a dozen horsemen. The latter, when they reached the prepared meeting place, reined back in order that their masters might speak alone. No record was kept of this fascinating encounter, although both Polybius and Livy provide us with an idea of what might have been said; but, if it were an attempt to patch up a peace, it failed. The two generals made their farewells and parted, to return to their individual lines and prepare for the battle to come.

The battle at Zama ended as Hannibal had feared. He had sought to compensate for his deficiency in cavalry by releasing his eighty elephants against the Roman infantry and breaking their formation, but Scipio was well prepared for this tactic; the Romans did not, in any event, value the use of elephants as a weapon of war, and the animals were quickly mastered. Hannibal was defeated, his army was annihilated, and he was compelled to flee, not drawing rein, according to Polybius, until he had again reached Hadrumetum, whence he returned to Carthage.

Upon the conclusion of the war, Hannibal, despite being publicly accused of having misconducted it, was still regarded in Carthage as a person of high influence. He was allowed to retain his military command and was additionally appointed civil magistrate, in which capacity he was required to undertake administrative and constitutional changes to end the existing oligarchic system of government. Inevitably, these reforms created enemies for him in high places and he was denounced to the Romans, in a charge which may or may not have been fictitious, of inciting Antiochus III of Syria to take up arms against them. His surrender was demanded by the Roman Senate and, in 195 BC, he fled to the court of Antiochus. Five years later, when the latter was defeated by Rome in a land battle at Magnesia, the surrender of Hannibal once again featured amongst the terms demanded of the Syrians by Scipio, and once again he escaped, on this occasion to enter the military service of Prusias of Bythnia, at that time engaged in war with a Roman ally, Eumenes II of Pergamum.

In an effort to dissuade Prusias from this campaign, the Romans despatched an envoy, Flaminius, to him, to express their displeasure at the war and their concern that the king should have given shelter to their arch-enemy, Hannibal. The detail of what happened next is obscure but Livy leaves no doubt that, after his first conference with Flaminius, Prusias posted a military guard over Hannibal's house. Plainly, the matter of Hannibal's presence had been a prime subject for discussion when the two men met, and the placing of Hannibal under house arrest could only have been done either because it was demanded by Flaminius or because the deed was initiated by Prusias to ingratiate himself with Rome. Livy saw the action in darker tones as the deliberate betrayal of Hannibal by his host, which would have ended, at worst, with his assassination or at best with his seizure and surrender to the Romans.

Hannibal himself had little doubt as to what was taking place and little faith in the loyalty of kings. He had constructed his house with seven exits to it, some of them cunningly concealed, so that, in the event of something of this nature happening, he would always have a means of escape: but, wrote Livy, 'the overwhelming power of kings leaves nothing undiscovered when they wish to

Site excavations at Carthage have revealed remains of the ancient city which, in 146 BC, was deliberately buried by Rome, with the covering earth symbolically strewn with salt. A century later a new city was built upon its site by Julius Caesar. The photograph shows the remains of the Roman forum. (Ian Atkinson)

have it found out'. When Hannibal learnt of the presence of soldiers in his vestibule, he tried to escape by a side door but soon discovered that every exit was guarded. Again, he had foreseen such a happening and now called for a draft of poison, set aside for such an event. Let us, he said, as he drained the cup,

> . . . free the Roman people from their long standing anxiety, seeing that they find it tedious to wait for an old man's death [he was sixty-two years of age]. It is no magnificent or memorable victory that Flaminius will win over a man unarmed and betrayed. This day will surely prove how far the moral standards of the Romans have changed. The fathers of these Romans sent a warning to king Pyrrhus, bidding him beware of poison – and he was an enemy in arms, with an army in Italy: these Romans themselves have sent an envoy of consular rank to suggest to Prusias the crime of murdering his guest.

And so the life of Hannibal, the scourge of Rome, came to its end. It was, however, not the end of the power struggle between the two peoples. War erupted again in 149 BC and ended three years later, again with the defeat of the Carthaginians, whose hated capital city the Romans on this occasion levelled to the ground. They buried it deep in sand and scattered salt upon the site so that nothing should ever grow again where it had stood.

The plough is driven over the site of Carthage. (The Mansell Collection)

# HANNIBAL'S MARCH FROM THE RHÔNE

Hannibal's march from the Rhône may broadly be pegged by three identifying topographical features: his Rhône crossing place; the river valley he followed from the Rhône; and the high pass through which he emerged into Cisalpine Gaul. There are, in the heart of the Alps, numerous other features less easily identifiable and, in order not to cloud the discussion unnecessarily, I have chosen to ignore these. Each step of Hannibal's way has been hugely debated by historians down the ages and such detail has little relevance in the context of this book. I have, however, extracted from the works of twenty-four eminent historians their favoured choice for the three features I have mentioned above. The names of many of these historians are listed in my Bibliography. I summarise their choices below, the totals shown against each feature represents the numbers opting for it (the discrepancy in totals is due to the fact that not every historian made a choice for every feature):

**1. Rhône Crossing:**

| | |
|---|---|
| Roquemaure | 13 |
| Tarascon | 4 |
| Fourque | 2 |
| Pont l'Esprit | 2 |
| Total: | 21 |

**2. River Valley from Rhône**

| | |
|---|---|
| Isère | 17 |
| Aygues | 1 |
| Sorgues | 2 |
| Durance | 2 |
| Total: | 22 |

**3. Alpine Pass**

| | |
|---|---|
| Mont Cenis | 6 |
| Mont Genevre | 6 |
| Little St Bernard | 4 |
| Col du Clapier | 5 |
| Col de la Traversette | 3 |
| Total: | 24 |

The selections of the emperor Napoleon Bonaparte, who crossed the Alps prior to the battle of Marengo and discussed the Hannibal route in his St Helena *Memoirs*, were Roquemaure, the Isère and Mont Cenis.

# HANNIBAL'S WAR ELEPHANTS

The elephant has qualities rarely apparent even in man, namely honesty, good sense, justice and also respect for the stars, sun and moon.

Pliny[1]

Broadly, there are two species of elephant, Asian and African, and both are fast diminishing in number. Little more than two thousand years ago the habitat of the Asian elephant extended as far west as Iran and Iraq. Currently, its presence is restricted to isolated and largely disappearing colonies in such places as Burma, Malaya, southern China, some islands of the East Indies and in the forest areas of Mysore in southern India. Similarly, there were once many species of the African bush elephant, of which the majority had died out by about 1500 BC. This animal is now only to be found in sub-Saharan Africa. There is a historical debate, but not one that is always readily accepted by naturalists, that a smaller, North African species also existed until recent times. Sylvia Sykes, for example, in her *Natural History of the African Elephant*,[2] states firmly that, whereas the majority of elephants living in certain parts of Nigeria, were smaller and possessed characteristics which distinguished them from the typical *africana* herds resident elsewhere, their physical and temperamental differences were no greater than those between two neighbouring human tribes. The Department of Zoology at the Natural History Museum has remarked to the author that the general lack of material and skeletal record of the African bush elephant has made it difficult to comment constructively about connections between it and other sub-species.

Pliny the Elder (AD 23–79) is one of those who, writing at an early time, initiated the discussion: he hinted in his *Natural History*[3] that this smaller race was noted in AD 42 by Suetonius Paulinus, when the latter's campaign against some Mauretanian rebels carried him across the Atlas Mountains to the edge of the Sahara, where 'the Canarii live in the neighbouring forests, which are full of every type of elephant and snake'. Polybius (200–118 BC), a man of great intelligence and a respected contemporary author, had no doubt of the inferior size and spirit of the African elephant compared with the Indian. In words that convey a feel of personal experience he wrote[4] that the African animal

cannot stand the smell and trumpeting of the Indian elephants; moreover, so it seems to me, they are taken aback by their great size and strength, so that they turn tail before getting to close quarters.

In our own times, Sir William Gowers[5] has provided a persuasive paper which argues the existence of a smaller African animal (*Loxodonta cyclotis*) still to be found, albeit increasingly beleaguered, in detached, widely dispersed areas of northern Africa, but predominantly in the forests of Senegal, Sierra Leone and, importantly, the Belgian Congo, in the north-east corner of which an elephant training establishment existed for many years where the animals were domesticated and trained for transport and other work. Today, the habitat of these creatures is irregularly distributed. Gowers, writing in 1948, confirmed that he personally had sighted small herds of them in Uganda and was of the opinion that they were still to be discovered across a wide area of northern Africa, from the Atlantic coast to the Nile valley and possibly beyond.

In ancient times, the hinterland of the Red Sea coast provided a fertile breeding ground for elephants, their numbers being particularly prolific in the then wooded valley of the Baraka river. Indeed, a base for the trapping and training of war elephants, with a port for their subsequent transhipment, was established under Ptolemy II at nearby Ptolemais, close to the present-day town of Aqiq, south of Suakim. Today, elephants are rarely seen so far east, if at all. In 1868 the presence of a last remaining few, an old female and four males, was recorded on the adjoining Eritrean plateau, south of Asmara, by a zoologist accompanying Napier's expedition to Magdala. He appears to have shot them in the interests of science, to take their measurements.

The fact that Hannibal employed war-elephants during the prosecution of his sixteen-year campaign against Rome is established beyond doubt and whether they were of Asian, North African or sub-Saharan origin may at first sight appear to be a matter solely of academic interest. From a military viewpoint, however, the comparative size and strength of the animals would have been something of importance. The modern-day sub-Saharan African elephant, the largest living land animal, can weigh up to 8 tons and, measured to the shoulder, stands between 9 to 11½ feet, on average some 2 feet taller than the so-called Forest variety. Sykes[6] places the maximium recorded height of an African bull elephant as 13 feet 2 inches. The dimensions of the Indian elephant, on the other hand, fall between these two categories, with an average weight of 6 tons. Without taking sides in the debate about the existence or otherwise of a smaller northern species of African elephant, it is difficult to deny the recorded conviction of contemporary historians that the African elephant was smaller than the Indian. It is, of course, always conceivable that the size variation of the two African species was a matter of breeding, influenced by the quality of the respective feeding areas they enjoyed. There would also have been a natural military desire to select the largest and most formidable looking animals for battlefield duties.

A portrayal of the species of war-elephant employed by Hannibal is to be found on the reverse side of the issue of Carthaginian coins minted *c.* 220 BC, that is to say, only two years before the young general set forth on his historic march across the High Alps to Italy. It depicts an animal which by the concave shape of its back, the large size of its ear, the flatness of its forehead and its

*Above*: the African elephant. *Below*: the Indian elephant. (Author)

Bronze coin from the Chiana valley, *c.* 217 BC. (© British Museum)

roughened, heavily ringed trunk, all suggest that an African elephant, with the characteristics we recognise today, is meant to be represented here. On that basis, and assuming that the northern variety was similarly identifiable, it may be argued that Hannibal, in the main, employed African elephants. It would certainly have been administratively sensible for him to have done so since, as we have seen, a nearby and ready source of supply existed for Carthage at that time.

On the other hand, Pliny the Elder records from Cato's *Annals* (viii, 11) that 'the bravest animal to fight in the Carthaginian army was called *Surus*, the Syrian'. The Egyptians, in their wars with the Syrians throughout the previous hundred years or so, are known to have acquired numerous Indian war-elephants, either by purchase or captured in battle. They are also known to have been close allies of the Carthaginians at that time: it is thus quite probable that the Egyptians occasionally provided them with numbers of this larger animal. In this respect, the reverse side of an Etrurian coin dated 217 BC and attributed to the valley of the Chiana, in Umbria, depicts an elephant with the physical characteristics of the Indian species, with its lowered head, small ears, and convexly bowed back. It cannot be purely coincidental that, in that same year,

Hannibal rode an elephant through the marshes of Etruria to Arretium, and there defeated a Roman army under Flaminius. This animal is speculated to have been the sole survivor of his crossing of the Alps. It is thus feasible that the animal shown upon the coin was Hannibal's personal war-elephant, perhaps especially selected for his use because of its larger size and fighting qualities?

The driver illustrated on the reverse of the Carthaginian coin (220 BC) appears by his headgear to be African. Polybius,[7] on the other hand, refers to the *mahouts* (drivers) of the Carthaginian elephants as *indoi*, a name probably carried forward from the Indian campaign conducted by Alexander the Great against Porus in 326 BC. Since that date, Indian drivers and trainers were acknowledged as the experts and, indeed, were employed by the Pharaohs, even when using African animals. It is conceivable that the Carthaginians employed Africans for this purpose.

The number of war-elephants fielded by any of the protagonists would have been limited by simple logistics. Elephants are wasteful, heavy eaters and destroy or discard as much vegetation as they consume. In 1944, when the Indian battalion with which I was then serving emerged into the Myittha valley, after a lengthy march through the Chin Hills of Burma's western frontier, we intercepted and took possession of a valuable haul of twenty elephants, together with their *mahouts*, belonging to the Irrawaddy Steamship Company. They were on their way to assist the retreating Japanese with their transport problems. During their stay with us, and before being returned to Kalewa to assist with timber felling for the construction of assault craft to be used in the coming crossing of the Chindwin river, they were picketed around our battalion position. At night time, with their fore legs shackled by chains, they were allowed to forage in the jungle for fodder.

An outstanding memory of that experience was that sleep proved difficult for us all as the animals, pushing their way through the undergrowth, snorted and rumbled, rattled their chains, uprooted young trees and tore down branches in a quest for fodder to satisfy their vast appetites, for they are voracious eaters. Grown animals may consume between 250 to 350 kilograms (550 to 770 lb) of solid food each day. As may be imagined, they take a considerable time in locating the quantities they require, and this creates a logistical factor which has to be taken into account when employing them, whether as beasts of burden or, as one may imagine, as war-elephants. Only rarely are they suitable as baggage animals, for the load they can carry is small in proportion to their size and appetite. Similarly, unlike mules or other pack-animals, their bulk renders it difficult for them to go where other pack-animals can go. Hannibal discovered this to his laborious cost, when he reached the summit of the Alps before descending into Italy:[8]

> . . . in one day he had made a track wide enough to take the mule train and the horses; he at once took these across, pitched camp below the snow line and sent the animals out in search of pasture. Then he took the Numidians and set them in relays to the work of building up the path. After three days of

Elephant-motivated production line at work as logs are pulled or pushed from timber grounds to the wood yard. The first stage in the Chindwin production line. (Imperial War Museum, SE 3198)

this toilsome effort he succeeded in getting his elephants across, but the animals were in a miserable condition from hunger.

In general terms, the Roman army does not appear to have been attracted to the idea of using elephants in battle. Pliny[9] records that they made their appearance in Italy, never before having been seen in Europe, during the war with Pyrrhus in 280 BC. Pyrrhus had brought with him an army of 22,000 infantry, 3,000 horse and 20 elephants, strange and frightening beasts bearing armed men in castles on their backs. He largely employed them on the flanks of his army as protection against cavalry attack. The Roman soldiery, perhaps in a derogatory manner, nicknamed them 'Lucanian Cows', after the place where they first encountered them. There is some suggestion that the introduction of these animals to the battlefield was considered unsportsmanlike by the Roman military, rather as senior cavalry officers during the First World War initially disapproved of the introduction of the tank. Roman feelings towards elephants, in that sense, is revealed by their treatment of the animals captured by Lucilius Metellus from the Carthaginians in Sicily in 252 BC. The consul shipped the beasts from the island, across the Straits of Messina to the mainland, on rafts constructed from a layer of planks resting on rows of wine jars lashed together. The animals were then employed in gladiatorial contests and killed for entertainment in the Circus, because the citizens of Rome 'were at a loss to know what to do with them'.

Pliny the Elder recognised the fundamental vulnerability of the elephant as a weapon of war. He did not have to seek far for his evidence for, in 250 BC, during the First Punic War, the Carthaginians under Hasdrubal had suffered severe casualties at Palermo, and lost sixty of their war-elephants, when the latter became confused in the Roman earthworks and turned in panic upon their own men. This sort of behaviour was a dangerous battlefield weakness quickly discerned by both Marcus Claudius Marcellus and Scipio Africanus. Elephants, Pliny[10] wrote

> . . . once tamed, are used in war and carry *howdahs* full of armed soldiers on their backs. In the East they make a major contribution to warfare, scattering battle-lines and trampling down armed men. Yet these beasts are terrified by the slightest shrill sound made by a pig. When wounded and frightened they always yield ground and cause no less destruction to their own side.

Livy,[11] in his detail of the battle of the Metaurus in 207 BC, at which Hasdrubal Barca was killed, describes in vivid terms the brutal remedy employed to regain control when the terrified animals reversed upon their own troops in this manner. It resulted, he tells us, in more elephants being killed by their own riders than by the enemy, for the *mahouts*

> . . . used to carry a mallet and a carpenter's chisel and when one of the creatures began to run amuck and attack its own people, the keeper would put the chisel between its ears at the junction between head and neck and drive it in . . . It was the quickest way to kill an animal of such a size once it was out of control; and it was Hasdrubal who first introduced it.

The war-elephant was used tactically in a variety of ways. We have already seen how Pyrrhus employed them on the flanks of his army in order to discourage cavalry attack. At Raphia in 217 BC, during the Fourth Syrian War, Antiochus III of Syria brought an army of 62,000 infantry, 6,000 horse and 102 Indian elephants into battle against Ptolemy IV of Egypt, who confronted them with some 50,000 infantry, 5,000 horse and 73 African forest elephants. Ptolemy's elephants were terrified by the smell, the trumpeting, and the greater size of the Indian animals, against whom they could not compete when it came to close combat. Polybius[12] describes an elephant confrontation in vivid words:

> The armed crews of the elephants put up a beautiful fight and the elephants themselves an even finer one, shoving with all their might and clashing head to head. For the way elephants fight is this: with their tusks interlocked they press against each other's head, circling, till one, overpowering the other, pushes his trunk aside and gets on his flank; then he jabs him with his tusks as bulls do with their horns.

Livy[13] writes of a later battle at Magnesia. He remarks that the fifty-four elephants then fielded by Antiochus were of 'impressive size' and were made to appear even more so by the frontlets they wore and the crests of aigrette feathers with which they were adorned; but nothing could surely have been more daunting than the towers upon their backs, each manned by four armed soldiers, besides the driver. The Syrian king positioned a formation of sixteen animals behind his cavalry, under his Master of Elephants, Philippus, so that they might quickly follow in support of the horse when these were released in attack. The remainder he stationed in the centre of his front line, grouped in pairs and located between every tenth section. The Romans, on this occasion, had likewise armed themselves with a supporting squadron of elephants, but these they held back behind their *triarii* because, in Livy's words, 'they were only 16 in number and African elephants cannot stand up to Indian even when the numbers are equal, either because the latter outmatch them in size – they are in fact very much larger – or because they are superior in fighting spirit'.

Another example of the battlefield employment of elephants occurred in 326 BC, when Alexander the Great's passage of the Hydaspes, at Haranpur in India, was delayed by Porus, king of the Pauravas. The latter held all fords across the river with pickets supported by elephants, their presence causing the Greek cavalry horses to become frantic, both in the water and upon Alexander's rafts as he endeavoured to force a crossing. This inbred fear of a horse for an elephant provided the latter with a natural and important role in battle, namely, protecting infantry against cavalry attack, particularly on the flanks of a massed formation.

On the other hand, the animal's uncertain behaviour in close combat with experienced infantry frequently rendered it a liability, unless equipped with defensive leather blankets to ward off the javelin attacks to which it was so vulnerable. This protective device was employed by Antiochus I during the Syrian War of 270 BC but there appears nothing to suggest that Hannibal provided his animals with anything similar. Indeed, the Carthaginians, and in particular Hannibal, seem so rarely to have exploited the tactical strengths of the elephant in battle and to have so often ignored its weaknesses. It is notable that neither Polybius nor Livy make any suggestion that the Carthaginian war-elephants were fitted with armed *howdahs* and crews during the Punic Wars, thus provoking the thought, once again, that the African species of animal employed by them – and by Hannibal – were smaller than the Indian variety and not large enough to carry this unwieldy contraption on their backs.

For their part, Roman generals quickly learned how to counteract the fear and confusion at first created by the appearance of these animals on the battlefield. At Zama,[14] Scipio Africanus, during his decisive encounter with Hannibal, drew up his legions in three successive lines, arranged according to *hastati*, *principes* and *triarii*, but positioned so that the cohorts did not touch. In this way a space was left between the detached companies through which the elephants driven by the enemy might be admitted without throwing his own ranks into confusion. He filled the intervals thus created with light armed skirmishers, so that his front might show no gaps, and these troops had orders to fall to the rear or to the flanks at the first onset of an elephant assault. By this means, as the animals passed through his line of battle, their flanks were exposed to the javelins and slingshot of his auxiliary troops. Another, more simple technique was for slingers to direct their fire on the approaching enemy elephants, thus driving them back into the body of their own troops. A variation of this latter tactic was for slingers to be mounted in chariots each fitted with a lighted stove, upon which red hot sling bullets were prepared and cast at the unfortunate animals being driven towards them.

The elephant proved itself to be a successful instrument of war when employed against raw troops and untrained tribal armies; but every military action almost inevitably produces a corresponding military reaction. When the grotesque and terrifying shapes of the first armoured tanks appeared out of the mists at the battle of Cambrai, in November 1917, to overrun the German trenches, they scored an instant success. They punched a hole 4 miles wide in the Hindenburg line, penetrated to a depth of miles, and captured 10,000 German troops with 200 guns: but, within ten days, the Germans had reorganised, counter-attacked and recovered the ground they had lost. The Roman army, with its high standards of efficiency and discipline, reacted in the same manner to Hannibal's war-elephants. His possession of them may have paid dividends at Trebbia (217 BC), where he stationed them 'half on the left flank, half on the right' in order to discourage, successfully so it happened, an enemy cavalry attack: but his ability to repeat these tactics subsequently was progressively diminished by Roman counter tactics.

The European experience with elephants in warfare probably commenced during the campaign between Alexander the Great and Darius, king of Persia, more than 100 years earlier than the Hannibalic War. A great deal of military experience in their use must thus have been gained during these intervening years; but, as we have seen, the Roman army remained seemingly wary about employing them. Thus, it is not easy to understand why Hannibal should so determinedly have brought them with him on his almost legendary five-month march from New Carthage in southern Spain, across the Ebro and the Pyrenees, thence, in the face of an opposed crossing, across the wide waters of the river Rhône to the snow-covered summit of the High Alps. Almost immediately, he found himself reduced to one in number. Perhaps his aim was to impress his Celtic allies, and potential enemies, in Transalpine and Cisalpine Gaul. It is difficult to argue that they brought him any great military advantage.

Table 6: The Elephant in Hannibal's War. (Refs: Livy, *The War with Hannibal*; Polybius, *The Rise of the Roman Empire*)

| Serial No. | Year BC | Event | No. of elephants | Reference |
|---|---|---|---|---|
| 1. | 219 | Hannibal's Spanish campaign against the CACCAE and the CARPENTANI. | 40 | Livy, xxi, 5 |
| 2. | 218 | Hannibal leaves elephants with Hasdrubal as he crosses the PYRENEES. | 21 | *ibid.*, xxi, 22 |
| 3. | 218 | Hannibal's elephants cross the river RHÔNE. | 37 | *ibid.*, xxi, 28 |
| 4. | 218 | Hannibal gets his elephants across the Alps, number uncertain. | | *ibid.*, xxi, 30–8 |
| 5. | 218 | Surviving elephants take part in the battle of the TREBBIA 'half on the left flank, half on the right . . .'. | | *ibid.*, xxi, 55 |
| 6. | 218 | Post-TREBBIA, '. . . rain, sleet and intolerable cold carried off many of the pack animals and nearly all the elephants . . .'. Seven died. | | *ibid.*, xxi, 58 |
| 7. | 217 | In the APENNINES: again many men and animals, including seven elephants, perished – is Livy confusing these two events? | | *ibid.*, xxi, 59 |
| 8. | 217 | Hannibal rode the one surviving elephant through the marshes at ARRETIUM. Here he lost an eye through some infection. | 1 | Livy, xxii, 2 Polybius, iii, 74 |

| Serial No. | Year BC | Event | No. of elephants | Reference |
|---|---|---|---|---|
| 9. | 216 | The Carthaginians decide to send Mago with reinforcements for Hannibal, including forty elephants. | | Livy xxiii, 13 |
| | | In the end, Mago sent to SPAIN and Hasdrubal (bro.) was sent with an equal force to SARDINIA. | | *ibid.*, xxiii, 32 |
| 10. | 216 | Elephants present at siege of CASILINUM. | | *ibid.*, xxiii, 18 |
| 11. | 215 | Reinforcements from Carthage, under command of Bomilcar, and comprising troops, elephants and supplies, land at LOCRI. Numbers unstated. | | *ibid.*, xxiii, 42 |
| 12. | 215 | Hanno joins Hannibal at NOLA with the elephants and reinforcements from LOCRI. | | *ibid.*, xxiii, 43 |
| 13. | 215 | Battle at NOLA with Roman forces under Marcellus, 6 elephants lost, 4 killed, 2 captured. Hannibal sends Hanno back to BRUTTIUM 'with the forces he had brought with him'. | | *ibid.*, xxxiii, 46 |
| 14. | 212 | Battle on Sicilian river HIMERA between Hannibal's general Muttines and Marcellus. Eight elephants killed or captured. | | *ibid.*, xxv, 40 |
| 15. | 211 | Hannibal marches to relief of CAPUA with thirty-three elephants. | 33 | *ibid.*, xxvi, 5 |
| 16. | 210 | Romans (Marcellus) withstand elephant attack at LUCANIA. | | *ibid.*, xxvii, 3 |
| 17. | 209 | Again heavy attack by elephants thrown back in battle at APULIA by Romans under Marcellus. | | *ibid.*, xxvii, 14 |
| 18. | 207 | Again in LUCANIA, at Grumentum, the elephants were outclassed in a 'disordered' battle: 4 captured, 2 killed. | | *ibid.*, xxvii, 42 |

| Serial No. | Year BC | Event | No. of elephants | Reference |
|---|---|---|---|---|
| 19. | 207 | The METAURUS: 'More of the elephants killed by their riders than by the enemy . . .'. | | Livy, xxvii, 49 Polybius, xi, 1 |
| 20. | 205 | Reinforcements from Carthage, with seven elephants, sent to Mago with instructions to move nearer Rome and join up with Hannibal. | 7 | Livy, xxix, 5 |
| 21. | 203 | Varus and Cornelius defeat Mago's army in Insubrean Gaul by repulsing his elephant attack. | | *ibid.*, xxx, 18–19 |
| 22. | 202 | Hannibal defeated at battle of ZAMA (N. Africa) by Scipio: the latter's anti-elephant tactics swayed the battle. | 80 | *ibid.*, xxx, 32 |

# THE TRASIMENE BATTLEFIELD

The battlefield is officially located on the north shore of Lake Trasimene and lies in a natural amphitheatre which covers the ground between Malpasso and the little town of Tuoro. Even today, despite the many farms which exist there, it is possible to see that its floor, although flat, would have been broken and covered with shrub and ideal country for an ambush of the nature designed by Hannibal. Hills to the north of the battlefield bend in an arc to include both Malpasso and Tuoro. Malpasso provides an entrance to the Umbrian hills from the fertile Val di Chianza, along the upper part of which Hannibal would have marched as he avoided the Roman forces at Arretium. The battlefield itself, where the massacre of Flaminius's army took place, today appears larger than it would have been in 218 BC, for the waters of the lake have subsided and much land has been reclaimed. Indeed, in 1996, the waters of Trasimene, the largest lake in central Italy, had fallen to such a degree that the tourist steamer service had at one time to be suspended.

Hannibal arrived at the Malpasso entrance to the arena on the afternoon of 23 June and encamped, so local tradition claims, where Tuoro is to be found today, in the rough area of the town cemetery. More than 100 cremation pits, such as have been found on other Carthaginian sites, are to be seen along the line of the wall in the *Via del Fornello* in Tuoro, providing vivid confirmation of the scale of the fighting which took place. From here an excellent panoramic view of the battlefield may be obtained.

Visitors to the battlefield site will find it well laid out by the local authority, with specially prepared descriptive stands. At the beginning of the foothills to its north, standing on high ground behind a farmhouse, stands a brick monument (see p. 68), provided with the following inscription:

> Qui il destino parvere decido inesorabilmente
> con una delle piu grandi battaglie della storia
> sui primato civile Mediterraneo
> permettendo ad Annibale
> a nome di Cartagine
> di spocare l'inestincuibile odio ciurato

La tragedia di questa antica Caporetto [*]
fu vinta a Zama
con fede incrollabilee con tenace valore
che dopo XX secoli ognora illumina il mondo
a monito dei lontani nepoti

XXIV GIUGNO MCMXX

This may be loosely translated as follows:

In this place, where Hannibal vented his unremitting hatred of Rome, destiny resolved, through one of the most important battles of history, supremacy in the Mediterranean.

The tragic outcome of this ancient Caporetto was later reversed at Zama, with sturdy faith and unshakeable valour. After 2,000 years, let this serve as an example to future generations of the world.

24 June 1920

[*]   Caporetto was a battle of the First World War at which the Italian army, fighting on the side of the allies, was soundly defeated by the enemy. When the memorial was erected, the memory of that disaster would still have been very fresh.

# NOTES

## CHAPTER I

1. Trs. by Peter Green. As in *Livy, The War with Hannibal* (London, Penguin Classics, 1965, repr. 1972)
2. Polybius, ii, 13.
3. Livy, xxi, 5; see also Polybius, ii, 36.
4. *ibid.*, xxi, 16.
5. These, of course, are Livy's words. Rome was as yet unaware that Hannibal was on his way and the walls of Rome were never to be attacked during Hannibal's War.
6. B.H. Liddell Hart, *The Way to Win Wars, The Strategy of Indirect Approach* (London, Faber & Faber, 1929).
7. He accompanied Scipio Aemillianus to Carthage during the Third Punic War.
8. Livy, xxi, 18.
9. F. de Bourrienne, *Memoirs of Napoleon Bonaparte*, ed. Edgar Sanderson (London, Hutchinson & Co., 1889), xix, 239.
10. J.F. Lazenby, *Hannibal's War* (Wiltshire, Aris & Phillips, 1978), viii, fn. 37, 298.

## CHAPTER II

1. *Julius Caesar*, Act III, sc. i, l. 273.
2. As quoted in *Design for Military Operations – The British Military Doctrine* (1989), prepared under the direction of the Chief of the General Staff.
3. Polybius, ii, 36. Hannibal was only 27–8 years of age at this time.
4. Livy, xxi, 18.
5. *ibid.*, xxi, 11.
6. *ibid.*, xxi, 21.
7. Polybius, ii, 14.
8. Livy, v, 35.
9. Polybius, iii, 34.
10. Appian (*The Hannibalic War*, 1,4), on the other hand, includes a total of thirty-seven.
11. John Peddie, *The Roman War Machine* (Stroud, Alan Sutton Publishing, 1994): see Chapter 4, for an explanation of the problems of distance related to time on the march.
12. Polybius, iii, 35.
13. Gavin de Beer, *Alps and Elephants* (London, Geoffrey Bles, 1955), vii, p. 47.
14. Polybius, iii, 44.
15. Livy, xxi, 30.
16. Polybius, iii, 38.
17. Hanno was a common-place surname which, confusingly, is frequently met.
18. Polybius, iii, 60.
19. *ibid.*, iii, 49.
20. There are, doubtless, many more.
21. Polybius, iii, 54.
22. Livy, xxi, 38.
23. Polybius, iii, 56: Polybius claimed to have seen these totals listed on a monument erected at Lacinimus, in southern Italy, and strongly defended their accuracy.
24. Livy, xxi, 38.
25. Polybius, iii, 60.

## CHAPTER III

1. Polybius, ii, 24.
2. *Napoleon's Memoirs*, ed. Somerset de Chair (London, 1946), V, p. 45.
3. Polybius, iii, 16.
4. Livy, v, 54.
5. Strabo, *The Geography*, ii, 5, 3, 2.
6. Pliny the Elder, *Natural History*, iii, 53–5.

7. Livy, xxxix, 2.
8. Alta Macadam, *Rome* (London, A. & C. Black, 1994), p. 13.
9. Livy, i, 44.
10. Arnold J. Toynbee, *Hannibal's Legacy* (2 Vols, London, Oxford University Press, 1965), II, iii, p.185.
11. K.D. White, *Roman Farming* (London, Thames & Hudson, 1970), 11, p. 68.
12. Polybius, ii, 23.
13. *ibid.*, ii, 24.
14. See Table 1, p. 47.
15. Toynbee, *Hannibal's Legacy*, II, iii, Annex 10, p. 466.
16. Geoffrey Rickman, *The Corn Supply of Ancient Rome* (Oxford, Clarendon Press, 1980), i, p. 10.
17. Livy, xxv, 13.
18. *ibid.*, xxx, 3.
19. Rickman, *The Corn Supply*, v, p. 104.
20. Livy, xxv, 20.
21. White, *Roman Farming*, 11, p. 66.
23. Livy, viii, 7 and 8.
24. A matter discussed in my work *The Roman War Machine*, iv, pp. 61–2.

## CHAPTER IV

1. *Design for Military Operations – The British Military Doctrine.*
2. Clausewitz, Carl von, *On War* (1832, repr. Penguin Classics, 1968)
3. It will be recalled that Sempronius Longus had been sent to garrison Sicily and, if circumstances permitted, to carry the war to Carthage in Africa.
4. Polybius, iii, 68.
5. Livy, xxi, 49.
6. *ibid.*, xxi, 52.
7. Livy, xxi, 48.
6. *ibid.*, xxii, 1.
8. White, *Roman Farming*, 11, p. 52.
9. Strabo, *The Geography*, 5, 1, 12.
10. Polybius, iii, 79.
11. *ibid.*, iii, 82.
12. *ibid.*, iii, 86.
13. *ibid.*, iii, 96.
14. Strabo, *The Geography*, 5, 2, 9.
15. Polybius, iii, 78.
16. Livy, xxii, 2.

17. Polybius, iii, 79.
18. A very rough estimate based upon the knowledge that Hannibal entered the battle of Cannae (217 BC) with some 50,000 men.
19. Livy, xxii, 2.
20. *ibid.*, xxii, 3.
21. Polybius, iii, 79.
22. In the Second World War, flour (*atta*) carried by Indian troops during the early days of the 1942 monsoon campaign frequently burst its wrapping and was reduced to an unusable paste.
23. Polybius, iii, 79.
24. Livy, xxii, 11.
25. *ibid.*, xxii, 4.
26. Polybius, iii, 80–1.
27. For further details see Toynbee, *Hannibal's Legacy*, Vol. I, ii, pp. 11–12.
28. *ibid.*, iii, 82: but always remembering that Livy depended heavily upon an account of events written by Quintus Fabius Pictor.
29. Livy, xxii, 4.
30. Polybius, iii, 83.
31. Over such a distance, presumably by trumpet.
32. The tribal composition of Hannibal's Celtic contingent is nowhere stated but the death of Flaminius at the hands of an Insubrian cavalryman provides a partial hint.
33. Polybius, iii, 86.
34. Livy, xxii, 9.

## CHAPTER V

1. Clausewitz, Carl von, *Principles of War*, trs. and ed. by Hans W. Gatzbe (London, The Bodley Head, 1943).
2. Livy, xxi, 38.
3. Polybius, iii, 89.
4. *ibid.*
5. Polybius, iii, 38.
6. For a discussion on this strategy see Liddell Hart, *The Way to Win Wars*.
7. Polybius, iii, 106.
8. Livy, xxii, 33.
9. These were the beadles of Roman public officers of high rank. A praetor was entitled to six, and a consul

twelve; presumably a dictator, on that scale of progression, would have been authorised eighteen or twenty-four.

10. Livy, xxii, 11.
11. Polybius, iii, 88.
12. *ibid.*, iii, 87.
13. See Toynbee, *Hannibal's Legacy*, Vol. I, p. 183, n. 1: the potential menace to Rome along this coast had led her to claim control of Antium (Anzio), a beachhead successfully seized and exploited by the Allies in early 1944, during the Second World War. Four long established coastguard colonies in this area during the Hannibalic war were: Antium, Terracina, Minturnae, Sinuessa. Salerno, the site of yet another Allied landing, was a *post-*Hannibal Roman colony.
14. Pliny, *Natural History*, 19, 3, 4 and Lionel Casson, *Ships and Seamanship in the Ancient World* (Princeton University Press, 1971), 12, p. 281.
15. Appian, *The Roman History*, vii, 16.
16. White, *Roman Farming*, p. 470, n. 66.
17. Polybius, iii, 89.
18. Livy, xxii, 14.
19. Appian, *Roman History*, VII, iii, 14.
20. Livy, xxii, 17.
21. Polybius, iii, 100.
22. Livy, xxii, 18.
23. Polybius, iii, 102.
24. *ibid.*, iii, 101.
25. Livy, xxii, 23.
26. *ibid.*, xxii, 27.
27. Polybius, iii, 195: it would be interesting to know how much Fabius saw of what was happening. Could he have been aware of the ambush positions?
28. *ibid.*, iii, 106: that is to say that their term of office was officially extended.
29. Clausewitz, *On War*.
30. Toynbee, *Hannibal's Legacy*, Vol. I, p. 499.
31. Polybius, iii, 107.
32. *ibid.*
33. Livy, xxii, 39.
34. Polybius gives command of the right wing to Hanno, Livy to Maharbal. Possibly Maharbal commanded the Numidian cavalry under Hanno.

35. H.H. Scullard, 'Cannae', *Oxford Classical Dictionary* (London, Oxford University Press, 1949, repr. 1968), p. 163.
36. Polybius, iii, 113; Livy, xxii, 36; Appian, *Roman History*, VII, iii, 17.
37. Scullard, 'Cannae', p. 163.
38. Toynbee, *Hannibal's Legacy*, Vol. II, p. 68.
39. Livy, xxii, 49.
40. Polybius, iii, 117.
41. Livy, xxii, 52.

## CHAPTER VI

1. FM Viscount Montgomery of Alamein, *A Concise History of Warfare* (London, Collins, 1968), i, p. 11.
2. Livy, xxii, 51.
3. Appian, *Roman History*, vii, 23.
4. Livy, xxii, 61: Carthaginian generals were crucified for their military failings.
5. Polybius, iii, 62.
6. Livy, xxii, 56.
7. See Valerie Maxfield, *The Military Decorations of the Roman Army* (London, Batsford, 1981), p. 104: an unusually high decoration, which had seemingly been awarded to two other men only, Romulus and Cornelius Cossus.
8. Livy, xxii, 57.
9. Polybius, ii, 24.
10. This figure is reached by calculating backwards from Hannibal's reported fighting strength at Cannae.
11. John Hill, *China Dragons* (London, Blandford, 1991), Appx C, p. 173: 2 R Berkshire Regiment, operating in Burma between December 1944–May 1945, suffered 398 battle casualties, 94 killed and missing, 304 wounded.
12. Appian, *Roman History*, vii, 26.
13. Livy, xxiii, 21.
14. Polybius, iii, 15.
15. Livy, xxi, 5.
16. Appian, *Roman History*, vii, 21.
17. Livy, xxiii, 5.
18. *ibid.*, xxiii, 11.
19. It was to last for a further fourteen years and more.

20. Livy, xxiii, 32.
21. Livy, xxii, 56: The presence of a Carthaginian fleet here at this moment, together with the earlier, pre-Trasimene, report of a fleet off Pisa (see Chapter IV, p. 65), makes it difficult for us to believe that Hannibal's situation was being so ignored by Carthage as Livy would have us understand.
22. *ibid.*, xxiii, 32: seemingly in excess of 30,000 but largely untrained.
23. Perhaps replacements for the many 'dear friends' for whom Hannibal shed a tear at Cannae.
24. The mention of war-elephants at this stage may be an error on Livy's part. It is, of course, conceivable that the fleet reported lying of the Aegates Isles may have managed to put something ashore.
25. Livy, xxiii, 33.

## CHAPTER VII

1. Liddell Hart, *The Way to Win Wars*, p. 154.
2. Toynbee, *Hannibal's Legacy*, Vol. II, iii, 66.
3. Livy, xxiv, 9.
4. *ibid.*, xxiii, 36.
5. *ibid.*, xxiii, 42.
6. *ibid.*, xxiii, 37: Longus could have marched from Tarentum or have formed part of the army of Laevinus, then in Apulia.
7. It should be remembered that Hanno's army, newly arrived, was largely, if not entirely, comprised of sorely needed Carthaginian reinforcements. Their loss must have been a grievous blow to Hannibal.
8. Livy, xxiii, 17.
9. *ibid.*, xxiv, 10.
10. As in Toynbee, *Hannibal's Legacy*, Vol. II, pp. 315 and 682.
11. Livy, xxiii, 46.
12. Puteoli was fortified and garrisoned by Fabius, at the end of 214 BC.
13. Livy, xxii, 37.
14. *ibid.*, xxii, 31.
15. *ibid.*, xxiv, 8.

16. Fabius is clearly here referring to the absence of Otacilius in Africa and at sea, whilst Bomilcar was landing troops at Locri.
17. Pliny, *Natural History*, iii, 86–92.
18. Pyrrhus, 276 BC; Rome, 250–242 BC.
19. Livy, xxiv, 5.
20. *ibid.*, xxiv, 11.
21. *ibid.*, xxiv, 20.
22. It will be remembered that Compsa, in the Aufidus valley and in the heart of the Apennines, was initially set up by Hannibal as a secure base *post* Cannae. This was therefore a significant Roman recovery.
23. Livy, xxiv, 6.
24. *ibid.*, xxiv, 35.
25. *ibid.*, xxiv, 40.
26. *ibid.*, xxiv, 20.
27. *ibid.*, xxiv, 36.

## CHAPTER VIII

1. Polybius, i, 37.
2. See page 33.
3. Dionysius, 368 BC: Pyrrhus, 277/276 BC: Rome, 241 BC.
4. Agrigentum, an ancient city of considerable beauty, where it was said by a contemporary philosopher that its people built as if they lived for an eternity, and ate as if there were no tomorrow.
5. The elders of Camarina drained the defensive swamp which partially surrounded the town. As a consequence, when it was later overrun by the enemy, the saying 'let sleeping dogs lie' originated.
6. Polybius, i, 37.
7. Archimedes was born *c.* 290–280 BC.
8. Livy, xxiv, 34.
9. *ibid.*
10. Polybius, ix, 26.
11. Livy, xxiv, 29.
12. *ibid.*, xxv, 13.
13. See Livy, xxvii, 25: he mentions that, upon the recapture of Tarentum by Rome, Livius was considered for reward because of his five-year defence of the citadel during Hannibal's siege.

14. Polybius, viii, 26.
15. Appian, *Roman History*, vii, 33.
16. *ibid.*
17. Livy, xxv, 11.
18. Polybius, viii, 34.
19. Livy, xxv, 27 .
20. *ibid.*, xxv, 27.
21. *ibid.*, xxv, 31.
22. *ibid.*, xxv, 40.
23. *ibid.*

## CHAPTER IX

1. de Bourrienne, *Memoirs of Napoleon Bonaparte*, xix, 239.
2. Polybius, iii, 35.
3. Livy, xxii, 19.
4. *ibid.*, xxiii, 26.
5. *ibid.*, xxiii, 29.
6. *ibid.*, xxiii, 11.
7. *ibid.*, xxiii, 41: Bomilcar was the father of Hamilcar, serving with Hasdrubal.
8. *ibid.*, xxv, 33.
9. Cicero, *pro Balbo*, 34.
10. See Table 4, p. 122; also Toynbee, *Hannibal's Legacy*, p. 650.
11. That is to say, one whose tenure of command of an army had been extended beyond his elected year.
12. Livy, xxvi, 1.
13. Polybius, ix, 3–4.
14. Toynbee, *Hannibal's Legacy*, Vol. II, ii and vi, 5. This account of Q. Fulvius's march is related in detail in Livy, xxvi, 9, but Toynbee (Vol. II, iii, Annex 3) argues in strong terms that the annalist is guilty of 'a positive falsification of the facts'. There are, however, two factors which may be judged to speak for Livy. One, importantly, is the sheer number of legions present at the siege of Capua (three armies of two legions): thus Fulvius could surely have been spared in such a crisis. The other is the fact that Polybius makes no mention of Fulvius's presence at Capua during this period. I have, therefore included it, whilst recognising its uncertain nature.
15. Livy, xxvi, 11–12.

16. *ibid.*, xxvi, 12.
17. *ibid.*, xxvi, 16.
18. Polybius, ix, 26.
19. Livy, xxvi, 19.
20. *ibid.*, xxvi, 42: for the purist, it must be said that these figures differ slightly from the various totals already provided for us by Livy, showing a deficiency of 2,000 foot and 300 horse.
21. Polybius, x, 8.
22. A lagoon is a stretch of salt water separated by a sandbank from the sea which feeds it.
23. Livy, xxvi, 43.
24. Yet another Mago, here the military commander of New Carthage.
25. Polybius, x, 15.
26. Livy, xxvi, 47.
27. *ibid.*, xxvi, 51.

## CHAPTER X

1. Polybius, x, 36.
2. Livy, xxiii, 48.
3. Montgomery of Alamein, *Warfare*, xix, p. 323.
4. Livy, xxvii, 19.
5. Polybius, ix, 26.
6. Livy, xxvii, 13.
7. After the return of Sicily to Roman influence in 210 BC, a band of 4,000 Sicilian outlaws was shipped across the straits to Rhegium by Valerius Laevinus as they were detrimental to the recovery of the island. Their numbers were then further increased by Bruttian deserters: Polybius ix, 27; Livy, xxvi, 40.
8. These officers would have accompanied the consuls so as agree their respective areas should it have been decided to occupy the hill.
9. Livy, xxvii, 27.
10. *ibid.*, xxvii, 34.
11. *ibid.*, xxvii, 42.
12. *ibid.*, xxvii, 38.
13. *ibid.*, xxvii, 46.
14. Polybius, xi, 14.
15. Livy, xxvii, 49.
16. Livy, xxvii, 50: the distance from Canusium to the Metaurus, as the

crow flies, would have been some 240 miles. This statement by Livy implies a march of at least 40 miles a day, over a period of fourteen days, with a battle in between: most unlikely! As a comparison, the standard annual test of the King's African Rifles, a famous marching regiment, was 100 miles in three days, achieved by marching 20 miles every alternate eight hours, but this would have been difficult to sustain.

17. *ibid.*, xxviii, 46.
18. *ibid.*, xxviii, 12.
19. *ibid.*, xxviii, 36.
20. *ibid.*, xxix, 4.
21. *ibid.*, xxix, 27.
22. Appian, *History of Libya*, 23: 30,000 killed, 2,400 prisoners; Livy, xxx, 6: 40,000 killed, 5,000 prisoners.
23. Livy, xxx, 16.
24. The financial compensation varies by sum and kind according to the annalist.
25. Appian, *Libya*, 31; Livy, xxx, 23; Polybius, xv, 1; Cassius Dio, 17.
26. Livy, xxx, 20: we are tantalisingly left uninformed by Livy as to where his shipping came from, for it is estimated he returned home with 12,000 men, with animals.

## CHAPTER XI

1. Thomas Burnet, *Dies Virae, dies illa*, item 203, as in *Oxford Book of English Prose*, chosen and edited by Quiller-Couch (Oxford, 1925).
2. Trs. by Peter Green. As in *Livy, The War with Hannibal* (London, Penguin Classics, 1965, repr. 1972).

3. *Design for Military Operations – The British Military Doctrine.*
4. *ibid.*
5. Polybius, iii, 8.
6. Livy, xxx, 22.
7. Polybius, ii, 36.
8. Livy, xxi, 5.
9. *ibid.*, xxiii, 27.
10. *ibid.*, xxiii, 11–13.
11. Polybius, ix, 22.
12. Vegetius, Preface to Book III.
13. Livy, xxi, 22.
14. Winston Churchill, *The Second World War* (6 vols, London, Cassells, 1951), Vol. IV, xlv, p. 735.
15. Livy, xxvi, 40.
16. *ibid.*, xxii, 52.
17. Appian, *Hannibalic War*, 58–9.
18. Livy, xxx, 20.
19. Polybius, xi, 19.

## APPENDIX B

1. Pliny, *Natural History*.
2. Sylvia Sykes, *The Natural History of the African Elephant* (London, British Museum, 1971).
3. Pliny, *Natural History*, v, 14.
4. Polybius, v, 84.
5. Sir W. Gowers, 'African Elephants and Ancient Authors' in *African Affairs* (July, 1948).
6. Sykes, *African Elephant*.
7. Polybius, iii, 46–7.
8. *ibid.*, iii, 55.
9. Pliny, *Natural History*, viii, 16.
10. *ibid.*, viii, 27.
11. Livy, xxvii, 49.
12. Polybius, v, 84.
13. Livy, xxvii, 40.
14. Frontinus, *Stratagems*, II, iii, 16.

# BIBLIOGRAPHY

## MAIN HISTORICAL SOURCES

Appian. *The Hannibalic War*
Cassius Dio. *The History of Rome*
Cicero. *A Roman History*
Frontinus. *Stratagems*
Livy. *The History of Rome*
Pliny the Elder. *Natural History*
Polybius. *Histories*
Strabo. *The Geography*
Vegetius. *Military Matters*

## GENERAL

Casson, Lionel. *Ships and Seamanship in the Ancient World*, Princeton University Press, 1971

Chevallier, Raymond. *Roman Roads*, London, 1989

Churchill, Winston S. *The Second World War*, 6 Vols, London, Cassells, 1951

Clausewitz, Carl von. *Principles of War*, trs. and ed. by Hans W. Gatzbe (London, The Bodley Head, 1943)

——. *On War*, 1832, repr. Penguin Classics, 1968

Cloudesley-Thompson, J.L. 'The Lucanian Cows' in *The School Science Review*, Vol. 128 (1954)

Clutton-Brock, Juliet. *Domesticated Animals*, London, Heinemann, 1981

de Beer, Gavin. *Alps and Elephants*, London, Geoffrey Bles, 1955

de Bourrienne, F. *Memoirs of Napoleon Bonaparte*, ed. Edgar Sanderson, London, Hutchinson, 1889

de Chair, Somerset (ed.). *Napoleon's Memoirs*, London, 1946

Dodge, T.A. *Hannibal*, 1891, repr. London, Greenhill Books, 1994

Fantar, Mohamed Hassine. *Carthage, La cité punique*, Tunis, Alif – Les Éditions de la Méditerranée, 1995

Gowers, Sir W. 'African Elephants and Ancient Authors' in *African Affairs* (July, 1948)

Hill, John. *China Dragons*, London, Blandford, 1991

Lazenby, J.F. *Hannibal's War*, Wiltshire, Aris & Phillips, 1978

Liddell Hart, B.H. *The Way to Win Wars*, London, Faber & Faber, 1929

——. *Scipio Africanus, Greater Than Napoleon*, 1926, repr. London, Greenhill Books, 1992

Macadam, A. *Rome*, London, A. & C. Black, 1994

Maxfield, Valerie. *The Military Decorations of the Roman Army*, London, Batsford, 1981

Mommsen, T. *History of Rome*, tr. W.D. Dickson, 1901

Montgomery of Alamein, FM Viscount. *A Concise History of Warfare*, London, Collins, 1968

Peddie, John. *The Roman War Machine*, Stroud, Alan Sutton Publishing, 1994

Proctor, Dennis. *Hannibal's March into History*, London, Oxford University Press, 1971

Rickman, Geoffrey. *The Corn Supply of Ancient Rome*, Oxford, Clarendon Press, 1980

Scullard, H.H. 'Hannibal's Elephants' in *Numismatic Chronicle*, Vol. 8 (1948), 157–68

——. 'Hannibal's Elephants Again' in *Numismatic Chronicle*, Vol. 10 (1950), 271–83

————. '*Cannae*', *Oxford Classical Dictionary*, 1949, repr. London, Oxford University Press, 1968

Sykes, Sylvia. *The Natural History of the African Elephant*, London, The British Museum, 1971

Torr, Cecil. *Hannibal Crosses the Alps*, Cambridge University Press, 1924, rev. 1935

Toynbee, Arnold J. *Hannibal's Legacy*, 2 Vols, London, Oxford University Press, 1965

Walbank, F.W. 'Hannibal's Elephants' in *Journal of Roman Studies* (1956), 37–45

——. *A Historical Commentary on Polybius*, 2 Vols, Oxford, 1957 and 1967

White, K.D. *Roman Farming*, London, Thames & Hudson, 1970

# INDEX